SELFHOOD

Social Psychology Series
John Harvey, Series Editor

Selfhood

Identity, Esteem, Regulation

Rick H. Hoyle
University of Kentucky

Michael H. Kernis
University of Georgia

Mark R. Leary
Wake Forest University

Mark W. Baldwin
University of Winnipeg

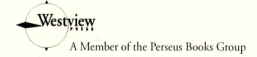

Westview PRESS

A Member of the Perseus Books Group

Social Psychology

Copyright © 1999 by Westview Press, A Member of the Perseus Books Group

Published in 1999 in the United States of America by Westview Press, 5500 Central Avenue, Boulder, Colorado 80301-2877, and in the United Kingdom by Westview Press, 12 Hid's Copse Road, Cumnor Hill, Oxford OX2 9JJ

Library of Congress Cataloging-in-Publication Data
Hoyle, Rick H.
    Selfhood : identity, esteem, regulation / Rick H. Hoyle ... [et al.].
        p.   cm.—(Social psychology series)
    Includes bibliographical references and index.
    ISBN 0-8133-3109-9 — ISBN 0-8133-3110-2 (pbk.)
    1. Self.   2. Identity (Psychology).   3. Self-esteem.   4. Self-management (Psychology).   I. Title.   II. Series.
BF697.H65   1999
155.2—dc21   98-40333
                                                                               CIP

The paper used in this publication meets the requirements of the American National Standard for Permanence of Paper for Printed Library Materials Z39.48-1984.

10   9   8   7   6   5   4   3

Contents

Tables and Figures

Tables

Figures

Preface

The empirical research literature on the self is vast and growing rapidly. Among the contributors to that literature are some of the most gifted scholars, past and present, in the social and behavioral sciences. For those reasons, the idea of writing a book on the self was at the same time daunting and exciting. In the end, excitement prevailed, and we set out to pen a volume that would be comprehensive, faithful to the research literature, and, most importantly, interesting to read.

Our principal aim in writing the book was to summarize in an integrative fashion the findings from empirical research on the self conducted in the tradition of experimental social psychology. We chose a style and a level of detail that should be appropriate for upper-level undergraduates and graduate students in the social and behavioral sciences; however, we attempted to make the book thorough and complete enough to be useful for researchers and practitioners unfamiliar with the empirical research literature on the self. As reflected in the title, we organized the literature with reference to three prominent themes in social-psychological research and theory on the self: identity, esteem, and regulation. Under the rubric of identity, we cover sources of identity, levels of identity, and the experience of identity—self-concept. With regard to esteem, we discuss sources of self-esteem and a number of relatively new ideas about different forms of self-esteem. We also present research on behaviors motivated by the desire for temporary increases in self-esteem. Finally, we cover a number of motives and strategies related to the ongoing activity of self-regulation. Collectively, these themes (and the model within which we embed them) provide a framework that encompasses most of the topics relevant to the self that have been studied by social psychologists.

New findings relevant to the self appear in scientific journals almost daily. Thus any attempt to characterize the accumulated knowledge about the self will, relatively quickly, become somewhat incomplete. Fortunately, the Internet and the vast store of information to which it provides access has provided a means whereby new information can be disseminated broadly and quickly. The recently organized International Society for Self and Identity maintains a site on the World Wide Web (http://www.wfu.edu/~leary/self/self.htm) that offers brief articles about the self, abstracts describing ongoing research on the self, and lists of investigators working on the self and their forthcoming publications. We invite readers to consult this and other similar resources to keep abreast of the latest research findings relevant to selfhood.

Rick H. Hoyle
Michael H. Kernis
Mark R. Leary
Mark W. Baldwin

Acknowledgments

Even in this age of e-mail, fax machines, and next-day delivery, collaborative efforts such as this one pose coordination problems that require patience and diligence from research assistants, secretaries, and computer consultants. Collectively, we express our gratitude to the staff members at our individual institutions who facilitated this long-distance collaboration. We are especially grateful to our editor at Westview, Cathy Murphy, who not only supported the idea of four authors at different institutions in two countries writing one book but encouraged it.

A risk involved with this sort of endeavor is that the final product will read as if different people wrote different parts instead of taking on the seamless quality of a well-written book. We were able to minimize this risk and improve the overall quality of the book by virtue of the helpful suggestions provided by several of our colleagues. Charles Carlson (University of Kentucky), Constantine Sedikides (University of North Carolina), and James Shepperd (University of Florida) read a complete draft of the book and provided numerous suggestions that helped us improve the flow of the writing and increase the comprehensiveness of our coverage. In addition, Patricia Frazier (University of Minnesota) read and commented on a draft of Chapter 3. Also important were the efforts of Michele Fejfar (University of Kentucky), who pored over drafts of all the chapters as well as the references and made important contributions to the accuracy and clarity of the final draft.

Finally, we wish to include the following individual acknowledgments:

I am grateful for research support during the writing of this book in the form of a grant from the Social Sciences and Humanities Research Council of Canada. I am also grateful to Bruce Daniels and Hugh Grant for their camaraderie and social support, often in the form of advice about advanced statistics and golf.—M.B.

I would like to thank my mother, who (as she puts it) "gave" me self-esteem, and my wife, Vicki, who nourishes it. During the writing of the book, I was supported by grant SBR-9618882 from the National Science Foundation.—M.K.

Much of the writing and editing was completed during a sabbatical year, and I gratefully acknowledge the generous contribution of the University of Kentucky. Also, I was supported, in part, by grants from the National Institute on Drug Abuse (DA-05312 and DA-09569) and the Center for Substance Abuse Prevention (SP-07967). Squeezing the writing of a book into an already overextended schedule is no easy feat. Indeed, it only works when friends and family pitch in and take care of matters that would otherwise go unattended. My colleagues in social psychology at the University of Kentucky—Monica Harris, Sung Hee Kim, Margo Monteith, and Richard Smith—were exceptionally gracious and understanding of my detachment from day-to-day duties during the final stages of writing. My graduate students, particularly Michele Fejfar and Sharon Williams, were understanding and independent. Mostly, however, it was my family who bore the brunt of my distraction, and I am deeply indebted to them. My sons, Matthew and Michael, themselves budding authors, provided much-needed encouragement and perspective. And without the understanding and support of my wife, Lydia, this book, along with most of the other worthwhile endeavors in my life, would never have happened.—R.H.

R.H.H.
M.H.K.
M.R.L.
M.W.B.

1

Selfhood

The Self is a haunting problem.
—*Allport (1961a, xvi)*

The self is a dynamic psychological system, a tapestry of thoughts, feelings, and motives that define and direct—even destroy—us. Minus the self, there is little more to human beings than meets the eye: frail, relatively hairless creatures ruled by instinct and circumstance. But clearly there is more. It is the self that distinguishes homo sapiens from even its closest evolutionary kin. Because of humans' unique capacity for self-reflection, a complex web of emotion, intention, and evaluation gives rise to the most salient aspect of human experience—selfhood.

Much has been written about the self, most of it during the latter half of the twentieth century, a period during which citizens of the free world have embraced self-esteem and the pursuit of self-interest as fundamental entitlements. The self is a frequently featured topic in wide-circulation magazines (one is even titled *Self*): "High self-esteem is the greatest gift you can give yourself," boasts one article (Burns 1990); "Why Americans Should Be Wary of Self-Esteem," warns the title of another (Lasch 1992). Similarly, scholarly journals in fields as diverse as psychology, sociology, philosophy, education, and business routinely feature reports of research on the self and related phenomena.

This widespread interest in the self has produced a large amount of information—and misinformation—about the self. As the volume of scholarly work on the self has increased, so has the appearance of articles and books based on intuitive but unsubstantiated claims about the self. Such publications typically offer simplistic but palatable accounts of selfhood; however, the reader who samples more than one likely will be left with more questions than answers (e.g., the magazine articles noted earlier that, on the one hand, portray self-esteem as "the greatest gift" and, on the other, caution readers to "be wary of self-esteem"). With this book, we hope to tip the scales in favor of careful, empirically informed analyses of the self.

In particular, we feature research findings and conceptual developments relevant to an understanding of the self produced by social psychologists since the mid-1970s. As has been true of virtually all research streams in social psychology during that era, the conceptual models and research strategies we describe reflect the influence of the cognitive revolution in psychology, that is, the tendency to view human beings as active, decisionmaking information processors who shape their environment as much as they are shaped by it. Our presentation is divided into eight chapters—two that establish a context and framework for our treatment and six dedicated to the organizing themes: identity, esteem, and regulation.

We begin this chapter by elaborating on the notion of selfhood. Then we make a brief foray into the past for the purpose of documenting the evolution of intellectual inquiry regarding the self. We conclude the chapter with an overview of our coverage of selfhood in the remainder of the book.

Selfhood

The term "selfhood" is not our own, though it captures the essence of our treatment of the self better than more commonly used terms such as "self-concept," "identity," or simply "self." M. Brewster Smith (1978), in his presidential address to the American Psychological Association, used the term "selfhood" to refer rather loosely to "what it means to be human" (p. 1053). Because our focus is on aspects of the self and related phenomena that are subject to empirical scrutiny, our use of the term is somewhat narrower than Smith's. By **selfhood** we mean *the thoughts, feelings, and behaviors that arise from the awareness of self as object and agent.* The object-agent distinction is an important one, and we devote considerable attention to it in the next three chapters. For now, it might be helpful to think of the **object** aspect of self as concerned with "being," and the **agent** aspect of self as concerned with "doing." "Being" refers to descriptive features of the self such as identity and self-esteem, whereas "doing" refers to behaviors and ways of thinking aimed at asserting, protecting, or repairing identity or self-esteem. A principal force that contributes to—even necessitates—these experiences and activities is the uniquely human capacity for reasoned self-reflection.

The distinction between self-as-object and self-as-agent provides a fitting segue into our brief consideration of the history of intellectual inquiry about selfhood. Intellectual interest in the self started much earlier than the discipline of psychology, within which most empirical inquiry is now done. Early intellectual treatments were largely philosophical and wrestled with profound and fundamental questions, many of which remain unanswered, such as the origin and location of the self and how it is that the self can be both object and agent. As the intellectual treatment of selfhood made its way from philosophy through sociology into psychology, the focus and methods of inquiry changed. In order to better understand why and how researchers in social psychology study selfhood, it is important to have at least a general appreciation of the history of intellectual inquiry about selfhood. Toward that end, in the next section we highlight significant contributors and schools of thought that set the stage for contemporary thinking by social psychologists about selfhood.

A Brief History

The legacy of intellectual inquiry about selfhood is long and is strewn with names that would be familiar to even the most casual student of the humanities or social sciences. Indeed, if the enduring importance of a construct or phenomenon can be judged by the amount of attention it has received throughout history from inquiring scholars, then selfhood must be considered supremely important. Philosophers Descartes (1962, 1986), Kant (1934), and Dewey (1890) wrestled with the role of self-consciousness in human emotion, will, and thinking. Sociologists Cooley (1902, 1925) and Mead (1914, 1934) attempted to integrate the individual and society by portraying the self as an internalization of social experience. And philosopher-psychologist William James (1950, 1961) described the self as rich and differentiated with emotional and motivational consequences for the individual. However, the seeds of this enduring fascination with selfhood were sown much earlier.

Scholarly interest in the self antedates the birth of most of the disciplines that now consider selfhood a fruitful topic of research. As early as the fourth century B.C., Plato (1951) described the soul, or self, as the source of all human activity (Viney 1969). Aristotle portrayed the self in much the same way and has been described as "the first to make a systematic enquiry into the nature of the ego" (Altschule 1957, 24). Perhaps as a result of the anti-intellectualism that characterized the Middle Ages, the search for the self dwindled to a minor point of occasional intellectual debate until the latter half of the seventeenth century.

The philosophers of seventeenth-century Europe shaped philosophical and scientific inquiry in major ways. As the climate grew more favorable for unrestrained intellectual pursuit, the self resurfaced as a central question—and problem—for notables such as Descartes (1962), Hobbes (1948), and Locke (1960). In many respects, the current Western view of human consciousness and will is a reflection of the great thinkers of this era.

During this period the self also became an issue of importance for the layperson in the form of a concern for individuality. The pursuit of self during this era was an attempt to distinguish the inner "true" self from the outer "apparent" self (Baumeister 1987). This distinction is particularly apparent in the introspective writings of René Descartes (1962, 50): "I recognized that I was a substance whose essence or nature is to be conscious. Thus, this self, that is to say the soul, by which I am what I am, is entirely distinct from the body and is even more easily known."

Soon after the appearance of Descartes' famous account of his search for self, the Englishman Hobbes (1948) published his *Leviathan,* in which he laid the groundwork for present-day "doctrines of self-esteem and self-regard as pivotal motives" (Allport 1954, 14). Hobbes portrayed the self in terms of sensory experience and was among the first to describe, and endorse, the basic pursuit of self-interest (Viney 1969). Hobbes's influence, particularly his concern for the sensory experience of self, can be seen clearly in the later works of James (1950) and Cooley (1902). Indeed, ideas from his treatise on self-interest are well represented in contemporary theories of self-related motivations (e.g., Greenwald 1980; Kunda 1987).

John Locke provided the clearest link between the philosophers of the seventeenth century and later thinkers who more directly influenced contemporary conceptualizations of the self. Locke (1960) described the self as a by-product of sensory experience, wholly defined by the phenomenology, or subjective experience, of the individual: "The self is not determined by identity or diversity of substance, which it cannot be sure of, but only by identity of consciousness" (p. 196).

According to Kant (1934), the self as conceived by Locke and Hobbes, the empirical self (i.e., self-as-object), was to be distinguished from the pure ego (i.e., self-as-agent). The empirical self involved a synthesis of sensory experience, perhaps encoded in memory, yet influenced by new experiences.[1] The pure ego, also known as "the knower" (Schopenhauer 1948), the "I" (Condillac 1930), "agent" (James 1950), or "experiencer" (American Psychological Association Committee 1918), was seen as the core of human existence. James (1950) grappled with the nature and function of the pure ego in his classic chapter on the self. He noted that "ever since Hume's time, it [pure ego] has been justly regarded as the most puzzling puzzle with which psychology has to deal; and whatever view one may espouse, one has to hold his position against heavy odds" (p. 330).

Contrary to James's commentary, the pure ego has, for the most part, remained the subject matter of philosophy (e.g., Popper and Eccles 1977),

---

[1]This notion of the self is very similar to that described by contemporary theorists (e.g., Kihlstrom and Cantor 1984; Markus and Kunda 1986).

not psychology. It is the empirical self, "the known," that has attracted the greatest attention in psychology. Indeed, James's treatment of the empirical self has influenced much current theory and research on the self (e.g., Gergen 1971; Markus and Nurius 1986).

An Early Model of Self-Concept

James (1961) drew a sharp distinction between the "Me," the empirical ego, and the "I," the pure ego. The former he divided into three "constituents of the Self": the material self, the social self, and the spiritual self. The material self included the individual's body and possessions. Of this self James (1950) noted, "The old saying that the human person is composed of three parts—soul, body and clothes—is more than a joke" (p. 292).

An individual's social self was described by James (1950) as "the recognition which he gets from his mates" (p. 292). In essence, James argued that the individual has as many social selves as he or she has meaningful acquaintances. His description of the social self foreshadowed a number of early (Prince 1929; Ribot 1895; Sidis and Goodhart 1904) and more recent multidimensional models of the self-concept (e.g., Gergen 1972; Hoelter 1985; Markus and Kunda 1986; Marsh and Shavelson 1985).

The final constituent part of the empirical self proposed by James (1950) was the spiritual self, or consciousness—the "self of all other selves" (p. 297). According to James (1950, 298–299), "this central part of the self is felt. . . . It is something with which we have direct sensible acquaintance, and which is as fully present at any moment of consciousness in which it is present, as in a whole lifetime of such moments." By introducing the spiritual self, James set the stage for treating the emotions that accompanied self-awareness—"self-complacency" and "self-dissatisfaction," and activities generated by them—"self-seeking" and "self-preservation."

James (1950) devoted much intellectual effort to pursuing the agent of the activities and feelings associated with self-awareness. Conceding to the seeming futility of the search for "I," he at one point questioned whether it is better to attempt to conceptualize the "I" or simply to consider it as "a law yet unexplained." In the end, James concluded that the "I" and the "me" are conceptually inseparable—"the indecomposable unity of every pulse of thought" (p. 371). Much later, Hilgard (1949) reiterated the futility of attempts to distinguish between self-as-object and self-as-agent. According to Hilgard, it is as if the self were "between the two mirrors of a barber-shop, with each image viewing each other one, so that as the self takes a look at itself taking a look at itself, it soon gets all confused as to the self that is doing the looking and the self which is being looked at" (p. 377).

Evidence of the impact of James's (1950, 1961) clear thinking and elo-quent writing about the self on contemporary models of the self is abun-dant. He portrayed the self as malleable, multifaceted, and conscious. The malleability, or variable experience of the self, is increasingly apparent in research inspired by cognitive psychology (e.g., Markus and Kunda 1986; Schwarz et al. 1991). It is now taken for granted that the self has many in-terrelated parts (e.g., Donahue et al. 1993; Markus and Kunda 1986; Mar-kus and Nurius 1986; Linville 1985). James's idea of the self as readily ac-cessible to the individual (i.e., conscious) is not as prevalent in contemporary models (cf. Wicklund 1979). This departure from the strictly phenomenological self portrayed by James (1950) can be traced primarily to the work of sociologists Cooley and Mead and philosopher John Dewey.

Focus on Social Experience

Dewey (1887, 1890) portrayed the self as an emergent internalization of social feedback and societal values. He proposed that "the self has no meaning except as contrasted with other persons" (1887, 327) and that "the self and the world are correlative, and have the same content" (1890, 59). Dewey's influence on self theory is seldom acknowledged, but the simi-lar views held by his colleague Charles Cooley and, later, George Herbert Mead elevated to prominence Dewey's notion of a social self.

Cooley is perhaps most noted for introducing the concept of the "look-ing-glass self." "Each to each a looking-glass reflects the other that doth pass," wrote Cooley (1902, 184). Considered a champion of the symbolic interactionist school, Cooley saw the self as "totally bound up with other people" (Wicklund 1979, 190). For Cooley, "a separate individual is an ab-straction unknown to experience, and so likewise is society when regarded as something apart from individuals" (1902, 1). In a fascinating paper, "A Study of the Early Use of Self-Words by a Child," Cooley (1908) traced the emergence of the self in a young child through analysis of the prevalence of references to self and others.

The child's first few words pertain to important others (e.g., "dada" and "mama") and presumably provide the impetus for the emergence of self. As the child matures, "the shadow on the wall and the reflection in the look-ing-glass" (1908, 232) become important points of focus and lead to the first signs of self-awareness; however, Cooley noted that "they are much less interesting at first than the shadows and reflections of others" (p. 232). The child soon comes to use the words "I," "me," and "mine" in an imita-tive fashion, then as a personal referent—the first sign of a consciousness of self.

George Herbert Mead, another member of the symbolic interactionist school, addressed more directly the social self and the evaluative implications of it. Like Cooley, Mead (1934) proposed that "the self is essentially a social structure, and it arises in social experience" (p. 140). In many respects, Mead was even more adamant in his conviction that the self cannot exist apart from the social world: "What I want particularly to emphasize is the temporal and logical pre-existence of the social process to the self-consciousness of the individual" (1934, 186). "We do not assume that there is a self to begin with. Self is not presupposed as a stuff out of which the world arises. Rather the self arises in the world" (1982, 107). Mead did not see the self as an internalization of the reflected appraisal of others, as did Cooley. Instead, he saw self and society as inseparable.

In *Mind, Self, and Society,* his most thoroughgoing treatment of the self, Mead (1934) argued that the self is "essentially a cognitive rather than an emotional phenomenon" (p. 173). He contrasted this view with that of Cooley and James, who portrayed the self in terms of sensory experience and emotions. A final statement from Mead (1934) serves to summarize his perspective on the self and to illustrate the degree to which he anticipated contemporary social-cognitive perspectives on the self: "The essence of the self, as we have said is cognitive: it lies in the internalized conversation of gestures which constitutes thinking, or in terms of which thought or reflection proceeds. And hence the origin and foundations of the self, like those of thinking, are social" (p. 173).

Resurgence of Interest in the Self

Pepitone (1968) wryly noted that "in the history of psychology the self has been in and out like the style-changes of *haute couture*" (p. 347). Indeed, as the influence of the symbolic interactionist waned in the decades after publication of major works by Cooley and Mead, attention to the self as a mediator of social behavior diminished. By the 1950s, the self was apparently "dead" in psychological theory (Pepitone 1968); however, the 1970s and, to an even greater extent, the 1980s saw a resurgence of interest in selfhood. In a review of research during this period of resurgence, Hales (1985) noted an increasing frequency of statements such as "social psychologists appear to have backed into a focus on the self" (Greenwald and Ronis 1978, 55); "the self has become acceptable" (Stryker 1977, 5); and "apparently, the study of self-evaluation is becoming one of the major and critical interests in social psychology" (Miller and Suls 1977, 16). During these years, many midrange theories in social psychology (e.g., cognitive dissonance, social comparison, attribution) were modified to include the "motivational significance of self-esteem preservation" (Hales 1985, 237).

In addition to the increasing frequency of references to self in discussion of empirical research, the appearance of works such as the multivolume set *Psychological Perspectives on the Self* (Suls 1982, 1993; Suls and Greenwald 1983, 1986), *The Self and Social Life* (Schlenker 1985b), *The Self in Social Psychology* (Wegner and Vallacher 1980), and Greenwald and Pratkanis's (1984) influential chapter "The Self" both signaled and fueled the reemergence of the self as a primary focus in the explanation of social behavior. These works (including the 32 chapters in the multivolume set) are, in most cases, authored by social psychologists—an indication of the rubric under which research on selfhood now falls.

The Self as Social and Cognitive

According to John Stuart Mill (1878), "The phenomenon of Self and that of Memory are merely two sides of the same fact. We may, as psychologists, set out from either of them, and refer the other to it" (p. 174). This insightful observation by Mill anticipated the current view of self among cognitively oriented social psychologists. The influence of cognitive psychology on self research and theorizing is clear in several major contributions during the past twenty years (e.g., Epstein 1980; Greenwald and Pratkanis 1984; Markus 1977; Markus and Nurius 1986; Rogers, Kuiper, and Kirker 1977). By adapting theory and methods proposed and refined by researchers pursuing the study of language and memory, cognitively oriented social psychologists exerted a swift and enduring impact on the way the self is conceived and approached for research. Where once there was a lack of clarity in theory and method, there is now a relatively well-accepted paradigm for conceptualizing and studying the self (cf. Hermans 1996).

The concept of schema seems to be the unifying theme of social-cognitive treatments of selfhood. Indeed, during the 1980s the notion of self-concept was virtually supplanted by that of "self-schema." The self-concept typically is portrayed as a passive structure composed of descriptive information about oneself, whereas a self-schema is viewed as an active information-processing structure. The disparity between these two conceptions is even clearer in statements by the researchers who subscribe to them. For instance, Rosenberg (1979) described the self-concept as "the totality of the individual's thoughts and feelings having reference to himself as an object" (p. 7), whereas Rogers, Kuiper, and Kirker (1977) described the self-schema as "deeply involved in the processing, interpretation, and memory of personal information" (p. 677). As the study of selfhood has broadened and intensified, descriptions of the self have taken on the character of a dynamic, interactive, *causal* aspect of personhood.

Summary

This brief history of intellectual interest in the self provides important context for our treatment of selfhood. It is important to recognize that the enduring influence of early theorizing about the self is clear, although the bulk of the theory and research we review throughout the book was generated during the most recent quarter century. Yet there is a dramatic difference between early and contemporary work on the self. Contemporary researchers rely heavily on empirical methods, whereas their predecessors exercised greater freedom in speculating about the structure and function of the self without empirical corroboration. This recent reliance on empirical methods has given rise to a profusion of quantitative data on the self, and the stage is set for dramatic advances in our understanding of the self and the processes in which the self is implicated. As we illustrate in the chapters that follow, the age-old fascination with the mysteries of the human self continues unabated.

Overview of the Book

The stage is now set for a detailed examination of selfhood—those elements of the human experience that stem from the capacity to self-reflect and regulate behavior. In the next chapter we pose a working definition of the self. The definition is detailed and specific, and we elaborate and illustrate each aspect of it. Characteristic of our treatment of the self in this book, we stay close to the empirical research literature, relying heavily on social-psychological research on the self and self-referent phenomena. With our working definition as backdrop, in the remaining chapters we present an organized and detailed review of social-psychological research on the self. As reflected in the title of the book, our presentation is organized according to three broad, overlapping emphases in the research literature: *identity*, *esteem*, and *regulation*. In Chapter 3 we explore the various sources of identity, focusing primarily on aspects of social life that shape identity. This is followed by a complementary chapter on self-concept that provides detailed coverage of contemporary models and methods inspired by the cognitive revolution in psychology. Chapter 5 and Chapter 6 deal with material that is typically gathered under the rubric of self-esteem. Chapter 5 focuses on individual differences in self-esteem, whereas Chapter 6 discusses cognitive and behavioral strategies that serve to maintain or temporarily enhance self-esteem. Chapter 6 also begins our coverage of regulation, introducing one of several motives that derive from the motivation to regulate our thoughts, feelings, and behavior as they reflect on the self. Additional motives that implicate the self are addressed in Chapter 7. Chapter 8 focuses on specific strategies by which self-referent thoughts, feelings, and behavior are regulated. Finally, in the Afterword we bring our treatment of selfhood to a close by stepping back from the research we have reviewed and briefly reflecting on the state of our current understanding of the self and self-referent processes as well as avenues for broadening and extending that understanding.

2

The Self-System

All models are wrong but some models are useful.
—Box (1979, 202)

What *is* the self? Collectively, social and behavioral scientists have made significant progress in characterizing the self. Spurred by the cognitive revolution in psychology, empirical research in the late 1970s and early 1980s laid the groundwork for what is now an impressive body of knowledge about the self. Although the theoretical model of the self that is emerging from this body of knowledge is incomplete, and most certainly wrong in some of the particulars, it serves the useful function of orienting an increasingly large number of self researchers toward a common set of questions.

A fundamental characteristic of this emerging model of the self is the almost constant interplay between the self-system and the social environment. In this chapter, we attempt to capture the essence of this interplay and provide a framework for our subsequent review of the burgeoning research literature on the self, using an explicit definition of the self-system. After stating the definition, we elaborate on each key concept through comparisons with familiar physical systems. In this chapter, we refer sparingly to findings from specific research studies; however, abundant support for most aspects of the definition will emerge from our integrative review of research findings in the chapters that follow.

We define the self, which, for reasons that will become apparent, we refer to as the "self-system," as follows:

> The **self-system** is an interactive, self-regulating *system* of self-referent thoughts, feelings, and motives. It gives rise to an enduring experience of physical and psychological existence—a phenomenological sense of continuity and predictability. The self is *reflexive* and *dynamic* in nature: responsive yet stable, complex yet unified; both private and public, conscious and nonconscious, variable and fixed.

11

Given our introductory remarks, it is perhaps surprising that the word "social" does not appear in our definition. But, as closer examination will reveal, the importance of social experience is apparent at every turn.

Self-Regulating System

What do we mean by the statement that "the self-system is an interactive, self-regulating *system* of self-referent thoughts, feelings, and motives"? A key word in this statement and our definition is "system." Indeed, it is this idea on which the remainder of our definition rests. In describing the self as a **system**, we mean that it is composed of multiple components that are meaningfully organized into a stable, cohesive, functioning whole. Like other systems, the self-system can be characterized as follows:

- It serves a small number of **basic functions**.
- It is **organized**.
- It is **self-regulating**.

In the interest of clarity, let us digress for a moment to consider a familiar bodily system—the cardiovascular system.[1] Its *basic function* is the transportation of various substances in a fluid medium to and from cells throughout the body. Structurally, it consists of interdependent parts—the heart and the blood vessels, the latter comprising arteries, veins, and capillaries. These parts are *organized* in such a way that the basic function of the system is served efficiently and effectively. Oxygen-carrying blood moves through arteries away from the heart and is distributed throughout the body, and oxygen-depleted blood moves through veins from throughout the body back to the heart. The cardiovascular system is said to be *self-regulating* because the volume of blood circulated to and from different destinations in the body and the speed with which it is circulated are adjusted in response to a complex interaction of signals from bodily tissues and the sympathetic and parasympathetic nervous systems. For instance, blood pressure, which is vitally important to the basic function of moving fluids through the body, must stay within limits the body can tolerate—too high and vessels rupture; too low and circulation stops. In a properly functioning cardiovascular system, blood pressure is regulated by processes that are sensitive to these limits, such as fluctuations in the size of the blood ves-

---

[1]We rely heavily on Anthony and Thibodeau's (1984) excellent primer on anatomy and physiology, *Structure and Function of the Body,* and a basic treatment of cardiovascular functioning by Carlson (1988) for information presented in this section.

sels, variability in the volume of fluid in the system, and the strength and rate of the heartbeat (Anthony and Thibodeau 1984).

Let us now consider these same basic characteristics of a system as they manifest in the self-system.

Basic Functions

All systems serve at least one basic function, and without at least a basic understanding of a system's function(s), it is not possible to characterize it in any kind of meaningful way. Perhaps surprisingly, given the long history of intellectual inquiry about the self, there is not a widely recognized list of basic functions served by the self-system. On the basis of the empirical research literature in social psychology, we see at least three **basic functions of the self-system**.

- **Planning and interpreting behavior.** The self provides a basis for planning and evaluating behavior in the form of standards. These **standards** include internalized *values* (Greenberg, Pyszczynski, and Solomon 1986), *principles* (Carver and Scheier 1982), and *goals* (Higgins 1987; Markus and Nurius 1986; Taylor, Neter, and Wayment 1995) that function to motivate the individual to engage in particular actions and avoid others in light of prevailing circumstances. For instance, Greenberg et al. (1986) posit that internalized standards of culturally valued behavior provide a context for behaving in ways that contribute to feelings of value and worth. And Higgins (1987) proposes that behavior is evaluated against self-beliefs that correspond to one's own and significant others' desires and sense of obligation. McAdams (1995; see also Graziano, Jensen-Campbell, and Finch 1997) refers to these collectively as Level II concerns of the person, deriving jointly from personality traits and contextual forces such as time, place, and role.
- **Monitoring.** The self serves as a monitor of the degree to which the individual is adequately fulfilling basic organismic needs. Two such needs are *social inclusion* (Baumeister and Leary 1995) and *cultural adherence* (Becker 1962). In the case of each of these basic human needs, personal self-esteem has been posited as a gauge of the degree to which that need is adequately fulfilled. With regard to social inclusion, sociometer theory (Leary and Downs 1995) proposes that, as a gas gauge indicates how much fuel is in the tank, self-esteem indicates how adequate and fulfilling are a person's social relations. In terms of cultural adaptation, terror management theory (Greenberg, Pyszczynski, and Solomon 1986) posits that self-esteem arises from viewing oneself as a valuable adherent to a cultural

worldview.[2] In each case, thoughts and feelings that arise within the self-system serve a monitoring function in the service of basic, survival-oriented needs.

• **Information processing.** Third, cognitive aspects of the self-system provide a coherent context within which information about oneself and social experience is understood and utilized. Greenwald (1980) eloquently stated this function as follows: "Ego [i.e., self], as an organization of knowledge, . . . serves the functions of observing (perceiving) and recording (remembering) personal experience; it can be characterized, therefore, as a personal historian" (p. 603). In an even stronger statement of this function, Combs and·Snygg (1959) suggest that "the phenomenal self . . . is the frame of reference in terms of which all other perceptions gain their meaning" (p. 145). How is this function accomplished? In a review of research on the self in information processing, Kihlstrom et al. (1988) concluded that "the self is one of the richest, most elaborate knowledge structures stored in memory" (p. 150). Although it now appears that self-knowledge is not qualitatively different from knowledge about other objects (Klein and Kihlstrom 1986), the sheer volume of self-knowledge and the ease and frequency with which it is referenced render it uniquely central in memory and thinking (Greenwald 1980). For instance, in the seminal experiment regarding the self in information processing, Rogers et al. (1977) showed that people remember words encoded with reference to the self better than words encoded with reference to particular qualities of the words themselves. Complementing this evidence of a *self-reference effect* was Markus's (1977) demonstration that self-knowledge is structured and organized and figures prominently in judgments about the self and interpretation of information relevant to the self. These foundational findings, described more fully in Chapter 3, along with a substantial body of research findings published subsequently, clearly and directly implicate the self in information processing.

Organization

Unlike the components of bodily systems, which can be touched, manipulated, even replaced, components of the self-system are intangible. That is

---

[2]Unlike sociometer theory, which portrays self-esteem largely as an indicator, terror management theory views self-esteem as both an indicator and a valued commodity for which the individual directly strives.

not to say that they are not real or consequential. Indeed, the parts we have identified—thoughts, feelings, and motives—are as real and consequential in everyday life as a limb or an organ. At issue in the present context is the degree to which these parts are, like the parts of any functioning system, organized.

Perhaps owing to the cognitive revolution in psychology, which has profoundly affected research methods as well as theorizing during the past two decades, most of the evidence regarding the organization of the self-system has focused exclusively on thoughts. Markus (1977) argued that, by inference, self-referent thoughts are organized because the self functions to organize social experience (i.e., the information processing function detailed earlier). She described the self-system as a set of interrelated cognitive structures that both reflect the individual's experience and affect the individual's planning and understanding of subsequent experiences (Markus and Sentis 1982). These substructures include various forms of self-representation— from individual differences (e.g., "self as woman"), to relationships (e.g., "self with best friend"), to particular situations (e.g., "self at school")— that become associated in memory as they are brought to mind simultaneously in social experience.

Considerably less empirical research has focused on the place of feelings and motives in the self-system. One possibility is that they are implicit in the "cognitive" structures that are the building blocks of cognitively oriented accounts of the self-system. This possibility is considered in Markus's (1983) call for an "expanded view" of self-knowledge. The expanded view would move beyond the relatively passive self-as-object models of the self-system that focus on self-knowledge (often to the exclusion of feelings and motives; e.g., Kihlstrom et al. 1988) to an expanded conceptualization in which knowledge structures, because they affect expectations for future action (Markus 1983; Markus and Nurius 1986) and evaluations of those actions (Higgins 1987), *include* affective information and prescribe desires and goals that motivate action and inspire self-improvement (e.g., deCharms 1968; Deci and Ryan 1995; White 1959).

Yet even with the issue of where feelings and motives fit into the self-system somewhat resolved, fundamental questions about the organization of the self-system remain unanswered. For instance, it is not yet clear exactly what the structure of the self-system is like. Terms such as "complexity" (Linville 1985), "compartmentalization" (Showers 1992a), and "differentiation" (Donahue et al. 1993) suggest particular ways and degrees to which self-knowledge may be organized (these ideas are elaborated in Chapter 4), but there is, at this point in time, no explicit hypothesis as to how or where the thoughts, feelings, and motives that make up the self-system are arrayed.

Perhaps an even more fundamental question concerns how these knowledge structures come to be organized, in whatever form they might take, into a system in the first place. For a plausible explanation and to highlight the nature of the problem, we turn to an example from the natural sciences, in which biologists, mathematicians, geologists, and physicists attempt to understand the laws that give rise to a wide range of complex systems—from molecules to galaxies (e.g., Yates 1987). In an enlightening essay, biologist Arthur Iberall (1987) described how the emergence and flow of rivers can be understood on the basis of a few well-reasoned assumptions (e.g., water flows downhill) and a few well-understood processes (e.g., rainfall, evaporation). Given the assumptions and raw materials, the processes give rise to a relatively stable and predictable but complex system. States Iberall, "Natural systems are not like man-made systems. They are self-organizing . . . within boundary constraints. Within the field so loosely constrained, they sort themselves out in both form and function" (p. 33). In line with Iberall's statement, we suggest that the self-system, in the course of cognitive and social development, "sorts itself out" according to a small number of lawful processes that most certainly involve social experience. As will be apparent in later chapters, social psychologists have made great strides during the past two decades toward explicating the involvement of the self-system in personal and social experience. Thus, we might optimistically conclude that plausible models of the organization of the self-system are forthcoming.

Self-Regulation

Another basic property of a system, and therefore of the self, is self-regulation. By **self-regulation** we mean the system functions in such a way that, under normal circumstances, it remains within adaptive limits on critical indicators without outside intervention. Recalling the example of the cardiovascular system presented earlier, blood pressure is a critical indicator, and the design of the cardiovascular system ensures that, under normal circumstances, blood pressure is neither too low nor too high.[3] A properly self-regulating system, physical or psychological, functions at or near *homeostasis*—relative constancy—most of the time (Cannon 1929).

What are the critical indicators of homeostasis within the self-system? As noted earlier, it would appear that self-esteem, though perhaps not an end in itself, gauges the degree to which the individual is socially accepted and culturally adapted. More generally, negative self-directed emotions such as guilt and shame may indicate instability or incongruence within the self-system (Higgins 1987). And elevations in physiological arousal (e.g., ten-

---

[3]Of course, self-regulation can fail (e.g., hypertension), in which case the influence of forces outside the system (e.g., medicine, dietary constraints) is required.

sion, anxiety) accompany disharmony between self-representation and behavior (Cooper and Fazio 1984). Two characteristics of these indicators are of note. First, emotions and arousal instigate and influence behavior, which, as described below, is a primary means of restoring homeostasis within the self-system. Second, these indicators can, to some degree, be traced to the neurology and physiology of the body (Caciacoppo, Berntson, and Crites 1996). Thus there is a clear link between the self-system and certain bodily systems, thereby implicating both psychology and biology in self-regulation.

The mechanisms or strategies that function to maintain homeostasis within the self-system fall into two broad categories: interpersonal and cognitive. *Interpersonal strategies* reflect calculated behavior, whereas *cognitive strategies* involve strategic thinking. These strategies are detailed in later chapters, so, for purposes of the present discussion, we touch on them only briefly here. Interpersonal strategies involve choosing situations, interaction partners, or specific behaviors that are likely to lead to affirmation of personal goals, values, and principles (e.g., Carver and Scheier 1982; Swann, Stein-Seroussi, and Giesler 1992). Cognitive strategies involve managing information in such a way that it "fits in" with knowledge structures in the self-system. For example, explanatory maneuvers that allow one to feel responsible for good performances and blame someone or something for failures (e.g., Arkin and Baumgardner 1985) are cognitive strategies that serve a self-regulatory function. In tandem, interpersonal and cognitive strategies of self-regulation effectively hold the self-system within healthy limits on critical indicators.

Personhood

According to our definition, the self-system, along with personality and physical characteristics, "defines the person." A brief discussion of aspects of the person that we view as distinct from (though related to) the self will bring our notion of the self-system into sharper relief. Consistent with McAdams's (1995) model of the person, we view personality as antecedent to the self. To understand the basis for this assertion, consider the three levels of personhood proffered by McAdams:

- **Level I: traits.** These are "broad, decontextualized, and relatively nonconditional constructs . . . a dispositional signature" (p. 365). Collectively, they represent what classically is known as personality (e.g., shyness, dominance). Their influence on the behavior of the individual transcends circumstances such as time and place and, because these more immediate concerns can be highly salient, may not influence behavior at all (Caspi and Moffit 1993).

- **Level II: personal concerns**. These include "personal strivings, life tasks, defense mechanisms, coping strategies, domain-specific skills and values, and a wide assortment of other motivational, developmental, or strategic constructs that are contextualized in time, place, or role" (p. 365). The overlap between this level of personhood and the self-system as we have described it is apparent.
- **Level III: evolving identity**. This is our term for what McAdams describes as "the person's identity as an internalized and evolving life story" (p. 365). Here, McAdams is referring to the larger concerns of personhood that deal with meaning and purpose in life. Specifically, individuals define themselves with reference to a set of values and strivings that provide personally meaningful context for their thoughts and actions.

McAdams's (1995) eloquent analysis of personhood clearly places personality in the background and the self in the foreground of personal experience, a position that would characterize any treatment of the self (such as ours) that is primarily social in orientation. Nevertheless, it is not uncommon to see the terms "personality" and "self" used interchangeably or the self portrayed as a facet of personality (e.g., Markus 1983). As McAdams's analysis and our definition make clear, the self-system is influenced by personality but is not synonymous with it.

Similarly, physical attributes, though consequential in the thoughts, feelings, and motives that constitute the self-system, are distinct from it. *Perceptions* of physical attributes, *evaluations* of physical appearance, and *feelings* of physical health and vitality are clearly part of the self-system, but these are *interpreted* notions of the body, not the body itself. We should note that we part company with some self theorists in drawing the distinction between the physical body and the psychological self. James (1950) saw the body as the most fundamental component of the material self, which, in his model, corresponds to possessions. (He described the body as "intimately ours.") Use of the term "self" in this manner risks construing the notion of self in such broad and encompassing terms that it loses integrity as a distinct object of empirical research. An alternative view, one that is consistent with our view of the self as a psychological construct, is that perceptions, evaluations, and feelings associated with one's body, but not the body per se, are part of the knowledge base that forms the structure of the self-system.

This internalization of the interpreted sense of body, along with a large measure of additional subjectively encoded information about oneself (e.g., intellectual ability, social skill), contributes to what we term the "enduring experience of physical and psychological existence." Here we are referring most directly to the notion of consciousness of oneself as a complex, multifaceted being, related to and dependent on other people, places, and objects, but distinct from them. Admittedly, there are various levels of consciousness, and it would appear that even the simplest of living species can distinguish itself from the environment. Clearly, the experience of consciousness in human beings far exceeds this rudimentary form of self-recognition to include not only the capacity to self-reflect, a capacity shared with other primate species (Gallup 1977), but the capacity to set goals, plan behavior, foresee consequences, and guard the integrity of the self (Sedikides and Skowronski 1997).

Continuity and Predictability

Voicing an observation that is as profound as it is obvious, Allport (1943) stated, "The existence of one's own self is the one fact of which every mortal person—every psychologist included—is perfectly convinced" (p. 451).[4] We would extend Allport's observation to include the perhaps more obvious observation that the self is *always* present (though, as Wicklund 1979, notes, not always influential)—a psychological and phenomenological constant. One might lose an organ or a limb, but the self cannot be excised from the person. The self is continuous, though not unchanging, across time and circumstances and, as a result, it anchors personal and social experience. Of course, the self undergoes change. But amid even the most profound changes in the self-system is the reassuring truth that the "I" that gave way to slumber last evening is the same "I" that greeted the new day this morning.

The implications of this continuity are perhaps best understood by considering what subjective experience would be like were the self not continuous across time and circumstances. Imagine facing a challenging task with no sense of how likely it is you will fail or how others might treat you if you do (Bandura 1997). Or consider how volatile social life would be without a consistent basis for choosing interaction partners and social situations (Swann 1985; Swann, Stein-Seroussi, and Giesler 1992). Indeed, on what basis would people contemplate, evaluate, and plan social behavior apart from a continuous experience of self? Continuity in the experience of self and reflexivity are essential qualities of the self-system.

---

[4]In sharp contrast, Epstein and Koerner (1986) state, "People have always . . . invented inner agents, mental processes, traits, and cognitive structures which—grammatically, anyway—seem to explain things. The self-concept and its close relatives, self-knowledge, and self-awareness, are a subset of the many inventions of this sort which have been handed down to modern psychology" (p. 27)

Reflexivity

A characteristic that sets humans apart from all other species is the ability to self-reflect. By self-reflection, we mean more than the pervasive and rudimentary capacity of living organisms to distinguish between self and environment, or even the ability of some nonhuman primates to recognize themselves and use this recognition as a basis for reasoning (Sedikides and Skowronski 1997). The degree of reflexivity of the human self-system is remarkable, and the consequences of that reflexivity are profound.

Rosenberg (1990) defined **reflexivity** as "the process of an entity acting back upon itself" (p. 3). The processes and consequences of reflexivity can be divided into two broad categories: reflexive thinking and reflexive action. Rosenberg (1990) refers to these processes, respectively, as reflexive cognition and reflexive agency.

- **Reflexive cognition** refers to the uniquely human capacity to bring all cognitive processes of which we are capable to bear on ourselves. Just as people can remember and think about other objects of which they are aware, they can remember and think about the self.
- **Reflexive agency** refers to the ability to act on oneself so as to cause one's own behavior. Just as people can manipulate circumstances or other people to produce intended outcomes, they can manipulate the thoughts, feelings, and motives that constitute the self-system.

The process by which humans think and behave reflexively involves self-awareness. As noted earlier, many, if not all, living organisms evince a rudimentary level of self-awareness. The unique qualities of human self-awareness are perhaps best understood when compared with self-awareness in other species. In a provocative treatment of self-awareness, Sedikides and Skowronski (1997) integrated principal assumptions of evolutionary psychology with findings from research on self-awareness in primates and humans. This integration led them to distinguish between three levels of self-awareness. We position these along a self-awareness continuum, depicted in Figure 2.1. The most rudimentary form of self-awareness, **subjective self-awareness**, involves the fundamental distinction between self and environment. This level of self-awareness, which is a nonconscious characteristic of all living organisms, contributes to the basic survival of the organism by allowing it to manipulate and maneuver within its environment (Lewis 1992).

A more sophisticated level of self-awareness, one documented only in humans and certain nonhuman primates, is objective self-awareness. **Objective self-awareness** is conscious and cognitive. By virtue of objective self-awareness, an organism can think about itself and be aware that it is

FIGURE 2.1   Levels of Self-Awareness

Subjective	Objective	Symbolic
All living organisms	Humans Chimpanzees Orangutans	Humans

SOURCE: The symbolic self in evolutionary context, by C. Sedikides and J. J. Skowronski. 1997. *Personality and Social Psychology Review* 1: 80–102.

doing so (Sedikides and Skowronski 1997). In addition to humans, chimpanzees and orangutans evince the capacity for objective self-awareness, which seems to depend on interactions with others. This latter point is illustrated in Gallup's (1977) classic research on chimpanzees. To demonstrate self-recognition, Gallup anesthetized young chimpanzees, placed red marks on one eyebrow and one ear, then, when they had fully recovered, exposed them to a mirror. The chimps not only noticed the red marks on their body; they used the mirror as a means of inspecting the marks, thereby showing clear evidence of self-recognition. In subsequent research, Gallup demonstrated that chimps raised in isolation from birth did not develop a rudimentary self-awareness until they were housed with other chimps for a few months. This intriguing program of research illustrates two important points about self-awareness, first, that humans are not unique in their capacity for objective self-awareness and, second, that social interaction is critical to the development of a sense of self-awareness.

Further along the self-awareness continuum is **symbolic self-awareness,** the uniquely human capacity to form, refer to, and communicate an abstract representation of oneself (Sedikides and Skowronski 1997). Symbolic self-awareness gives rise to the symbolic self, which is an elaborate knowledge structure that underlies most of the phenomena that we have grouped under the selfhood rubric. Symbolic self-awareness and the resultant symbolic self are central to interpersonal communication, goal setting, goal-directed action, self-evaluation, self-referent emotions (e.g., guilt, shame), and self-protective strategies (Sedikides and Skowronski 1997; see also Rosenberg 1988). Indeed, the contents of the remainder of this book are primarily an elaboration on the strategies and experiences that result from symbolic self-awareness.

The reflexivity made possible by self-awareness is both a blessing and a curse. Awareness of self and the ability to project the self backward and forward in time is critical to survival in a complex social world. Sedikides and Skowronski (1997) noted a number of survival-oriented advantages to reflexivity such as the ability to plan behavior based on past experience and the ability to internalize in-group values and attitudes, thereby increasing cooperation within groups and raising the likelihood of success in competition between groups. The downside to this capacity for reflexivity is the relatively constant reminder of oneself. The same ability that allows people to plan their behavior by projecting themselves forward in time reminds them that they could fail or fall short of what others expect (Markus and Nurius 1996). And, although self-reflection can prolong the afterglow of praise for a job well done, it can serve as a constant reminder of significant losses or failures (Pyszczynski and Greenberg 1987).

Because of this downside to self-awareness, the symbolic self, which has taken center stage in the lives of twentieth-century humans, is sometimes a burden (Baumeister 1987). Most people bear the burden of self through strategic and adaptive application of cognitive and behavioral strategies of self-regulation (Carver and Scheier 1982); however, some are unable to do so and resort to drastic measures, such as masochism or suicide, to escape the burden of self (Baumeister 1988, 1990).

Dynamic Properties

Reflexivity coupled with the richness and uncertainty of social life renders the self a dynamic system. By **dynamic**, we mean that the self-system routinely and continuously compensates for or adjusts to information from outside the system. Such information, which arises during social encounters as well as through impersonal mechanisms of feedback (e.g., reports of test scores), can be relevant to identity, competency, or control. For instance, finding out that a new acquaintance perceives one to be politically conservative when one is, in fact, liberal requires social behavior that asserts and reaffirms one's political identity. Similarly, faring poorly on an important examination when one ordinarily performs well requires casting the performance in a light that diminishes its impact on self-perceptions of competency. And, learning that one was treated unfairly in the job-selection process might motivate behaviors designed to bolster feelings of control over future outcomes. In each of these instances, motivated strategic behavior or thought serves the purpose of restoring a temporarily unsettled self-system to a state of equilibrium.

The research literature in social psychology includes many examples of the dynamic properties of the self-system. For instance, when people are provided with psychological test results that contradict their self-view, they discredit the test and their subsequent self-descriptions are negligibly affected by the feedback (Markus 1977). What happens if people are not provided such an opportunity to respond to feedback that contradicts their self-views? When competent people learn of a poor performance in a public forum, and they are not asked to respond to the feedback, their self-esteem, ironically, increases (Greenberg and Pyszczynski 1985). This *compensatory self-inflation* appears to be an instance of self-regulation initiated within the self-system when behavioral strategies of self-regulation are not possible. Indeed, the self-system can be set into action by the mere presence of other people with particular characteristics: Young women's ratings of their own attractiveness are more positive after viewing a photograph of an unattractive woman than after viewing a photograph of an attractive woman (Brown et al. 1992). Such contrast effects provide compelling evidence that the self-system is responsive to the social environment. At a more general level, people might *disidentify* with—or render irrelevant to their identity—people or activities that consistently contribute to devaluation of the self, thereby becoming "psychologically insulated" from the threat to the self-system posed by the people or activities (Steele 1992). These findings are representative of research that demonstrates the dynamic functioning of the self-system (see also Fazio, Effrein, and Falender 1981; Morse and Gergen 1970). Taken together, the results of these research studies establish the sensitivity of the self-system to social information, and the impressive ability of the system to adjust to that information.

(Apparently) Contradictory Features of the Self

The final part of our definition points up several apparent contradictions or inconsistencies in the structure and functioning of the self-system. For instance, though the self-system is responsive to an ever changing social matrix, it is, at another level, quite stable over time. Although there is great variety in the thoughts, feelings, and motives that constitute the self-system, there is considerable evidence of unity. Some aspects and activities of the self-system are not directly influenced by other people, whereas others rely almost exclusively on the perceived opinions or evaluations of other people. Although people are aware of much of the content of the self-system, there are self-referent thoughts, feelings, and motives of which people are not fully aware. And, though the content of self-knowledge may seem to vary across situations or relationships, it actually is relatively fixed. These seeming contradictions or inconsistencies are only apparent, and a deeper consideration reveals that they are adaptive characteristics of a complex, flexible, and resilient system.

Responsive Yet Stable

If, as the symbolic interactionists assert, the self is entwined with social life, then it is reasonable to ask how people maintain a relatively stable view of themselves in a social arena that is constantly changing. As noted in the earlier sections on self-regulation and dynamic qualities of the self-system, the key to stability of the self-system is its responsiveness to the social forces that routinely impinge upon it. This responsiveness contributes to stability because the self-system is not passive when affected by social forces, a characteristic that would lead to change in the self that mirrors change in the social environment (cf. Baumgardner 1990; Brockner 1983). Rather, the self-regulating characteristic of the self-system gives rise to cognitive and behavioral strategies that countervail in the face of social inputs that challenge the self.

A compelling example of this tug-of-war between the self-system and the social environment is the spontaneous self-concept—self-knowledge available to a person in a particular context upon self-reflection (McGuire and McGuire 1982). When children are asked to describe themselves, they are most likely to mention self-aspects that distinguish them from other individuals in the immediate social environment. For instance, the greater the proportion of other-sex people living in the home, the more likely children are to mention their sex when asked to describe themselves (McGuire and McGuire 1981). This and other similar findings support the distinctiveness postulate, which states that the most salient aspects of self-knowledge in a particular social setting will be those characteristics that distinguish the individual from others in that setting or in typical social settings (McGuire and Padawer-Singer 1976). For present purposes, the distinctiveness postulate is an example of the responsiveness of the self-system to the social environment and of the manner in which that responsiveness contributes to stability as opposed to change in self-knowledge.

Another take on responsiveness and stability is self-verification theory (Swann 1983). According to self-verification theory, people seek to confirm their self-concepts because stability of self-conception underlies stability of social life. Perceived stability of social life contributes to perceived control over social outcomes. So strong is this need for perceived control that people who view themselves negatively, when given a choice, choose to interact with people who evaluate them unfavorably rather than with people who evaluate them favorably (Swann, Stein-Seroussi, and Giesler 1992). Thus the choice of interaction partners is one means by which the self-system, in an ongoing struggle with potentially contradictory social forces, remains stable.

In summary, the self is, at the same time, responsive to social forces but stable in the face of highly variable social inputs. The apparent contradiction between these two characteristics is resolved when the nature of the responsiveness is made clear. With rare exception, the self is not battered about by prevailing social winds. Rather, individuals exert control over the social forces that impinge upon them and, when those forces challenge their self-conceptions, social and cognitive strategies of self-regulation can act to raise rather than lower confidence in those self-conceptions.

Complex Yet Unified

The self-system comprises a complex web of thoughts, feelings, and motives. Research indicates that particular thoughts, feelings, and motives become associated in memory to varying degrees, rendering coherent clusters of self-referent information (e.g., Markus and Wurf 1987). These clusters have been variously referred to as *self-schemas* (Markus 1977), *self-aspects* (Linville 1985), *self-views* (Pelham and Swann 1989), *self-attributes* (Higgins, Van Hook, and Dorfman 1988), *components* (Donahue et al. 1993), and *domains* (Hoyle 1991). The information they typically comprise can be conceptualized in various ways. For instance, the different social roles individuals adopt (e.g., student, spouse, team member) may give rise to coherent clusters of self-knowledge relevant to the enactment of those roles (e.g., Stryker 1987). Alternatively, self-aspects can be conceptualized in terms of salient dimensions of personal and social experience such as physical appearance, social competence, and general competence or ability (e.g., Harter 1985a; Hoyle 1991). In Chapter 3 we detail how self-aspects emerge from social experience, and in Chapter 4 we discuss the implications of different numbers and arrays of self-aspects.

Private and Public

Not only does the self comprise multiple facets, only a subset of which are engaged at any point in time, but those facets can be experienced or reflected on from different perspectives (Buss 1980; Fenigstein 1987; Higgins 1987). Two general perspectives that figure prominently in social-psychological accounts of the self and self-referent phenomena are private and public. The **private perspective** involves self-reflection in the purest sense. It is the individual's experience or understanding of self in light of his or her personal values, ideals, and standards. The **public perspective** is the experience or understanding of self with reference to the values, ideals, or standards of other people. We must be careful not to portray these two modes of self-reflection as independent (Tetlock and Manstead 1985; Wicklund and Gollwitzer 1987). Indeed, it is hard to imagine personal values, ideals, or standards, no matter how strongly embraced, that were not formed or adopted in interactions with significant others (Stryker 1987). Similarly, it is hard to imagine that an individual's understanding of the values, ideals, or standards of a significant other are not colored by his or her personal values, ideals, and standards (Greenwald 1980). The line between private and public experiences of self is fuzzy, indeed.

In addition to private and public perspectives on the self, there is private and public *knowledge* about the self (Froming, Walker, and Lopyan 1982; Scheier and Carver 1981, 1983). **Private self-knowledge** is information about oneself to which observers are not privy, such as undisclosed thoughts, feelings, and motives. **Public self-knowledge** encompasses thoughts, feelings, and motives disclosed (intentionally or not) during conversation, on apparel, or by choice of social setting or interaction partner. Private self-knowledge is implicated in self-regulatory strategies that concern fidelity to personal goals and values (Carver and Scheier 1981), whereas public self-knowledge is implicated in the wide variety of impression management strategies identified by social psychologists (Leary 1995).

Conscious and Nonconscious

Traditional methods of assessing characteristics of the self-system have involved self-report measures of various kinds. As a result, researchers were for many years restricted to studying characteristics of the self that people can reliably report (Wylie 1974). Perhaps because psychology is strongly committed to empirical methods of inquiry (i.e., one should not "stray far from the data"), theorizing about the self tended to focus on characteristics of the self that are available for introspection (e.g., Allport 1955; Rogers 1951). Only recently have investigators begun to develop strategies of assessment that extract information about the self-system of which respondents are not readily aware, thereby rendering nonconscious characteristics of the self available for empirical study. Information produced by these strategies, which are described and illustrated in Chapter 4, indicates a number of important nonconscious characteristics that have significantly influenced contemporary accounts of the self.

Perhaps the most influential methodological advance in the study of the self is the application of research strategies developed for the study of information processing to the study of self-referent phenomena (Kihlstrom et al. 1988). These strategies include such tacks as priming, word associates, response latencies, and various forms of recall, which, when creatively applied, provide a compelling basis for drawing inferences about information processing structures and mechanisms. Each of these methods allows researchers to tap into aspects of the self-system of which people might not be aware. Pioneering applications of these strategies by Markus (1977) and Rogers, Kuiper, and Kirker (1977) signaled a new era in the study of the self. Indeed, findings from studies that used the information processing approach form the foundation for contemporary treatments of the self such as ours (see reviews by Greenwald and Pratkanis 1984; Kihlstrom et al. 1988). One virtue of these strategies is the access they provide to nonconscious self-referent phenomena such as selective processing of self-referent information

(Markus 1977) and the role of self-knowledge in processing of information not explicitly relevant to the self (Rogers, Kuiper, and Kirker 1977).

Other approaches—variations on the self-report method—also show promise as means of tapping nonconscious aspects of the self. For instance, statistical variability in repeated assessments of self-esteem gauges stability of self-esteem, a characteristic that people seem unable to accurately report about themselves (Kernis, Grannemann, and Barclay 1992). As illustrated in Chapter 4, self-ratings on adjectives (e.g., *competent, kind, failure*) as they apply to various self-aspects (e.g., "me as student," "me with my friends") can be arrayed as a Self-Aspect x Trait matrix and analyzed in various ways to provide a picture of the degree of differentiation of self-knowledge (e.g., Donahue et al. 1993; Linville 1985; Showers 1992a). Such information appears to be nonconscious and, therefore, inaccessible via traditional self-report instruments (Nisbett and Wilson 1977). More importantly, nonconscious aspects of the self-system such as stability and differentiation have important implications for social interaction and well-being.

Variable and Fixed

How can the self be both variable and fixed? This seeming contradiction is resolved in an elegant model of the self-concept offered by Markus and Kunda (1986). Their model was inspired by a schism in the empirical literature on the stability of self-concept. Whereas results of some research in that literature indicate that self-concept is relatively fixed (e.g., Markus 1977; Swann and Read 1981), other research findings suggest that the self-concept is quite variable (e.g., Alexander and Knight 1971; McGuire and McGuire 1982). In Markus and Kunda's model, this schism is bridged by the notion of a working self-concept. The *working self-concept* is one of a universe of specialized self-conceptions that, together, constitute the self-concept as typically defined. The particular working self-concept that is active at a particular moment depends on the social forces impinging on the person, the personal resources he or she has recruited to interact or problem solve, and the immediately prior working self-concept. Importantly, the working self-concept engaged in a particular circumstance is but one of a relatively stable constellation of working self-concepts. Thus, at the situational level, the self appears variable, whereas across situations, the self appears stable (see also Damon and Hart 1986; Pelham and Wachsmuth 1995).

Putting It All Together

The self-system is a rich, dynamic psychological system that exerts substantial influence over people's understanding of themselves and their world. As a system, the self is multifaceted and organized, reliably performing a limited number of basic functions that contribute to survival in a complex social world. Humans' extensive capacity for self-reflection, coupled with the self-regulating nature of the self-system in an ever changing social arena, gives rise to a dynamic, fluid system of thoughts, feelings, and motives that is stable yet flexible.

We now turn to a consideration of people's subjective experience of the self-system—how they understand and define themselves.

3

Identity

Identity is the storied self—*the self as it is made into a story by the person whose self it is.*

—McAdams (1995, 385)

Because of the diversity in how the self can be described, social psychologists have been interested in the processes whereby people select what kinds of information to emphasize when thinking about themselves. Ponder for a moment the number of things you do in the course of an average day. For example, you probably make a lot of choices—what to have for breakfast, what clothes to wear, which friends to spend time with, and maybe what form of entertainment to get involved in during any spare time. You undoubtedly take part in all sorts of activities, from reading a book to engaging in some form of exercise to washing the dishes after a meal. You probably have many different kinds of interactions, such as arguing with a family member, complying with an employer's demands, or gossiping with a neighbor.

Importantly, the way people make sense of such actions determines what, if anything, those actions say about their identity. Action identification theory (Vallacher and Wegner 1985) specifies that any action can be construed or interpreted in an almost unlimited number of ways. Going bicycling, for example, can be construed as "exploring the countryside" or "getting a workout" or, more simply, "pedaling from A to B." Thinking of a bicycle trip as pedaling from one place to another is fairly irrelevant to a person's self-image. Thinking of it as "getting a workout," on the other hand, would probably lead the person to monitor how hard he or she is pedaling and to think of himself or herself as "athletic" rather than, for example, "adventurous." Whether deliberately or unintentionally, people take the raw data of experience and transform it to be part of their sense of self.

The most straightforward way to study identity is to ask people to describe themselves. In the Twenty Statements Test (Kuhn and McPartland

1954), for example, research participants are asked to write twenty sentences beginning with "I am . . ." As illustrated in the set of completed statements shown in Table 3.1, people typically report a whole range of self-aspects, including their personality traits ("truthful," "helpful"), physical characteristics ("girl," "tall for my age"), social roles ("friends with anybody"), and opinions and preferences ("I like several boys/girls").

Some descriptions emphasize the person's membership in social groups or categories, such as being a woman or a man, being African-American, or being Scottish—*social identities* that provide a "we-feeling" and give a sense of belongingness and similarity to other members of the same group. At the same time, people also report aspects of their *personal identity*, involving their unique characteristics, such as traits and preferences, that define how they differ from others (Tajfel and Turner 1986; Turner et al. 1987).

Self-descriptions can include both general aspects that characterize the person most or all of the time and situationally specific aspects that describe the person in particular situations. For instance, it is not difficult for most people to describe themselves in general terms, such as being honest, having a short temper, and so on. Yet knowledge about the self is typically considerably more detailed than that, and it usually includes representations of what kind of person one is in different situations. A person might

TABLE 3.1   Response from an 11-Year-Old Girl in the Sixth Grade to the Question, Who Am I?

My name is _____ .
I'm a human being.
I'm a girl.
I'm a truthful person.
I'm not pretty.
I do so-so in my studies.
I'm a very good cellist.
I'm a very good pianist.
I'm a little bit tall for my age.
I like several boys.
I like several girls.
I'm old-fashioned.
I play tennis.
I am a *very* good swimmer.
I try to be helpful.
I'm always ready to be friends with anybody.
Mostly I'm good, but I lose my temper.
I'm not well-liked by some girls and boys.
I don't know if I'm liked by boys or not.

SOURCE: From The Development of Self-Conceptions from Childhood to Adolescence, by R. Montemayor and M. Eisen. 1977. *Developmental Psychology* 13: 314–319. Copyright 1977 by the American Psychological Association. Adapted with permission.

say, for example, "I am easygoing when I'm with friends, but I get angry and aggressive when I get stuck in traffic." For this reason, many people feel that general trait descriptors do not adequately capture the complexity of their own behavior, insisting that they can be either easygoing or angry, energetic or relaxed, honest or dishonest, depending on the situation (Sande, Goethals, and Radloff 1988).

The Socially Constructed Self

As we have shown, people construct a sense of self by selecting certain types of information about their own behaviors and drawing inferences about what they mean about themselves and their place in the world. Upon closer examination, it becomes apparent that this process of constructing a sense of self is something people do not typically do alone; rather, they do it in their interactions with other people.

Even a person's most basic sense of his or her own existence seems to depend on interactions with others. Recall Gallup's (1977) studies, in which he put makeup on anesthetized chimpanzees. In one of his experiments, a number of the chimpanzees had been raised alone, kept apart from other chimps from birth. Without the benefit of a history of ongoing interaction with others—playing, fighting, competing, and cooperating—these chimps had not developed a rudimentary self-awareness. When one of them would look in the mirror, it would not recognize that the ape with the red spot on its eyebrow was in fact itself; it would bob back and forth, make threatening gestures, and generally treat the mirror reflection the way it would act toward another unknown chimp.

Gallup and his colleagues then went one step further. They took two of these isolated chimpanzees and housed them together in the same cage for a few months. After this period, which allowed the chimpanzees to experience themselves in interaction with each other, the chimps started to show the beginnings of self-recognition. A third, however, who had been kept in isolation, did not.

So it seems that interaction with others is an important requirement for the establishment of the most basic sense of self. Let's examine some of the ways in which our interpersonal world shapes and defines our identity.

Interpersonal Sources of Selfhood:
From Intersubjectivity to Reflected Appraisal

A core sense of self arises at a young age from experiences of intersubjectivity, a state of connection and mutual understanding that emerges during interaction with another person (Neisser 1988; Stern 1985). Intersubjectivity involves a sense of coordination between one's own and others' actions. It first develops in the common experiences of early infancy—being cuddled by parents, looking into their eyes and being looked at in return, playing peek-a-boo games, and the like—which involve nonverbal and emotional give-and-take between infant and caregiver. Gradually the infant learns to share with others a range of subjective experiences, such as intentions, attention to something in the environment, or emotional states. Infant and adult might communicate that they both are excited and happy, or sad and sleepy, for example, and the way in which the infant's experiences mesh with the caregiver's responses helps the infant to clarify and recognize his or her own behavior and internal states.

Here are the beginnings of how social interaction defines identity: Intentionally or unintentionally, the adult can influence the infant's developing sense of self by selecting and emphasizing certain aspects of the infant's experience. When the child takes a tumble, for example, the parent can reflect back the silliness and fun of the situation, or, conversely, the danger and fear that the child might be feeling, and the child may use this communication to frame his or her own experiences.

A reasonable degree of match between the child's experience and the adult's feedback is necessary in order to establish a state of intersubjectivity; different types of mismatches, such as when the caregiver fails to reflect the same emotional tone or energy level that the infant is feeling, can make the infant quite distressed and may lead to the development of a disrupted sense of self (Stern 1985). Along these same lines, Bowlby (1969) described how children learn the interaction patterns commonly experienced with a caregiver, particularly with respect to how emotionally available and responsive the adult will be. A core sense of self-worth also is shaped by these interactions: Whereas a child who receives warm, accepting reactions from other people will be likely to develop a secure sense of his or her goodness and worth, a child who is often ignored, or whose experiences of intersubjectivity are tinged with an element of hostility or rejection by the caregiver, may begin to develop a negative or insecure sense of self-worth.

Symbolic Interactionism and the Reflected Self

The nature of intersubjectivity moves to a new level as the child learns to speak. With the development of language comes the ability to interact with others in terms of symbols, including a symbolic or conceptual self. Children gradually begin to use the pronouns "I" and "me" and to recognize their own existence as an object in the world (Cooley 1908). At the same time, generally between the ages of two and four years, they come to the realization that other people have minds and thoughts of their own.

Then, putting it all together, they come to entertain the notion that *these other people can think about me!* When a boy's mother says, "You put away your toys—good boy!" for example, he can understand that she is thinking about him as an obedient son and has positive feelings about him.

Some of the most influential writers on this topic of perspective taking and identity were Cooley (1902) and Mead (1934). As noted in Chapter 1, Cooley likened the process of self-reflection to looking in a mirror. He said that people first imagine the way they must appear to other people, and then they consider the likely evaluation or judgment those people have of them. What people conclude about how other people evaluate them might be based on actual statements or reactions those people make, or they might just be assumed or inferred based on past interactions.

Mead (1934) elaborated on this process, writing that "the individual experiences himself as such, not directly, but only indirectly, from the particular standpoints of other individual members of the same social group, or from the generalized standpoint of the social group as a whole to which he belongs. For he . . . becomes an object to himself only by taking the attitudes of other individuals toward himself" (p. 138).

Different social perspectives can be used in thinking about the self. One can experience one's self in terms of how one relates to a specific person, such as a particular friend, teacher, or companion. Or one can imagine how one would be seen by some **reference group** whose acceptance one desires ("I wonder what the cool people at the tennis courts thought of my new plaid socks?"). Mead described a second stage in the establishment of identity, though, in which the person goes beyond imagining how he or she appears to specific other people. Over time, on the basis of experience with many different audiences and a variety of contexts, the individual organizes, and then generalizes, the attitudes of particular others. Rather than thinking "Mom thinks I'm lazy" and "Uncle Joe thinks I'm lazy" and "my pal Ned thinks I'm lazy," the person forms the generalization that "people think I'm lazy." Mead termed this abstracted social perspective the **generalized other** and saw it as the internal representation of the larger community in which one takes part.

Mead's (1934) emphasis was on the social functions of reflexivity—how learning to see ourselves through others' eyes helps us navigate our interactions with them. He described social interaction using the metaphor of playing on a baseball team. In order to play successfully, a player must first understand the rules of the game and the kinds of events that one can reasonably anticipate happening. Part of this understanding is knowing what each player is likely to do in a given situation—the pitcher throws the ball toward home plate; if the batter hits the ball, the fielders try to catch it and throw it to the player tending first base, and so on. Critical to a successful baseball team is that each player can anticipate what the others will do;

otherwise the player on first base might not be looking in the right direction at the right time when the ball is thrown. Each player on the team thus learns his or her own role, and also learns to anticipate how the other members of the team will orient their behavior toward him or her. Successful orientation of a complex activity like this requires the ability to take the others' perspective and imagine what others are thinking about oneself. A similar analysis could be made of any attempt to negotiate social interaction, for example, when conversing with a prospective employer, dating partner, or clergyperson. A great deal of cognitive effort usually goes into trying to anticipate how the other person will react to certain things one might say or do. Just talking with a friend involves anticipating how one's statements will be interpreted and what the friend will think of one as a result. Interactions with other people influence how we think about ourselves.

For example, conversations can bring to mind some subset of information from a person's pool of self-relevant knowledge. This process is illustrated in a study by Deutsch and Mackesy (1985). They had research participants pair up with each other and talk about the characteristics of different target people. Sometime later, the participants were then asked to describe themselves. Analysis of their self-descriptions showed that the categories and characteristics they reported when describing themselves tended to be the ones they had used when communicating to the other participant, that is, their self-portrayal was made up of the constructs that had come to the fore in the earlier conversation. The authors suggested that certain understandings and perspectives gradually become habitual, even taken for granted, when they are repeatedly part of the shared reality between friends.

An even more direct means by which social interaction can affect identity is through explicit feedback from others. When someone you know tells you that you are "smart" or "inconsiderate" or "a good cook," these comments can lead you to think about yourself in a new way. Whether or not one is persuaded by feedback of this nature depends in part on the kinds of factors studied in social-psychological research on persuasion: One is more likely to believe a person who is perceived as highly competent (e.g., a music teacher who says you have perfect pitch) or whose views are supported by others (Backman, Secord, and Pierce 1963; Eisenstadt and Leippe 1994). Also, one is more likely to attend to feedback from important or significant people in one's life (Rosenberg 1973).

The sense of self is shaped by interaction with others, then, and these encounters continue to influence one's self even when the other people are no longer around, particularly if one anticipates interacting with them again (e.g., Hardin and Higgins 1996). We might imagine interactions with them, thinking about what we would say or do, how other people would see us and respond, and so on. Indeed, numerous writers have observed that even when we are sitting alone, with no one else around, our thoughts often involve conversations with or performances for a kind of "private audience" of other people (Baldwin and Holmes 1987). As with real flesh-and-blood audiences, our private audience can consist of all manner of different people, based on real and imaginary relationships; people carry on internal conversations with friends, family members, therapists, and even media figures (Gergen 1991; Schlenker 1985a). In one study, for example, university students who had a good friendship with their roommates also tended to engage in many positive imaginary interactions with them (Honeycutt and Patterson 1997). At times the experience might be of an abstract, generic audience, as captured in the notions of generalized other (Mead 1934) or "chorus" (Berger and Luckmann 1967, 151). These internally represented interactions and performances represent the internalization of the social world, and they are thought to be a major factor in the social construction of identity.

Consider the following experiment by Baldwin and Holmes (1987). Undergraduate women first were asked to perform a short exercise in which they spent a few moments imagining being with specific significant others. Some participants were told to imagine being with their parents; others were told to visualize being with two friends from campus. During this exercise they closed their eyes and were instructed to "picture the other person's face" and "imagine what it is like to be with this person." Ten minutes later in a different context, they were asked to rate their enjoyment of a number of written passages, one of which was a sexually permissive story taken from a popular women's magazine. (This story described a young woman contemplating having sex with a good-looking man whom she did not know well.) As the researchers predicted, women who had visualized their parents in the first phase of the experiment rated the erotic passage as less enjoyable and exciting than did those who had visualized their (presumably more permissive) college friends. This finding that the "private audience" shaped the participants' sense of self and sense of appropriate behavior was also supported by some anecdotal evidence. At the end of the experiment, one woman said that she had felt embarrassed that it was taking her so long to fill out the rating scale for the sexual passage. She reported that as she was trying to answer the questions about how exciting she found the passage, she began arguing intensely, in fantasy, with her mother about which number to circle. When asked, she said that it had not occurred to her that the earlier guided visualization of her parents might have been the source of her later conflictual fantasy.

Interpersonal sources of identity, then, involve experiences of intersubjectivity—starting in infancy and continuing throughout life. They also involve perspective taking, or imagining how one is seen by other people. The way one thinks and feels about oneself, and even the way one regulates one's behavior, is shaped by real and imaginary interactions with others.

Self-Presentation and Negotiating the Social Self

If our identity is shaped and maintained to a large extent by our interactions with others, does this mean that our sense of who we are is completely determined by feedback from others about how *they* see us? Are we at the mercy of others' opinions? Probably not, or at least not entirely. Research on the social construction of the self has *not* supported the simplistic prediction that people's self-views might perfectly mirror the views that others have; in fact, the correlation or overlap between the two generally is fairly low (Shrauger and Schoeneman 1979). That is, if a researcher asked you how you saw yourself and then asked your friends, family, coworkers, and others who know you well how they saw you, the two descriptions would not necessarily match. Many people are relatively inaccurate in judging the kinds of impressions they are making on others, in part because others' reactions are shaped by their own personalities, motives, and willingness to give honest feedback rather than by how they really feel (DePaulo et al. 1987).

However, in some instances the link between self-concept and social feedback is fairly strong. For example, on dimensions on which people feel very certain about their standing, a high degree of correspondence exists between self-views and the opinions of significant others (Pelham and Swann 1989). More importantly, the evidence from many studies is fairly clear that people's self-views are similar to how they *think* others see them— people's sense of who they are coincides reasonably well with their own hunch about what others think of them, even if it does not always match up with what others *actually* think of them (Shrauger and Schoeneman 1979).

Because of the potential for social influence on identity, most people try to control the kinds of impressions others form of them. People's identities are not merely bestowed on them by others, then; rather, they negotiate them (Swann 1985). Social psychologists have examined in some detail the processes by which people take an active part in the social construction of their own identity. Often people seek out relationships that provide social validation for their own self-conceptions. For example, in a study of life in a sorority, Backman and Secord (1962) found that women tended to interact more often with others whom they thought saw them as they saw themselves.

Far easier than trying to limit the people with whom we interact is to try to control more directly the impressions people form. Schlenker (1980) defined **self-presentation** as the conscious or nonconscious attempt to control identity-relevant images before audiences. Stated simply, the person begins with a self-image that he or she believes to be—or wants to be—true of the self and presents that self to some audience. He or she then looks for validation of this identity in the way others respond; the reactions of others provide a confirmation of the identity.

What kinds of information are presented to others? The selection of what aspects of self to present in any given situation is usually determined by a host of factors (Leary 1995). People typically wish to be seen positively by others, both to enhance their own feelings of self-esteem and to help them achieve interpersonal goals. On the other hand, sometimes they may try to lead other people to fear them by acting in an intimidating manner in order to increase their power in social relationships. Consider the schoolyard bully who tries to frighten other children into treating him well and giving him what he wants. Sometimes people may act helpless or weak in order to solicit assistance or pity from others. The range of potential self-presentations is substantial.

Some people think that self-presentation sounds like a manipulative, even deceitful practice. Sometimes it is, of course. Clearly, sometimes people's efforts to present a certain self are completely *strategic,* explicitly aimed at impressing or manipulating others in order to achieve some goal (Baumeister 1982; Leary and Kowalski 1990). After all, as we saw in the last chapter, one reason people think about themselves is to regulate their behavior in order to meet their goals, and many of those goals involve other people. Human beings are social animals. People like to feel connected to others, whether in close relationships with family members, friends, and lovers who know them well, or just in having a sense of belonging to a group or society as a whole (Baumeister and Leary 1995). People want to get things from other people, they want to be liked, and they want to cooperate with other people to achieve some common goal. People also compete with others, and sometimes try to manipulate or intimidate them, in order to meet their goals. People often try to present a certain public self that will help them achieve their goal of being liked, being feared, or getting a better job. When people recognize their efforts at self-presentation as frankly strategic, aimed at impressing or manipulating others in order to achieve some goal, they may experience a degree of "role-distance" (e.g., Goffman 1959) such that they perceive a clear distinction between their public presentation and their true self. Of course, certain kinds of people are more likely to engage in such strategic self-presentation, but everyone does it at one time or another.

For several reasons, though, self-presentational behavior often expresses the true, privately held views of self (Baumeister 1982; Leary 1995; Schlenker 1980). First, for any interaction to proceed smoothly, the participants must have a common understanding of who each other is and what kinds of behaviors can be expected from each. Often this information needs to be conveyed quickly and efficiently. A customer and a salesperson in a store, for example, need to be able to identify each other as such so that the customer doesn't walk around asking for assistance from one person after another. Similarly, a man and a woman on a first date need to establish some common ground in terms of expectancies, wishes, and preferences. Otherwise one might suggest going someplace where they can "be alone" while the other tries to arrange a meeting for their respective parents to discuss the dowry. To facilitate the process of defining how an interaction will proceed, people present themselves the way they want and expect to be perceived, to lead people to see them as a particular type of person and treat them in a certain way.

Second, people often present a certain self precisely as a way of seeking confirming feedback from others. Schlenker (1985a) pointed out that, although people may present a range of different images of self across different situations, they still have privately held identities that they hold to and try to validate. Social psychologists have studied extensively the processes whereby people "compare notes" to negotiate a social reality together. Festinger (1954), in his theory of social comparison processes, hypothesized that people often look to others to help define ambiguous or unclear aspects of their experiences. For instance, when eating a serving of "mystery meat" in a high school cafeteria, students may compare theories about what it is and try to reach consensus on whether it is safe to eat. Similarly, when trying on a new item of clothing, most of us will solicit the opinion of others to help us decide how good it looks. As many have argued, the same reasoning applies to people's sense of self: "There are many personal qualities—friendliness, respectability, moral courage—which can only be assessed by social means or mirrored in the reactions of others to us" (Jones 1964, 17). Interestingly, we not only solicit others' input, we may attempt to manage it. Indeed, research has shown that when social feedback is highly inconsistent with people's self-concept, they are likely to go out of their way to try to convince people to see them as they see themselves (Swann and Hill 1982).

For example, a woman might see herself as a well-educated, cultured individual. If something happens to threaten that self-conception, such as being treated by others as uninformed about literature, she may go out of her way to collect and display symbols of being well read. She might show up carrying a well-thumbed copy of the *New York Times Book Review* and drinking the cafe lattés that give her that certain air of sophistication. Research has demonstrated that people whose cherished self-conceptions are threatened in this way are indeed more likely than others to use symbols, props, and the like to bolster their claim to a certain social identity (Wicklund and Gollwitzer 1982).

Even when people are strategically self-presenting to achieve some social goal, they do not usually need to fabricate an utterly false image of themselves. People have many aspects to their identity, and the task of self-presentation often involves selecting from this repertoire of self-images a particular version to suit the communicative context of the moment (Leary

1995). A key factor in determining self-presentations is the issue of believ-ability: Although in principle people could fraudulently present themselves as movie stars, millionaires, or foreign dictators (and of course people sometimes do), there is always the difficulty that interaction partners either already know something that shows these self-presentations to be untrue or would be likely to find that out somewhere down the line. Public behavior represents a commitment to a certain identity, obligating the person to con-tinue to maintain this identity in future interactions (Goffman 1959). For this reason, people tend to present a social face that is generally consistent with their true sense of who they are. This is especially the case with core, central self-beliefs that people see as essential to their identities; these self-images are the ones most likely to come to mind and thus be included in public displays. People are unlikely to risk acting inconsistently with these important self-conceptions, as this could undermine their right to claim them in the future (Schlenker 1980).

How People Self-Present

Part of establishing and maintaining an identity, then, involves presenting self-images to others. People can do this in a variety of ways. First, there are many situations in which people often come right out and describe them-selves to others, telling about their traits, their opinions, their social roles, and so on. This kind of communication happens daily in job interviews and on plane trips. It is not uncommon for people on a first date to go into great detail describing their personal histories, relationship attitudes, and desires for the future.

Various psychologists have characterized this form of self-presentation as telling a story about oneself, or a **self-narrative**. Gergen and Gergen (1988), for example, reviewed a range of self-stories or accounts that people tell, whether explaining what they had been doing that day or trying to summa-rize a whole lifetime in a single life story. McAdams (1996; see also Berger 1963) suggested that most people try to fashion a reasonably coherent life story, starting at birth and continuing through the present and into the fu-ture. He places life stories at the center of identity and analyzes the content and organization of people's life stories as a literature professor might ana-lyze a novel. Some people might tell a story that has the classic form of a romance, for example, whereas others might tell of a tragedy in which a promising beginning led to a critical turning point that was followed by ul-timate defeat.

The idea of a self-narrative accentuates the fact that people experience an overwhelming amount of information about themselves in the course of a single day. When people think about themselves, then, they necessarily select certain events that seem particularly important or representative;

then they organize them into some sequence that tells a story. The way people perform this selection and organization—the way they tell the story—determines the identity they ultimately develop. In one study of this process, McAdams et al. (1997) examined the kinds of self-narratives told by adults who were highly generative, or devoted to the well-being of the next generation. They asked a sample of popular schoolteachers and other people who were highly giving to children to describe their life as if it were a book, consisting of chapters, heroes and heroines, high and low points, and so on. When the researchers analyzed the stories, they found that these adults were particularly likely to tell a narrative that followed a "commitment script." When they recalled major events in their lives that were negative or frustrating, they tended to tell a story about how initially negative situations were eventually overcome, leading to a happy or productive ending. They were no more or less likely than anyone else to report negative and positive events in their lives, but the way they linked them together seemed to help them persevere when the going got tough, by maintaining hope that things would work out in the long run.

People have a large degree of flexibility, then, in how they construct their self-narratives. Once again, social interaction plays a role in this process. It is clear that self-narratives are shaped, from early childhood on, in communication with others. Gergen (1991) pointed out that if a young girl describes her day in kindergarten with a rambling account of the day's images including her pencil, her friend's hair, and the school flag, this narrative might seem unsatisfactory to her parents, who might proceed to lead her to a "proper" story with a beginning, a middle, and an end. Indeed, research indicates that two-and-a-half-year-old children usually can tell a story about "what happened" in a way that incorporates adult values regarding what is important to remember, how the events should be ordered, and so on (Nelson 1993).

As with any kind of self-presentation, people generally tailor their self-narratives to show themselves in a good light. For example, social psychologists have studied the way people try to explain—or explain away—instances of behavior that do not quite fit their desired self-images. If a person sees self as competent in some domain—for example, as a good driver—and then suffers a failure or setback—for example, a car accident—he or she may try to preserve the desired image by shifting the responsibility away from self. The driver may blame the weather, another driver, or a black dog that ran into the road; in fact, he or she may try out a range of possible accounts until finding an explanation that everyone agrees is acceptable and portrays the outcome in the best possible light (Schlenker 1980; Snyder and Higgins 1988).

Many of these accounts involve shifting the focus from enduring aspects of self to short-term or external factors. The notion of **self-handicapping**

(Jones and Berglas 1978), for example, suggests that a person who fears failure on a potentially self-defining task may even seek out or invent obstacles, so that if the task does end in failure there is a ready excuse. On the night before his or her driving test, for example, a student driver might stay out late partying and may even go out of her way to tell her friends about it so that if the test does not go well there will be a story to tell that preserves the valued self-image. Similarly, research inspired by action identification theory (Vallacher and Wegner 1985), reviewed earlier in the chapter, has shown that people who fail at some task often try to tell a story that portrays their actions in terms that have fewer implications for identity—by saying, for example, that "when parallel parking I stopped too far from the curb" rather than "I am no good at parking."

Self-narratives are not merely told; they are lived, as the person keeps his or her life story moving from one chapter to the next. Accordingly, some writers have likened self-presentation to being an actor instead of a storyteller. If, as Shakespeare observed, "all the world's a stage, and all its men and women merely players," then one way to examine social interaction is as a kind of extended drama in which we all adopt roles and then perform them for each other. Goffman (1959) used this **dramaturgical approach** to analyze the ways people learn socially prescribed scripts and rituals, collect the costumes and props needed to support their part, and then act out their character as compellingly as possible. A business executive, for example, might wear a well-tailored suit, carry a notebook computer, and shake hands firmly while looking people directly in the eye. If the same executive dressed in ripped jeans, carried a battered guitar, and responded to an outstretched hand with a suspicious look, the impressions of the audience might be very different. Goffman described in great detail the way people verbally and nonverbally manage their performances so that their audience—the people observing them—is led to the desired view of who they are.

Not surprisingly, people's self-presentations vary according to characteristics of the audience (Leary 1995; Schlenker 1980). James (1950) originally observed that people often present different sides of themselves, depending on who their audience is at the time. He described this multiplicity in a man's social self by saying that he "has as many different social selves as there are distinct *groups* of persons about whose opinion he cares. He generally shows a different side of himself to each of these different groups. Many a youth who is demure enough before his parents and teachers, swears and swaggers like a pirate among his 'tough' young friends" (p. 294).

In his discussion of self-narratives, McAdams (1996) agrees with James that specific public renderings of the life story often are tailored for specific audiences: "The story I tell you about myself on a first date may be very different from the one I tell at the office the next day or the one I tell my therapist next week" (p. 307). He makes it clear, however, that one feature of a "good" or "functional" life story is that it is not pulled out of thin air in order to appeal to some audience but is solidly grounded in the person's true experiences and social situation.

Internalizing the Presented Self

As mentioned earlier, people's public self-presentations often correspond reasonably well with their privately held beliefs about who they are, partly because they *want* other people to see them as they really are. In addition, however, there are a number of ways in which people can come to believe privately in the public self they present. As the symbolic interactionist notion of the looking-glass self would suggest, research has shown that people's self-presentational behaviors often have the strongest impact on their private sense of self when the behaviors in question are performed in an interpersonal context.

These phenomena are illustrated nicely in a study by Tice (1992). She wondered whether performing some action in public, in front of an audience of some kind, might lead people to incorporate the behavior into their private sense of self. She set up a situation in which she asked eighty undergraduate students to portray themselves in specific ways—as introverted, sensitive, and thoughtful or as extraverted, outgoing, and socially skilled (depending on the experimental condition to which they were randomly assigned). The student participants' task was to try to portray themselves as having the trait she assigned to them by drawing on examples from their past experience to answer some general questions about their relationships, extracurricular activities, and so on.

Half of the participants performed this task in a very public situation. They were being watched by a graduate student and they started by giving their name, hometown, and other background information. The remaining participants were in a comparatively private condition. They were left alone to recite their answers into a tape recorder and were told that the graduate student who later listened to the tape would not be given their name or any other identifying information.

After responding to the questions and presenting themselves in either an introverted or an extraverted manner, participants were asked to rate their "true" personalities on scales measuring such qualities as talkative-quiet, friendly-unfriendly, and outgoing-shy. Results showed that, as predicted, people who self-presented publicly internalized their behavior more than people who did so anonymously. Those who had been instructed to publicly self-present as introverted started to see themselves as truly introverted, whereas those instructed to self-present as extraverted came to feel truly extraverted. In the private, anonymous condition, by contrast, people's ratings of themselves were not affected by the self-presentation exercise. Something about being seen by an audience, then, led people to internalize their behavior.

Tice (1992) added another wrinkle to the study because she wanted to be sure that these experimental effects reflected something real about the participants' self-views and did not result from a desire to appear consistent to the experimenter. After the self-ratings were done, participants moved their chairs to a waiting room in which another person—actually a confederate, or helper, of the experimenter—was waiting. They were left alone for three minutes and any conversation was recorded. Then, after the participant left, a tape measure was used to measure the distance between the chairs, to see how closely the participant had positioned himself or herself to the confederate. As shown in Figure 3.1, the behavioral indicators supported the self-ratings participants had given earlier. Those who had been in the public (but not the private) condition acted in a way consistent with their earlier

FIGURE 3.1   Distance Participants Sat from the Confederate, as a Function of Self-Portrayal and Public vs. Private Self-Presentation

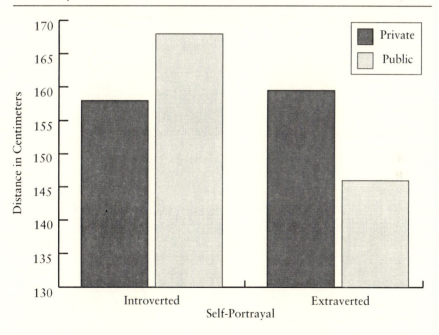

SOURCE: Self-concept change and self-presentation: The looking glass self is also a magnifying glass, by D. M. Tice. 1992. *Journal of Personality and Social Psychology* 63: 435–451. Copyright 1992 by the American Psychological Association. Adapted with permission.

self-presentation. Participants who had presented an extraverted face were twice as likely to start up a conversation and sat about eight inches closer to the confederate than those who earlier had presented an introverted self.

Tice (1992, Study 3) suggested several reasons why public behaviors lead to greater internalization than private ones. First, when self-presentations involved people drawing on their own store of personal memories (e.g., "that time I made everybody laugh" versus "those weekends when I stayed at home, curled up with a good book"), there was more internalization than in other conditions she created in which people merely read statements provided by others. This may be because of a process that has been labeled **biased scanning** (Jones et al. 1981). When people direct their attention to a certain subset of their past experience, this information subsequently affects how they think about themselves (cf. Markus and Kunda 1986).

More generally, presenting a public self of some kind can generate evidence, both external and internal, that leads people to see that role or self-narrative as accurately representing part of their true self. Bem (1972) proposed that a key process in identity construction is **self-perception:** Given that our own attitudes, personality traits, motivations, and so on may often be ambiguous or unclear to us, we are left in the position of inferring them on the basis of observations of our own behaviors. Thus a person who wanted to make a self-judgment in the domain of competitiveness would review his or her behavior in past competitive situations. If he or she usually behaved very competitively, and particularly if this behavior was freely chosen when other options (e.g., cooperation) were available, the self-inference may be of having the trait of competitiveness. As the notion of biased scanning implies, though, this self-perception process can be strongly influenced by whatever kinds of information are closest at hand or come most readily to mind. If the person has spent the last week enacting the role of "hard-driving, competitive business executive," easily recalled information about high-powered meetings, hostile takeovers, and long hours at the office may inform the self-perception process. Except in cases where obvious external pressures force a person to act in a certain way, it may be concluded that this behavior reflected his or her true self.

Internalization may also occur in a way similar to that described by actors, who often report that playing a part in a play or movie can involve getting so "caught up" in the role that it takes over their emotions temporarily (e.g., Gergen 1971, 55). Most people are not professional actors, of course, but becoming involved in one's day-to-day social roles, whether passionate lover, pious clergyperson, or angry protestor, might similarly lead to the generation of the feelings that go along with them. As Berger (1963) put it,

One feels more ardent by kissing, more humble by kneeling and more angry by shaking one's fist. That is, the kiss not only expresses ardor but manufactures it. Roles carry with them both certain actions and the emotions and attitudes that belong to these actions. The professor putting on an act that pretends to wisdom comes to feel wise. The preacher finds himself believing what he preaches. The soldier discovers martial stirrings in his breast as he puts on his uniform. In each case, while the emotion or attitude may have been present before the role was taken on, the latter inevitably strengthens what was there before. (p. 96)

A striking example of this was the classic Stanford Prison Experiment (Haney, Banks, and Zimbardo 1973), in which normal male college students were recruited to take part in a mock "prison" in the basement of the psychology building at Stanford University. Half were randomly assigned the role of prisoner; half were assigned the role of prison guard. Those playing the prisoner role were dressed in hospital gowns, and the "guards" were given badges, clubs, and reflecting sunglasses. Within a matter of days, the "guards" began to act aggressively while performing their role, going out of their way to dominate and humiliate the other men. Conversely, the "prisoners" began to react with submissiveness and passivity. After the experiment, participants reported that their sense of identity had begun to change during that short period of time. The guards began to feel more aggressive and sadistic, whereas the prisoners began to see themselves as weak. Even self-presentations that are clearly artificial and contrived, then, can come to shape and define the private sense of self.

In Tice's (1992) self-presentation study, behaviors had a greater impact on internalized self-perceptions in the public, compared to the private, condition. Tice argued that although biased scanning might occur in both circumstances, its effects might be magnified in the public situation because "metaphorically, people in the public condition may have felt as if someone were looking over their shoulder while they scanned their self-concepts" (p. 448). As depicted in the notion of the looking glass self, identity may be particularly influenced when one considers the perspectives and thoughts of others.

Tice (1992) also suggested that public commitment plays a role in internalization. She found that when people were reminded that they freely chose to participate in the self-presentation phase of the study, they were more likely to internalize their public behavior. Also, if participants expected to meet the graduate student "observer" again, their "true self" ratings were brought more closely into line with the self that was presented. This harkens back to the ideas raised at the beginning of this section: People typically present self-images that they are prepared to back up with future action. Indeed, there is an implicit norm in most, if not all, cultures that people should not pretend to be something they truly are not (Goffman 1959). If people choose to act in ways that diverge from their true identity, then they experience **cognitive dissonance**, a state of discomfort arising from having acted in an inappropriate or inconsistent manner (e.g., Aronson 1969). If it is possible to resolve the discrepancy by simply shifting a self-view somewhat so that the behavior no longer is inconsistent with it, people often will do so in order to relieve the discomfort (a detailed example is provided in Chapter 7). This allows them to maintain a uniform self, in which self-presentations, social feedback, and private self-image all converge on the same identity.

By the same token, once a person has established a degree of social reality for a certain self-image, he or she may come to expect that others will give appropriate feedback that validates that image. Berger (1963) gives the example of a man being promoted to an officer position in the army. At first he might feel like a bit of an imposter, even feeling embarrassed when soldiers of a lesser rank salute him. Over time, though, he will come to expect to be treated with deference and may even become angered if a private does not respond to him in the appropriate manner. Once having negotiated a certain valued identity, then, and having it confirmed by others, he is taken aback when the usual social validation is not forthcoming.

The Bigger Picture:
Cultural and Historical Influences

Now we turn to the bigger picture. Would people be who they are if they had grown up in a completely different culture or a different time period? Probably not. Because self-experience is to a large extent constructed in our interactions and communication with others, a host of social and cultural influences shape identity. Some research in social psychology has recently begun to take a cross-cultural or historical slant, therefore, in examining the way people make their self-concept intelligible both to others and to themselves against a backdrop of cultural assumptions, language practices, and social norms. When people tell stories about themselves, they draw on the stock of myths and plotlines they have heard and read since childhood, representing the culture's literary tradition. When they act out social roles, relying on scripts and routines that make up their cultural drama, they come to construe themselves using the specific identity categories that are embedded in the interactive patterns. All of this leads to a way of looking at identity that, while typically taken for granted within a given culture, can vary significantly from one cultural setting to the next.

Culture

Cross-cultural studies have shown that different societies contain very different views of what the "self" is. Shweder (1982) outlined a number of core questions about life for which different cultures provide different answers, ranging from What's me vs. what's not-me? and What's male vs. what's female? to the issue of how self relates to others: Am I independent, dependent, or interdependent? As Markus and Cross (1990) pointed out, the answers to these questions likely form the basis of self-experience.

In the West (i.e., Europe and North America), for example, it is taken for granted that each individual has a personal name that identifies him or her uniquely. In Bali (an Indonesian island), by contrast, people are designated according to such things as their social status and their position in their family ("firstborn," "father of," and so on). Based on these kinds of observations, Geertz (1975) asserted that the Western idea of people as "bounded, unique, more or less integrated" entities that are largely independent of their interpersonal relations is "a rather peculiar idea within the context of the world's cultures" (p. 48).

Triandis (1989) and Markus and Kitayama (1991; Kitayama et al. 1997) elaborated this contrast between Western and Eastern cultures, particularly Japan. In the West, identity is defined primarily according to characteristics of one's personal self—one's preferences, abilities, traits, and so on—that is, internal attributes that define how one is different from others. As such, Westerners (perhaps Americans in particular) are taught to develop an "independent self," which they try to assert in pursuit of their personal goals. In Asian cultures, grounded in traditions that emphasize the maintenance of a smoothly functioning social order, identity is instead centered on an "interdependent self," defined in terms of one's relations with others. Asians are taught to attend to the fundamental connectedness between themselves and other people, and to the different social contexts in which different kinds of behavior are appropriate. When Asian participants complete the Twenty Statements Test, for example, they are more likely than Westerners to report relational self-concepts such as being someone's daughter or being a certain other person's friend (Ip and Bond 1995; Rhee et al. 1995). Markus and Kitayama pointed out that proverbs from the two cultures demonstrate this difference of emphasis. In the individualistic West "the squeaky wheel gets the grease," whereas in collectivistic Japan "the nail that stands out gets pounded down."

A similar analysis can be made about how Western culture constructs the identities of different people in it. Men and women, for example, tend to have different views of themselves. Men are more likely to develop an "independent" self-concept that is focused on features that distinguish them from others; women tend to have "relational" or "interdependent" selves, in which relationships and connections to others are emphasized (Josephs, Markus, and Tafarodi 1992). Many of the differences between men and women in Western culture are likely due to the self-presentations that are rewarded and given consensual validation by others. Boys are encouraged to be assertive and independent; girls are rewarded for being nurturant and concerned about their relationships with others (Deaux and Major 1987).

Language

A critical medium of culture's influence is language. Recall the Deutsch and Mackesy (1985) study described earlier, in which people's self-concepts were shaped by the kinds of categories and labels that came up in conversation with someone else. Now imagine that effect multiplied by a lifetime of conversing with others using the specific set of categories that is emphasized in one's language and culture. For example, someone who is creative and intense and has an unconventional lifestyle might be described as an "artsy" type. How about a person who is worldly, socially skilled, reserved, and devoted to his or her family? If you were raised in an English-speaking culture, chances are you are more likely to see people in terms of whether they fit the former description, for which there is a label. If you were raised in China, however, the second description (of a *shì gu* person) would be a more commonplace way of characterizing people.

In a clever study, Hoffman, Lau, and Johnson (1986) sought to demonstrate the impact of culture and language on how people are viewed. They recruited participants who were fluently bilingual in English and Chinese and had them read a description of some person engaged in a range of ordinary activities. For some participants the descriptions were written in English and for others they were written in Chinese. Later, when participants were asked to report their impressions of the people they had read about, they tended to remember and draw inferences about different kinds of behavior depending on which language was being used. If reading in English, for example, they assumed that someone who was creative and intense would also have an unconventional lifestyle; if reading the same description in Chinese, where this "type" of person did not have a label, they did not "fill in the blanks" in this way. Conversely, if reading about a *shì gu* person in Chinese, their impression was organized around this label; if reading about the same person in English, they did not focus on the same information. It should not be surprising that a person who grows up in a certain culture, embedded in a set of understandings and social categories, has his or her self-perception shaped by this kind of linguistic influence.

Historical Factors

A number of recent analyses have examined historical changes in the way people experience themselves. A few centuries ago people seemed less concerned with issues of identity, self-knowledge, and so on (Baumeister 1987). During that era, people's social roles were largely defined for them. Those were not times of great social mobility or career choice—people's gender and family background often completely defined their social role. A person who was born and raised in the family of a peasant farmer was quite likely to be a peasant farmer too. And because there was not much movement from place to place, people knew each other's background and social position. As Berger and Luckmann (1967) described it,

> In such a society, everybody knows who everybody is and who he is himself. A knight *is* a knight and a peasant *is* a peasant, to others as well as to themselves. There is, therefore, no *problem* of identity. The question, "Who am I?" is unlikely to arise in consciousness, since the socially predefined answer is massively real subjectively and consistently confirmed in all significant social interaction. (p. 164)

The individual in today's society is confronted by a very different situation, typically including far more choices to make among different career paths, relationships, and social activities. Gergen (1991) gave a rich account of how selfhood has evolved over the last two centuries, showing the profound impact that changes in a culture can have. Nineteenth-century romanticism, for example, assumed that people experienced self as a deep, emotional interior, consisting of the person's immortal soul with all its values and deep-seated passions. Yet as early as eighteenth-century enlightenment, and then prominently in twentieth-century modernism, people increasingly began to identify more with their ability to reason, and with the beliefs, opinions, and conscious intentions that go along with that.

Gergen (1991) argued that both of these views of self—which are still quite active in shaping how we experience ourselves—are gradually giving way to a new form of selfhood, arising from the tremendous increase in the availability of communication technologies and the exposure they give us to multiple relationships and to cultures and worldviews different from our own. He suggests that many people in today's world are experiencing a sense of self as "saturated" with different ways of looking at themselves. The sense of self as a unified core of one's experience is dissolving as people increasingly recognize the degree to which their self is adapted to different situations and audiences—an epidemic of role distance, one might say. The self can be experienced quite differently from context to context or relationship to relationship, and this is not a problem (unlike in the earlier worldviews) because there is increasingly no core identity that must be preserved and promoted. Gergen suggested that although this postmodern self can be unsettling, particularly to those raised to think in terms of romantic or modern selves, it can also be liberating and can make one more flexible in adapting to the multiple and often conflicting demands of social life at the turn of the twenty-first century.

Sources of Identity:
Concluding Comments

Psychologists and philosophers have argued that the way people identify themselves makes a significant difference in their social and personal experience. Yet there seems to be little consensus about the most appropriate or functional form of self-construal. Humanists warn that people who define themselves according to their social roles and the way others see them risk living an inauthentic life in which they deny their true feelings and desires in order to make an impression on others. Erikson (1959) suggested that it is important to fashion one's own view of who one is and then commit to that identity. Existentialists (e.g., Fromm 1956; Rank 1936; Sartre 1956), on the other hand, say that although it might be comforting to adopt a fixed role identity in order to "fit in" to the social order, it entails the danger of losing sight of the fact that one is constantly creating that identity; agency is thus the core of the self. Others (e.g., Buber 1958) say that although it is important to avoid identifying with any fixed, socially defined self, it is nonetheless the case that self is experienced most directly in interpersonal relationships with others; thus, one should focus on having authentic relationships. Some religious writers advocate identifying with one's "higher self"—one's values and prosocial tendencies—rather than the "lower self" of physical desires. Others report that ignoring one's physical self might contribute to the development of depression. The French philosopher Descartes (1962), with his famous dictum, "Cogito, ergo sum" ("I think, therefore I am"), laid the groundwork for the notion that the most direct, irrefutable evidence of one's own existence is in the awareness of one's own thoughts. Conversely, Zen Buddhists suggest that overemphasizing and becoming attached to one's personal self is the root of much of human suffering; one should instead realize that there truly is no "self" to be known by introspection. Some existentially oriented psychoanalysts (e.g., Becker 1973; Laing 1965) would seem to argue the opposite, saying that uncertainty about one's existence is in fact the root of much of human suffering, including psychosis. Finally, social constructionists argue that all of these routes to self-construal are profoundly shaped by cultural preconceptions, language, and conversations with others.

It seems likely that each path to identity has its costs and benefits, strengths and weaknesses. The route one takes will depend at least in part on the degree to which one holds to the different values of comfort, security, happiness, authenticity, freedom, and so on that are assumed by these different views of identity. In the end, people draw on some subset of these sources of identity, and the resultant information about themselves contributes to the development and maintenance of a more or less stable, more or less coherent self-concept. It is to this self-concept that we now turn.

4

Self-Concept

One can neither see a self-concept nor touch it, and no one has succeeded as yet in adequately defining it as a hypothetical construct.

—*Epstein (1973, 283)*

Research on the self-concept is more abundant and perhaps more diverse than research on any other topic relevant to the self-system. This intense interest seems justified because self-knowledge—the principal element of the self-concept—is the raw material from which the self-system is formed and through which it functions. In this chapter we present theory and research on the self-concept in two major sections. In the first section, we focus primarily on the *content* of self-knowledge and how that content affects people's views of themselves and other people. In the second major section, we turn our attention to an emerging research literature that concerns how the *organization* of self-knowledge affects people's understanding of themselves and others. Research endeavors in both traditions are noteworthy for the degree of innovativeness and creativity apparent in their methodology and measurement. In order to provide a sense of the challenges that research on the self-concept poses, we describe and illustrate some of the means by which self-knowledge is assessed or inferred.

Varieties of Self-Knowledge

Most self-theorists agree with Allport's (1961b) suggestion that "the human mind is able to regard itself as an object in much the same way that it regards objects in the outer world" (p. 137). Accordingly, the study of how people think about themselves—their **self-concept**—draws heavily on more general models of human cognition. In those models, a distinction is made between two broad categories of knowledge—procedural and declarative.

This distinction has proven useful for understanding the nature of self-knowledge (Kihlstrom and Cantor 1984).

Procedural self-knowledge consists of all the different rules of thumb people use in thinking about themselves, including the processes introduced in previous chapters by which specific self-knowledge is manipulated and combined to construct a characterization of self—such as self-perception, action identification, and perspective taking. In later chapters, we describe additional instances of procedural self-knowledge when we look at the processes people use to evaluate themselves and regulate their behavior.

Declarative self-knowledge, in contrast, consists of the content of self-experience, including the characteristics, traits, roles, and so on that we use to describe ourselves. This collection of self-knowledge is traditionally what psychologists mean when they refer to the self-concept—a theory or coherent set of beliefs about the self (Epstein 1973). Most psychologists assume that people start with the basic data of self-experience: feelings, observations of their own behavior, memories of significant episodes with other people, and so on. Thoughts and memories that are similar or related in some way—for example, feelings of anxiety when meeting people, self-observations of trying to avoid social situations, and episodes of stammering when interacting with strangers—become associated in memory, along with some summary label such as "I am shy." The different memories and beliefs about self become organized and linked together in an associative network of memory. Over time, this network of knowledge can become elaborated with more and more confirming evidence until the person has a well-articulated view of self in this domain. This aggregation of knowledge is then called on when the person thinks about his or her behavior in a new situation, makes plans for the future, or tries to explain self to others. That is, declarative knowledge structures about the self both represent knowledge about the self and influence the way new information is processed.

Self-schemas, for example, are declarative knowledge structures based on repeated self-observation and feedback from others that organize the way people process new self-relevant information. In her landmark paper introducing the notion of self-schemas, Markus (1977) reported a number of studies showing some of the ways in which a firmly held self-concept in some domain influences the way that people deal with information about themselves and others. She had people rate themselves on a number of trait dimensions (e.g., *independent-dependent, leader-follower*), and rate how important it was to their own self-concept. She identified people as having a self-schema, or as being *schematic,* on some dimension if they considered the term to be highly descriptive and also important to their self-concept. People who rated the term as not particularly descriptive or did not see it as an important dimension to their self-concept were defined as *aschematic* in that domain. Such people appeared to lack a self-schema on that dimension.

This research and subsequent studies (see Markus and Wurf 1987 for a review) have demonstrated that self-schemas have a number of effects on thought and behavior. First, people process information that is congruent with their self-schema very efficiently and confidently. Markus (1977) found, for example, that people who thought of themselves as independent had very clear ideas about where they stood on this dimension. When asked to respond either "me" or "not me" to a list of words relating to independence (e.g., individualistic, unconventional) and dependence (e.g., conforming, submissive), they were able to make much quicker judgments than if they were rating themselves on characteristics for which they had no self-schema. They also were highly resistant to any new information that suggested their self-views might be erroneous; for example, they rejected as inaccurate a test that indicated they might in fact be dependent.

Second, self-schemas influence people's responses to self-relevant information, even information to which they are not consciously attending. In the classic "cocktail party" phenomenon, for example, people who are trying to listen carefully with one ear to a tape-recorded list of words get momentarily distracted if their own name is presented briefly to their other ear—much as your attention to a conversation partner at a party is disrupted by someone's mentioning your name on the other side of the room. Bargh (1982) found a similar effect in a study using trait adjectives instead of names. People who were schematic on independence were momentarily distracted when words related to independence were presented to the ear they were trying to ignore.

Third, self-schemas influence the way information is stored in memory and then later recalled. Markus (1977) found, for example, that people who were schematic on the trait of independence easily remembered examples of their own past behavior that demonstrated their independence. This ready accessibility of self-relevant memories affects the way people think about new experiences. One of the most thoroughly researched phenomena in the self-concept literature is the **self-reference effect** (Rogers, Kuiper, and Kirker 1977). Consider this scenario: Two people watch a movie and then discuss the lead character, whom they both liked. It soon becomes apparent that each person picked out and remembered different aspects of the character's personality. One noticed her independence and assertiveness (traits that match his self-view) and the other noticed the character's intelligence and resourcefulness (traits that are central to her self-view). This is an example of how self-concept affects the way people process information about themselves and others.

Studies of the self-reference effect typically involve asking participants to read a list of trait adjectives and make specific judgments about each one. For each word they are to answer a question about its relevance to their self-concept ("Does this word describe you?") or a question about some other aspect of the word, such as its semantic meaning ("Does this word mean the same as x?"). Later, participants are asked to recall as many of the words as they can. Typically, they are much better able to recall words that they had rated for self-descriptiveness. In extensions of this research, the self-reference effect was also apparent when participants were asked to relate the target word to past episodes from their own lives (Bower and Gilligan 1979).

Research has suggested a number of reasons for this. One is captured by the notion of familiarity. Recall the two people watching a movie together. If one has thought a lot about his own independence, he is better able to pick out another person's independence-related behavior, such as when the main character took a vacation by herself, and to quickly draw a confident conclusion about her independence on the basis of that information (Markus, Smith, and Moreland 1985). Also, in doing so the person will relate the person's behavior to his own similar experiences, such as when he last went traveling alone. This deeper processing and elaboration of the independent behavior, which the resourcefulness-schematic viewer did not do, makes the information relevant to independence stand out and influences the person's memory and impression of the character.

The Dynamic Self and the Activation of Self-Knowledge

A commonsense understanding of the self-concept suggests that it is a single idea: a concept of oneself, much like a concept of "elephant." As we saw in the previous chapter, however, identity is multifaceted, derived from many sources. Close examination of people's thoughts and feelings suggests that they do not usually think about themselves in terms of some general, unitary construct. Just like the proverbial blind men examining the elephant's trunk, ear, and left hind leg, most people tend to think about specific aspects of themselves—their trait of independence, their "parent" self, or their poise in social situations.

The assumption is that people have available to them a range of self-conceptions: the self-schemas that represent their core views of self as well as more tentative self-images based on recent self-perceptions or reflected appraisals. All of these self-conceptions may be linked together in a general self-concept, but at any given time, only a subset will actually be active in thought and memory, defining the **working self-concept** of the moment (Markus and Kunda 1986; also termed spontaneous self-concept, McGuire, McGuire, Child, and Fujioka 1978; and the phenomenal self, Jones and Gerard 1967). When attending a lecture, for example, one's student self-concept is presumably activated, whereas during a rock concert one's "party animal" self-concept comes to the fore (e.g., Kihlstrom et al. 1988). The notion of a single self-concept is gradually being replaced by an emphasis on this working self-concept, which is seen as constructed from self-knowledge that at the moment is relevant and apparent to the person. Once pulled into the working self-concept, a specific self-schema can influence how new experiences are perceived, interpreted, and remembered.

Researchers have been interested, therefore, in the factors that determine which self-aspects become activated for different people at different times, and what effects this activation has (e.g., McGuire and Padawer-Singer 1976). Partly, as just mentioned, it depends on the situation. The aspects of the self-concept that are most relevant or applicable (Higgins 1996) to one's current goals and activities are most likely to come to the fore. Another situational factor is *distinctiveness*, or the degree to which different self-aspects set one apart from others in the immediate environment. In a series of studies, McGuire and colleagues asked schoolchildren simply to "tell us about yourself." They then examined the spontaneous self-concepts that were reported. Responses tended to emphasize aspects of self that were distinctive in the current social context. In one study, for example, the researchers wondered whether being a member of a minority group would continually bring this group membership to mind. Indeed, in a study of 560 students from the northeastern United States, white students—who made up 82 percent of the local population—mentioned their race only 1 percent of the time; African-American students, on the other hand, mentioned their race 17 percent of the time (McGuire et al. 1978). In a second study, the distinctive self-aspects involved personal, idiosyncratic aspects of identity rather than social-group identities. Children of average height or weight were only half as likely to mention these characteristics as children who were quite tall or short, heavy or light (McGuire and McGuire 1981).

Sometimes specific *self-focusing cues* in the environment direct people's attention to themselves. An extensive literature has evolved based on the notion that people's overall level of self-awareness can vary from time to time and situation to situation. The original theory regarding this process stated that people's attention could be either focused outward, on the environment, or reflexively, on the self as an object in the world (Duval and Wicklund 1972). To the extent that people are thinking about themselves as an object, they are **self-aware**—and this turns out to make a big difference in how they think, feel, and behave. The research is deceptively simple. Research participants are given some task to do, such as filling out a questionnaire or trying to form an impression of a new person. As an experimental manipulation to increase self-awareness, half of the participants are seated in such a way that they can see their own reflection in a small mirror (supposedly left in the laboratory for a different study). Study after study has shown that a minimal stimulus like this typically leads participants to focus on themselves and on processing information in terms of its relevance to the self (Hull and Levy 1979). They tend to use more first-person pronouns (I, me), for example, and they show more evidence of the self-reference effect, remembering information in the environment that is relevant to their own self-concept. We take up the topic of heightened self-awareness in greater depth in Chapter 8.

Self-awareness sometimes involves the activation of specific aspects of self, such as public versus private self-knowledge. Research into self-awareness has shown that it is possible to activate one or the other type of self-knowledge, with predictable effects on people's thoughts and actions (Wicklund 1979). As described earlier, putting a mirror in front of people tends to focus their attention on private self-knowledge. Pointing a video camera at them, on the other hand, seems to focus their attention on public self-knowledge, producing a heightened awareness of how others see them (Buss 1980).

Finally, self-aspects can be triggered through a phenomenon known as *spreading activation* (Collins and Loftus 1975). This phenomenon is particularly germane to the question of how self-relevant knowledge is structured or organized in people's memory. The basic idea is that once one element of a particular self-schema (e.g., "outgoing") is primed, activation should spread through associative links to other self-schemas the person holds (e.g, "independent," "clumsy"). Higgins, Van Hook, and Dorfman (1988) examined this "wakening of associations" (James 1950) using a modified version of the Stroop task, a standard procedure borrowed from cognitive psychology (Stroop 1935). In the basic Stroop task, research participants are presented (generally on a computer screen or printed page) a series of words printed in a variety of colors. They are instructed to rapidly name the color of ink in which each word is printed and ignore the meaning of the word. Although this exercise seems simple enough, performance on it is significantly influenced by the content of the words. When the word is particularly relevant to the participant in some way (e.g., it represents a dimension on which the participant is schematic), there is an observable interference effect. Participants are measurably slower to name the color of these attention-grabbing words, presumably due to automatic processing of the task-irrelevant (but personally relevant) information.

Higgins et al. (1988) added a twist to the Stroop task to examine spreading activation from one self-aspect to another. Before each color-naming trial, subjects were shown a prime: either another self-descriptive adjective or a non-self-relevant adjective. If self-descriptive traits are in fact associated with each other in an organized self-schema, then priming one trait descriptor in this way should activate the other traits as well, via spreading activation. Thus evidence of organized associations among bits of self-knowledge would consist of a priming effect whereby presentation of one self-descriptive term (e.g., "generous") as a prime produces interference when the subject tries to color name a second self-descriptive term (e.g., "introverted").

Early studies using this approach showed little evidence of organization in the way self-aspects are associated, leading researchers to question the assumption that various self-aspects are well integrated in memory as one unified self-concept. Higgins et al. (1988; also Segal et al. 1988) found no increased interference effect when prime and target were both self-descriptive traits—which is when interference should have been observed if there is a tightly organized self-concept. Additional research, however, showed that the spreading-activation effect does occur under certain conditions and for certain individuals. Segal et al. (1988; Segal and Vella 1990) found the effect for depressed inpatients, supporting models that implicate organized, negative self-schematic structures in depression (e.g., Beck 1967; Kuiper, Derry, and MacDonald 1982). Higgins et al. (1988) found the spreading-activation effect in nondepressed individuals, but only for one set of self-descriptors—traits that were problematic for the subject because they represented domains in which the subject was falling short of evaluative standards. These authors argued that evaluatively important information might be the best-organized subset of self-knowledge. Finally, Segal and Vella (1990) also found the effect for non-depressed individuals, but only under conditions of heightened self-awareness, when the entire self-schema presumably was highly activated (Wicklund 1979). Although the evidence is somewhat mixed, then, it does appear that this adaptation of the Stroop task is one useful tool for examining the organization of self-knowledge, and research in this tradition continues.

Recently, DeSteno and Salovey (1997) proposed that evidence for organization among self-features should be found primarily for domains that are especially important to the individual, that is, in areas where the person is schematic. A person who is very achievement oriented, for example, might be expected to show a particularly high degree of organization among relevant self-aspects such as "hardworking," "talented," and "intelligent." These researchers asked participants to spend three minutes listing self-descriptive terms. They then coded each self-descriptor for whether it represented achievement issues or some other theme (e.g., affiliation). Finally, as an index of cognitive organization, they computed for each participant a clustering score to represent the degree to which achievement-related terms were written one after another, that is, whether the reporting of one achievement-related term led, via spreading activation, to a second, third, or even fourth term. As the researchers predicted, people who were highly schematic in the achievement domain (as measured separately) showed more clustering of achievement-related material in their self-descriptions.

As the Stroop and memory-clustering research shows, research has supported the idea that self-knowledge is organized within domains that are important or schema-relevant for the individual, although the evidence is weak for a tightly organized, unified general self-concept. As a result, research into the self-concept has examined the different domains that may tend to show evidence of structure and the ways that people differ in how this information is organized. We turn to some examples now.

Investigating Links Between Aspects of the Self-Concept

The Collective Self

Some aspects of people's self-concept involve their memberships in groups, such as race, nationality, gender, club memberships, occupational groups, and so on (Deaux 1993). These features of the self-concept are called **collective identity**. When a person's collective identity becomes activated, he or she tends to shift into a "we" (rather than "I") frame of mind, which accentuates similarities to other members of the group and differences from nonmembers (Simon, Pantaleo, and Mummenday 1995). This shift has been shown to contribute to a range of group-level phenomena, such as increased group cohesiveness among in-group members and increased competition with out-group members, as well as increased stereotyping of out-group members—seeing "them" as "all the same" (e.g., Turner et al. 1987).

In a study of this process, Trafimow, Triandis, and Goto (1991) focused people on either their collective or personal identities while they completed the Twenty Statements Test. They found a pattern of spreading activation, whereby thinking about one collective identity (e.g., male) led people to think of other collective identities (e.g., student), whereas thinking of a personal attribute (e.g., skeptical) led people to think about other personal characteristics (e.g., clumsy). Although this finding suggests that collective identities and personal attributes might be segregated in memory, Reid and Deaux (1996) presented additional evidence that people show a degree of integration as well, to the extent that personal and collective identities have relevance for one another. Remind people that they are Catholic, for example, and they will think of themselves as spiritual; remind them they are professors and they will see themselves as intelligent (e.g., Charters and Newcomb 1952).

This link between collective and personal self-representations can also lead to an interesting phenomenon known as **self-stereotyping**. A person who categorizes himself as a member of a group is more likely to behave in line with the stereotype he holds about that group. Levy (1996) studied the activation of stereotypes of old age in a group of participants sixty years of age or older. Levy first gave participants subliminal exposures to stereotype-relevant words, presented so quickly on a computer screen that they were not consciously visible. Some participants were shown words chosen to activate a negative stereotype of aging (e.g., "senile," "confused"); others were shown words to activate a positive stereotype (e.g., "wise," "enlightened"). Then they all read a story about a seventy-three-year-old woman and stated their impressions of her. Consistent with the idea that stereotypes can be activated outside of awareness (e.g., Devine 1989), participants in the negative prime condition were much more likely than those in the positive prime condition to say the woman was senile, dependent, and forgetful. A second phase of the study was included to examine self-stereotyping. Participants performed a set of memory tasks on which performance typically worsens with advanced age. Participants in the negative prime condition performed significantly worse on these tests than those in the positive prime condition. These results were not observed for younger participants. Thus, only when a stereotype was potentially self-relevant—and thus there presumably were preexisting links between the collective and personal identities—did its effects spread to people's working self-concepts, influencing their performance on the memory tests.

The Relational Self

As we saw in Chapter 3, people may experience very different senses of themselves depending on whom they are with. Numerous authors (see Baldwin 1992 for a review) have suggested that people's self-schemas may often be embedded in mental representations of relationships—so-called **relational schemas** or interpersonal schemas—that represent their self-characteristics not as separate, isolated entities but rather their sense of who they are when interacting with others (cf. Niedenthal and Beike 1997).

In one study of this sense of "self-with-other," participants were asked to list some (approximately 25) important people in their lives and to report how they saw themselves when with each person (Ogilvie and Ashmore 1991). Using a sophisticated statistical program, the researchers were able to analyze these responses and generate for each person a profile of the kinds of self-with-other he or she typically experienced. For one participant, the sense of self as peaceful and enthusiastic was clustered with her relationships with peers, whereas the sense of self as unsure, confused, and depressed was clustered with her father, who was largely absent when she was growing up. Participants in this research typically were amazed at how accurate the computer program was at revealing their typical ways of experiencing their interpersonal self.

Extending this idea, Hinkley and Andersen (1996; see also Baldwin and Holmes 1987) hypothesized that activating a certain relationship in memory should, therefore, lead to the activation of associated self-concepts. Reminding someone of a relationship in which she typically feels incompetent, for example, might lead her to feel incompetent in a current situation.

To test this hypothesis, these researchers first asked participants to think of one relationship in which they felt particularly good about themselves, and one in which they typically felt quite bad about themselves. They then asked participants to describe these two significant others in several sentences each. More than two weeks later, participants were contacted again and asked to come to the laboratory for a second, supposedly unrelated session. When they arrived, they were told they would be meeting a new person and were given some descriptive information about this new person. Unknown to them, there was actually no one for them to meet; the descriptions were based on the information they had given earlier. Some people read information similar to what they had written about a positive significant other; other participants read information similar to what they had written about a negative significant other. They were asked to visualize what it would probably be like to interact with this new person and were then asked to respond to a number of self-esteem scales to indicate how they were feeling about themselves. As the researchers hypothesized, participants' working self-concepts shifted in the direction of their self-with-other, becoming, for example, more positive when anticipating meeting someone who reminded them of another positive relationship.

This kind of effect may result from the activation of expectations about contingencies of interpersonal acceptance (Baldwin and Sinclair 1996). That is, many writers have hypothesized that because the desire for acceptance by others is an important motivation, people learn the if-then interpersonal contingencies relevant to maintaining this relatedness (e.g., Safran 1990; Sullivan 1953). One such contingency—played out daily in a variety of contexts—is the belief that if one fails, significant others often will react with criticism and rejection. Numerous writers have noted that a belief in this type of performance-contingent acceptance appears to play a role in depression and self-esteem disturbances (e.g., Kuiper and Olinger 1986; Rogers 1959). If so, there should be evidence for the spread of activation from the *if* part of the contingency (e.g., "if I fail") to the *then* part ("then others will reject me"). In Baldwin and Sinclair's study, undergraduates performed a lexical decision task, in which they read letter strings on a computer and tried to quickly identify whether each was a word or not. Sometimes these letter strings were words related to interpersonal acceptance—words such as *acceptance, cherished, rejection,* and *despised*—and sometimes they were related to rejection. Before each of these letter strings, they first read performance-related words such as *success* and *failure.* Consistent with the notion of evaluative contingencies, some people were faster to identify positive interpersonal outcomes such as *cherished* as words when given the context of success, and faster to identify negative targets such as *despised* when given the context of failure. As implied by the notion of self-with-other relational schemas, people with low self-esteem were particularly likely to show evidence of spreading activation from negative performance contexts to negative interpersonal outcomes.

Organization of Self-Knowledge

The application of theory and methods from cognitive psychology to the study of the self-system moved the focus of research beyond questions about the basic content of self-concept to questions regarding the organization of self-referent thoughts, feelings, and motives in memory. Such research might be considered "second-generation" self-concept research. Prior to the late 1970s, most data on the self-concept were procured using paper-and-pencil questionnaires that provided scores across a variety of preestablished domains. Although such data are useful for indexing the differential importance of frequently occurring domains of self-knowledge in respondents, they provide little insight regarding how self-knowledge in those domains, and others not commonly addressed, influence self-referent information processing. Second-generation research on the self-concept relies more on ad hoc and respondent-generated lists of attributes that are rated or sorted by respondents in such a way that mathematical or statistical strategies can be used to index implicit characteristics of self-knowledge (e.g., the self-with-other profiles described earlier). Although these methods can provide information similar to that in first-generation self-concept research, they have the advantage of providing information about how self-knowledge is arrayed in memory and, by inference, how it influences self-referent thoughts, feelings, and behaviors.

Substantive Self-Knowledge

The groundwork for prominent contemporary strategies of studying the self-concept was laid almost thirty years before the first published accounts of second-generation self-concept research appeared. Psychologists studying human sensation and perception developed mathematical models of the processes involved in recognizing and remembering visual shapes and patterns (Attneave 1954; Shannon and Weaver 1949). These models drew from theories about how information is processed to characterize basic human activities such as problem solving and movement (Attneave 1959; Wiener 1948). Information theories make two important assumptions that are fundamental to second-generation self-concept research: (1) information can be quantified and (2) judgments and decisions involving a collection of information are affected by the associations among individual pieces of information.

Working from these two basic tenets, Linville (1985) developed an influential model and method for studying the organization of self-knowledge.

According to the model, the self-concept is a multifaceted cognitive structure, and people vary in the degree of complexity evident in their self-concept. The **self-complexity** of a people's self-concept is defined as the number of different ways in which people conceptualize themselves—self-aspects (e.g, roles, emotional states, self with others) and the interrelatedness of those self-aspects. Linville further posited that self-complexity should influence the way people process self-referent information that arises during the course of everyday life and, therefore, affect their emotional reactions to such information. People with a relatively large number of independent self-aspects should be less affected by self-referent information (e.g., performance feedback) because, in the information-processing context provided by the self-system, the information—good or bad—would bear on only a small, relatively independent part of the whole system. Conversely, people with a small number of overlapping self-aspects would be more strongly affected by self-referent information because it activates (i.e., pulls into the working self-concept) a larger part of the self-system, and the activation spreads to interrelated self-aspects not directly implicated by the information but linked in memory.

An important contribution of the research on self-complexity is the means by which self-complexity is measured. Research participants are provided index cards on which are written words or phrases (e.g., *smart, clumsy*). Their task is to describe themselves by sorting the cards into groups according to which ones they believe belong together. In addition to these index cards, usually numbering around thirty, respondents are provided blank cards for creating duplicates of words or phrases they wish to include in multiple piles. The card sort provides the raw data for computing the H statistic (Attneave 1959; Scott 1969), which reflects the degree of redundancy in the use of information evident in the self-descriptive sort.

An alternative approach to generating the raw data for computing self-complexity is illustrated in Table 4.1. Using the Self-Description Grid (McKenzie and Hoyle 1996), a portion of which is shown in the figure, respondents "sort" a collection of trait adjectives with reference to a series of self-aspects either provided by the investigator or generated by each respondent. These data can then be used to compute the H statistic mentioned earlier. The computation of the H statistic is somewhat complex (see Attneave 1959, 5–8, 24–25 for an excellent tutorial); however, the idea behind the number is rather simple and bears elaborating. Referring again to Table 4.1, note that a hypothetical respondent has indicated with an X the self-aspects of which each adjective, in his or her view, is descriptive. Comparing across rows, one can see that the pattern of Xs is identical for some adjectives, whereas the pattern is unique for others. For instance, the adjectives *good* and *helpful* were used to describe the self-aspects *romantic partner, friend, son/daughter,* and *worker,* but not *student. Tired* and

TABLE 4.1   Example Self-Rating on a Portion of the Self-Description Grid

	A *Student*	B *Romantic Partner*	C *Friend*	D *Son/Daughter*	E *Worker*
Good		X	X	X	X
Lazy	X			X	
Helpful		X	X	X	X
Tired	X			X	X
Perfect					
Careless	X	X	X	X	X
Smart	X		X	X	X
Afraid		X		X	
Happy		X	X	X	
Clumsy	X			X	X

SOURCE: A self-administered measure of self-complexity, by K. S. McKenzie and R. H. Hoyle, 1996. Paper presented at the annual meeting of the Midwestern Psychological Association, Chicago, May.

clumsy were used to describe self as *student, son/daughter,* and *worker,* but not *romantic partner* or *friend.* Otherwise, there is no redundancy in the patterns that accompany the adjectives. If a unique pattern of usage was associated with each adjective, then the respondent would obtain the maximum self-complexity score. If, on the other hand, the same pattern of usage was associated with every adjective, then the respondent would obtain the minimum self-complexity score.

Self-complexity, measured in this way, has produced a number of intriguing findings that provided new insights into the self-system and self-regulation. In her seminal research on self-complexity, Linville (1985) conducted two studies. In one study, undergraduates performed the card sort described earlier before describing their mood on a series of items presented by computer. When the computer ostensibly stopped working, participants were asked to move on to the next phase of the study, which involved completing a task supposedly related to intelligence. When participants completed the task, the experimenter scored it and notified each participant that he or she had either performed very poorly or very well (feedback was randomly assigned). At that point, the computer appeared to start working, and the participants were asked to reenter the information about their mood. Comparisons of mood scores revealed that people low in self-complexity are more greatly influenced than their high complexity counterparts by performance feedback, particularly when it is negative.

In a second study, Linville (1985) enlisted a group of college women to complete the card sorting task and keep a diary of their mood for fourteen days. As predicted, self-complexity was inversely correlated with daily fluctuations in mood. That is, the more complex the participants' self-concept, the less extreme their mood swings during the two weeks of the study. The findings from subsequent research on self-complexity and mood suggest that they are not always associated (e.g., Emmons and King 1989; Rhodewalt, Madrian, and Cheney 1998). In fact, there is evidence to suggest that such fluctuations might be attributed more directly to self-esteem differences than to self-complexity per se (Campbell, Chew, and Scratchley 1991). Resolution concerning the conflicting findings relevant to this core prediction may lie in the correspondence between the frame of reference for the self-ratings and the outcomes being considered. For instance, when self-ratings focus on possible selves (Markus and Nurius 1986), the resultant self-complexity score is correlated with emotional reactions to feedback regarding likely future performance but not feedback regarding present performance (Niedenthal, Setterlund, and Wherry 1992). Conversely, actual self-complexity predicts reactions to evaluations of present performance but not likely future performance. This pattern of findings suggests that self-complexity is not an overarching individual difference that characterizes the self-system in all contexts (see also Salovey 1992). Rather, self-complexity may vary in different parts of the self-system, and it clearly varies according to the perspective from which the self is conceptualized.

More profitable applications of self-complexity have focused on self-complexity as an intrapsychic resource that serves as a buffer against the potential ill effects of negative life experiences. For instance, among adults (but not children; Jordan and Cole 1996) who recently experienced a high level of stressful life events (e.g., moved to a new residence, experienced death of a relative), those high in self-complexity evinced fewer depressive symptoms and fewer stress-related physical symptoms than their low self-complexity counterparts (Linville 1987).[1] People relatively high in self-complexity are more likely to avoid self-focused attention following a failure than people relatively low in self-complexity, indirect evidence that the effects of failure are less profound when the self is relatively complex (Dixon and Baumeister 1991). Among people who have recently experienced a relationship breakup, those with high self-complexity experience less distress in general, and those for whom the relationship self-aspect is relatively minor in the self-system and independent of other self-aspects experience fewer coping problems than their low self-complexity counterparts (Smith and Cohen 1993).

---

[1]Surprisingly, during periods of low stress, people low in self-complexity enjoy a slight advantage in adjustment. A possible explanation for this pattern was offered by Linville (1987): If low stress is accompanied by positive thoughts and emotions, then, because of the interdependence of self-aspects in the self-system of people low in self-complexity, the positive consequences of low stress would be experienced more broadly when self-complexity is low.

An alternative conceptualization of the degree to which self-aspects are interrelated is self-concept differentiation (Donahue, Robins, Roberts, and John 1993). **Self-concept differentiation** is defined as "individual differences in the tendency to see oneself as having different personality characteristics across one's roles" (Donahue et al. 1993, 834). One difference between self-concept differentiation and self-complexity is that the former focuses specifically on social roles, whereas the latter takes a broader view of the content that might characterize different self-aspects. Like self-complexity, self-concept differentiation is measured through a set of mathematical operations on an Adjective x Self-Aspect matrix of self-ratings (e.g., Table 4.1).

As was true of self-complexity, the computation of self-concept differentiation is rather involved. The computation is accomplished through the use of the statistical technique of factor analysis (Block 1961). To illustrate, consider the following circumstance: A woman rates herself on ten trait adjectives with reference to three social roles—student, daughter, and worker. Given those data, it is possible to derive three numbers, correlation coefficients, that reflect the degree of association between the three roles as rated by her on the trait adjectives. Using factor analysis, it is then possible to determine to what extent the associations among the roles might be caused by a single underlying source—an integrated identity. To the extent that the correlations cannot be explained by a single underlying source, the self-concept is differentiated.

This computational strategy is illustrated in Figure 4.1. In the figure are two Venn diagrams comprising three overlapping circles. Each circle

FIGURE 4.1   Two Levels of Self-Concept Differentiation Involving Three Self-Aspects

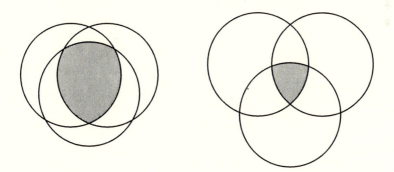

NOTE: Shaded area represents information shared by all three self-aspects. Self-aspects represented on the left are relatively low in differentiation compared to those represented on the right.

represents one of the three roles named earlier, and the area within the circle represents variability in the use of the ten adjectives to describe that role. The shaded area in each diagram denotes area of overlap of all three circles. In the Venn diagram to the left in the figure, the degree of overlap is high and self-concept differentiation, because it is reflected in the remaining area within the diagram, is low. In contrast, in the diagram to the right in the figure the degree of overlap is relatively low and, therefore, self-concept differentiation is comparatively high.

Donahue et al. (1993) posited that self-concept differentiation could be either an asset or a liability in terms of adjustment and coping. To the extent that differentiation reflects *specialization,* then greater differentiation should function like greater self-complexity to enable people "to respond flexibly and adaptively to different role requirements, which should improve interpersonal relationships and functioning within roles" (p. 835). On the other hand, greater differentiation might correspond to greater *fragmentation* of the self, "a lack of psychological integration stemming from unresolved intrapsychic conflicts" (p. 835). In two studies, Donahue et al. (1993) evaluated these competing predictions about self-concept differentiation. In an initial study involving college students, they found support for the fragmentation prediction. Greater self-concept differentiation was associated with lower self-esteem, more depressive symptoms, and lower satisfaction with role performance.

In a second study, these researchers found that self-concept differentiation of women at age fifty-two was positively correlated with anxiety and emotional instability and negatively correlated with emotional adjustment and well-being some thirty years earlier. In other words, poor adjustment appears to give rise to greater differentiation, or fragmentation, of the self-concept. Based on these findings, Donahue et al. (1993) concluded that differentiation of the self-concept, at least with regard to self-aspects grounded in social roles, reflects fragmentation and a lack of integration among aspects of the self-system.

This conclusion would appear to conflict with the predictions and findings involving self-complexity. Whereas self-complexity is portrayed as an asset, self-concept differentiation appears to be a liability. One obvious explanation for the disparity between the predictions and findings related to these two constructs concerns the manner by which they are measured. Both make use of sophisticated mathematical manipulations of data from a Self-Aspect x Adjective matrix (see Table 4.1), but they extract different information from that matrix. At present, the precise substantive meaning of the numbers produced by the mathematical manipulations is not clear, making it difficult to reconcile the apparently contradictory findings involving self-complexity and self-concept differentiation. Until a carefully considered interpretation of what those numbers mean is offered, it will remain unclear whether a complex or differentiated self-concept is an asset or a liability.

Evaluative Self-Knowledge

The two potentially self-descriptive adjectives *competent* and *crotchety* differ in at least two ways: (1) *Competent* is relevant to the achievement or ability domain, whereas *crotchety* is relevant to the social domain, and (2) the evaluative connotation of *competent* is positive, whereas *crotchety* is decidedly negative. Approaches to the organization of self-knowledge such as self-complexity and self-concept differentiation emphasize the substantive meaning and relevance of self-descriptive information. Other approaches focus on the evaluative meaning of self-descriptive information, capitalizing on the fact that most, if not all, self-knowledge has implications for self-evaluation (Greenwald, Bellezza, and Banaji 1988; cf. McGuire and Padawer-Singer 1976). The simple distinction between positive and negative self-knowledge provides the basis for a number of intriguing models of how self-knowledge is organized.

It is first worth noting that positive and negative self-knowledge are not simply two sides of the same coin. Indeed, the presence or absence of negative self-knowledge is more consequential in a variety of self-referent phenomena than the presence or absence of positive self-knowledge (Schwarz 1986). For instance, the disparity between one's actual and undesired (i.e., negative) selves is substantially better as a predictor of life satisfaction than is the disparity between actual and ideal (i.e., positive) selves (Ogilvie 1987). As the disparity between the actual and undesired selves increases, life satisfaction increases. In an attempt to explain this and other asymmetric patterns involving positive and negative self-knowledge, Malle and Horowitz (1995) proposed that negative self-knowledge is more tightly organized in memory and, therefore, more consequential for information processing than is positive self-knowledge. Results from a series of studies supported their proposal, demonstrating that negative self-knowledge is more strongly interconnected and more consistent than positive self-knowledge.

The distinction between positive and negative self-knowledge is sufficiently clear that the organization of the two types of evaluative self-knowledge can be examined separately. Indeed, it might be the case that self-complexity or self-concept differentiation has different implications for the two categories of self-knowledge. This possibility motivated Morgan and Janoff-Bulman (1994) to evaluate the separate contributions of positive and negative self-complexity to coping with traumatic life events. Instead of computing a single self-complexity score based on participants' sorts of all available adjectives, they had participants sort the positive and negative adjectives separately. Thus they were able to compute self-complexity scores for positive and negative adjectives as well as the full set of adjectives. Their findings supported the distinction between positive and negative self-complexity, which are only modestly intercorrelated (see also Woolfolk et al. 1995). Among participants who had experienced a traumatic life event, positive and negative self-complexity contributed independently to the prediction of coping and adjustment; higher positive self-complexity was an asset, whereas higher negative self-complexity was a liability. Among participants who had not experienced a traumatic life event, only negative self-complexity was relevant to adjustment; greater negative self-complexity was associated with poorer adjustment.

Other research focused on the distinction between positive and negative self-knowledge has pointed to negative self-complexity as more influential in adjustment than positive or overall self-complexity. In a series of correlational studies, Woolfolk et al. (1995) found that negative self-complexity, but not positive self-complexity, predicted self-esteem, depression, and negative emotions in general. They also found that both positive and negative self-complexity scores were influenced by the composition of the adjective list (e.g., proportion of positive or negative adjectives) that was provided to respondents. However, consistent with other research on positive and negative self-knowledge (e.g., Malle and Horowitz 1995; Segal et al. 1988; Segal and Vella 1990), they found that negative self-complexity performed with greater stability and predictability across studies.

Although the distinction between positive and negative self-complexity has proven useful, the strategy of treating positive and negative self-knowledge separately precludes consideration of whether the nature of the association between them affects thought and behavior. A model of self-concept organization better suited for such analyses is built around the notion of evaluative integration (Showers 1992a, 1992b). **Evaluative integration** concerns the degree to which positive and negative self-knowledge co-occur within self-aspects. If a particular self-aspect, say "student," is characterized by positive information only, whereas another self-aspect, say "athlete," is characterized by negative information only, then evaluative self-knowledge is *compartmentalized* across those aspects. On the other hand, if those two aspects of the self-system are characterized by a mixture of positive and negative information, then evaluative information is *integrated* across them. These two patterns of organization are depicted in Table 4.2. Note that the same evaluative information (i.e., 10 trait adjectives) is construed in a very different way in the two halves of the table. The implications of these two organizational patterns are important for understanding how valenced feedback is processed. Showers (1992a) reasoned that people who have a relatively positive view of themselves benefit from a compartmentalized organization because their generally positive view of themselves would not routinely be qualified by negative self-knowledge. People who

TABLE 4.2   Compartmentalized and Evaluatively Integrated Organizations of
Self-Knowledge

Compartmentalized		Evaluatively Integrated	
Student	*Athlete*	*At Work*	*At Home*
+ competent	– clumsy	– anxious	– clumsy
+ motivated	– insecure	+ competent	– insecure
+ helpful	– confused	+ creative	+ helpful
+ creative	– distracted	– confused	– distracted
+ active	– anxious	+ motivated	+ active

NOTE: + indicates positive valence and – indicates negative valence.

SOURCE: Compartmentalization of positive and negative self-knowledge: Keeping bad apples out of the bunch, by C. Showers. 1992. *Journal of Personality and Social Psychology* 62: 1036–1049. Copyright 1992 by the American Psychological Association. Adapted with permission.

have a relatively negative view of themselves, on the other hand, benefit from an integrative organization because such an organization would allow for tempering of their negative self-views by countervailing positive self-knowledge. Initial studies supported this reasoning, although the support for the argument that evaluative integration benefits people with a generally negative self-view was weaker and less reliable than the support for the advantages of a compartmentalized organization for people who generally view themselves positively.

Evaluative integration has been measured in a variety of ways, and the various approaches have provided complementary insights into the implications of various organizations of evaluative self-knowledge for self-referent information processing. In the initial research by Showers (1992a), research participants completed the card sort described earlier. Then the group of cards assigned to each self-aspect was subdivided into positive and negative groups. A tally of the number of cards in each subgroup within self-aspect provides the numbers necessary to determine the strength of the association between valence (i.e., positive-negative) and self-aspects. A stronger association indicates greater compartmentalization.

In a more fine-grained analysis of evaluative integration, Showers (1992b) asked participants to list words that describe them in social situations and to designate them as positive or negative. Evaluative integration was measured by indexing the frequency with which positive descriptors were followed by negative descriptors and negative descriptors were followed by positive ones. This particular pattern of integration, alternating valences, was associated with high self-esteem and, for certain self-aspects, a lack of negative emotions. Oyserman and Markus (1990) used a similar logic to investigate the effects of possible selves on delinquent behavior.

They operationalized *balance* in possible selves as correspondence between feared and expected selves. For instance, in a balanced organization the feared self "homeless" might be accompanied by the expected self "employed." Balance and alternating valences represent a particular form of evaluative integration that provides a cognitive context within which the potentially deleterious effects of failure can be avoided through memories of prior or anticipated successes (Taylor and Brown 1988). A final approach to operationalizing evaluative integration involves indexing the variability in positivity ratings assigned to a series of self-descriptive words or phrases. Research using this approach has demonstrated that evaluative integration is an asset during life transitions for people who generally feel good about themselves (Showers and Ryff 1996).

In summary, for most people under most conditions greater compartmentalization of positive and negative self-knowledge is associated with better adjustment (e.g., Showers 1992a); however, as research on evaluative integration broadens into more diverse populations and situations and focuses on specific patterns of evaluative integration (e.g., Showers 1992b), it is becoming clear that the effects of evaluative integration are not so straightforward. For instance, for some people, high evaluative integration is associated with greater stability of self-esteem (Rhodewalt et al. 1998). People negotiating a life transition benefit from greater integration of positive and negative self-perceptions of changes brought about by the transition (Showers and Ryff 1996). A compartmentalized organization contributes to quicker recovery from a sad mood under some conditions; however, when attention is focused directly on negative self-aspects, an integrated organization is more beneficial to recovery (Showers and Kling 1996).

Integrating the Findings on
Organization of Self-Knowledge

The new avenues of inquiry about the self made possible by second-generation approaches to thinking about and assessing the self-concept are exciting and promising; however, the early returns on research in this tradition raise almost as many questions as they answer. For instance, the answer to the basic question of whether a complex or a differentiated self-system is an asset or a liability remains unanswered: "It depends." More recent research in this tradition has begun to consider what conditions produce which outcomes. Although the mathematical and statistical indexes that currently dominate research in this arena are compelling, as noted earlier, there remains considerable mystery regarding exactly what psychological characteristics they represent. Perhaps they capture only a portion of the richness of variability in how self-knowledge is organized.

For instance, mathematical indexes such as self-complexity and self-concept differentiation may miss the integrative influence of higher-order self-aspects or self-narratives that provide an idiosyncratic, integrative context for seemingly disparate self-views (Harter et al. 1997). For example, the seemingly disparate views that one is both *passive* and *assertive* might be reconciled by holding to a higher-order view of oneself as *perceptive* regarding which type of behavior, passive or assertive, is appropriate in a given situation (Klein and Loftus 1993). As measures of self-concept organization become more sophisticated and better informed by research findings, the nature of the associations among the various indexes will become clearer and, as a consequence, the role of organization in psychological functioning and behavior can be stated more definitively.

Experience of Self-Knowledge

In addition to questions about the organization of self-knowledge, contemporary research on the self-concept has begun to focus on people's experience of self-knowledge. It might seem odd to ask how well people know themselves; however, recent research has clearly shown that not all people know themselves equally well. Moreover, the degree to which people know themselves clearly is tied to their self-esteem. Two fruitful programs of research on the experience of self-knowledge have provided keen insights into the association between self-concept and self-esteem. We now discuss each in turn.

Self-Concept Clarity

In an incisive analysis of the voluminous research literature on the reactions of high- and low-self-esteem people to evaluative feedback, Campbell (1990) proposed that people vary in the clarity with which they understand themselves. Campbell labeled this individual difference **self-concept clarity**, which is defined as "the extent to which the contents of an individual's self-concept (e.g., perceived personal attributes) are clearly and confidently defined, internally consistent, and temporally stable" (Campbell et al. 1996, 141). According to Campbell (1990), self-concept clarity is "an important concomitant of self-esteem" (p. 539) that helps to explain why low self-esteem people are more generally affected by social cues that implicate the self than their high-self-esteem counterparts (see also Brockner 1984)

One means of measuring self-concept clarity is using the Self-Concept Clarity Scale (Campbell et al. 1996), shown in Figure 4.2. Items such as item 7 tap the confidence aspect of self-concept clarity; the scale also

FIGURE 4.2   Items of the Self-Concept Clarity Scale

---

1. My beliefs about myself often conflict with one another.[a]
2. On one day I might have one opinion of myself and on another day I might have a different opinion.[a]
3. I spend a lot of time wondering about what kind of person I really am.[a]
4. Sometimes I feel that I am not really the person I appear to be.[a]
5. When I think about the kind of person I have been in the past, I'm not sure what I was really like.[a]
6. I seldom experience conflict between the different aspects of my personality.
7. Sometimes I think I know other people better than I know myself.[a]
8. My beliefs about myself seem to change very frequently.[a]
9. If I were asked to describe my personality, my description might end up being different from one day to another day.[a]
10. Even if I wanted to, I don't think I could tell someone what I'm really like.[a]
11. In general, I have a clear sense of who I am and what I am.
12. It is often hard for me to make up my mind about things because I don't really know what I want.[a]

NOTE: Scale ranges from 1 (strongly disagree) to 5 (strongly agree).

[a] Item reverse-scored so that disagreement is given a high score (to reflect greater clarity).

SOURCE: Self-concept clarity: Measurement, personality correlates, and cultural boundaries, by J. D. Campbell et al. 1996. *Journal of Personality and Social Psychology* 70: 141–156. Copyright 1996 by the American Psychological Association. Adapted with permission.

includes items that target internal consistency (e.g., item 1) and temporal stability (e.g., item 8) of self-concept. Scores on the Self-Concept Clarity Scale are positively correlated with self-esteem, positive affect, and extraversion, and negatively correlated with depression, anxiety, negative affect, and self-reflectiveness (Campbell et al. 1996). Thus, as predicted, people's self-reports of the clarity of their self-concept are associated with self-reports of self-referent affect and cognition—greater clarity is accompanied by more positive self-referent affect and cognition.

Self-concept clarity also can be measured by indexing certain characteristics of people's self-ratings. For instance, the confidence dimension of self-concept clarity has been assessed as the degree of extremity of self-ratings on bipolar adjective scales. For instance, ratings near the middle of a seven-point scale anchored on one end by *competitive* and the other by *cooperative* could be interpreted as lack of clarity regarding one's standing on that dimension. On the other hand, ratings near either extreme could be interpreted as evidence of greater clarity with regard to one's standing on that dimension. Consistent with this prediction, Campbell (1990) found that extremity of self-ratings (with regard to either pole of a bipolar scale) was positively correlated with self-esteem. Similarly, the temporal aspect of self-concept clarity can be indexed using statistical characteristics of respondents' self-ratings. The similarity of respondents' self-ratings over time, calculated in a variety of ways, is positively correlated with self-esteem (Campbell 1990; Campbell et al. 1996). Further corroborating the theoretical definition of self-concept clarity, the internal consistency of people's self-ratings—the degree to which people rate themselves similarly on different items that assess the same attribute—is positively correlated with self-esteem and correlated as predicted with a variety of measures of self-referent thoughts and feelings (Campbell 1990; Campbell et al. 1996). Together with the findings involving the Self-Concept Clarity Scale, these findings provide strong and consistent evidence of the link between one's experience of self-knowledge and the regulation of self-knowledge in the course of social life.

Self-Certainty

A second variable that reflects people's experience of their own self-knowledge is self-certainty (Baumgardner 1990). **Self-certainty** reflects the degree to which a person is confident about his or her self-views across a variety of domains. For instance, Person A and Person B both might describe themselves as "slightly above average" in intelligence; however, Person A might concede that sometimes he thinks he is actually a bit below average and other times he thinks he is well above average, whereas Person B might assert that she is slightly above average, plain and simple. In this example, although the two people see themselves as equally intelligent, Person B is more certain of that self-view than Person A.

Self-certainty is measured using the Latitude of Self-Description Questionnaire (LSDQ; Baumgardner 1990). Like many measures of self-concept, the LSDQ asks respondents to describe themselves on a series of trait adjectives (e.g., *intelligent, persistent, likable*); however, the LSDQ differs from traditional adjectival measures in important ways. First, the LSDQ is a decidedly social measure because it asks respondents to rate themselves with reference to their peers. Second, respondents not only estimate their standing on the trait adjectives but they also estimate the highest and lowest levels on the trait adjectives that might describe them. These latter estimates form the basis of the measure of self-certainty.

Two response patterns to an example item from the LSDQ appear in Figure 4.3. Completion of the measure requires respondents to consider their relative standing on each adjective in three ways. First, the respondent is asked to "decide if you think you have more than average, average, or less than average of the particular trait. Then mark on the scale with an X where on that continuum you see yourself" (Baumgardner 1990, 1071). In the two response patterns shown in the figure, both respondents rated themselves at the sixty-fifth percentile (i.e., as high or higher than 65 percent of

FIGURE 4.3   Two Response Patterns to a Single Item from the Latitude of Self-Description Questionnaire

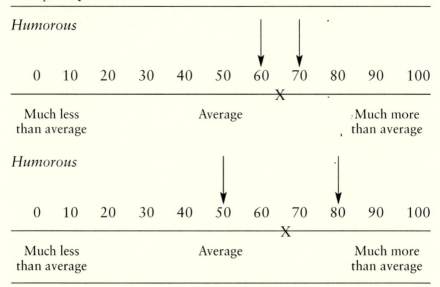

SOURCE: To know oneself is to like oneself: Self-certainty and self-affect, by A. H. Baumgardner. 1990. *Journal of Personality and Social Psychology* 58: 1062–1072. Copyright 1990 by the American Psychological Association.

the population) on the trait *humorous*. The second phase of responding to items of the LSDQ produces the measure of self-certainty. The respondent is asked to

> decide where you see your range on that trait. You probably found yourself a bit unsure of where to place the X in the first exercise. This is because we usually view ourselves as somewhat flexible on almost all traits (although some more than others). What you need to do is simply decide where that range is and mark the two endpoints with arrows. . . . When done, you should have two arrows, marking the endpoints of where you might fall, and one X, marking your best guess of where you do fall. (Baumgardner 1990, 1071)

Looking back to the figure, the first respondent sees himself as possibly falling as low as the sixtieth percentile or as high as the seventieth percentile on humor, whereas the second respondent can see herself falling between the fiftieth and eightieth percentile. The second respondent's latitude of self-description on the trait *humorous* is wider (30 percentage points) than the first respondent's (10 percentage points), indicating less certainty regarding her standing on the trait *humorous*. A total self-certainty score is created by averaging latitude widths across the twenty traits included in the scale; lower scores indicate greater self-certainty.

Research on self-certainty using the LSDQ (Baumgardner 1990) underscores the importance of considering people's experience of their own self-knowledge in research on self-concept and self-esteem. Self-certainty is positively correlated with global self-esteem. The more certain people are in expressing their self-concept, the higher their self-esteem. This association appears to hold regardless of whether the trait adjectives on which self-ratings are made are positive or negative, or concern social or intellectual traits. In summary, one way of understanding the link between self-concept and self-esteem is through a consideration of self-certainty. Greater certainty about one's self-concept contributes to higher self-esteem, and uncertainty about one's self-concept goes hand in hand with low self-esteem.

Self-Concept in the Social Arena

Self-concept is a rich and intriguing aspect of selfhood that rightfully has received a considerable amount of attention from social psychologists. A substantial and growing body of research findings provides an increasingly clear and detailed view of how the self-concept varies between people and across situations and how it functions in the regulation of thoughts, emotions, and behavior. As our understanding of self-concept has increased, its prominence in people's experience of themselves and the world around them has become more apparent. This prominence is aptly described by DeSteno and Salovey (1997):

> Of all the concepts that reside in memory, it can be argued that the self[-concept] reigns supreme with respect to individuals' daily functioning; without a coherent self-concept, we could not identify ourselves or, more important, even differentiate ourselves from other objects, animate or otherwise, in awareness. But the integrality of the self-concept extends well beyond this basic perceptual function. It is a representation of all that one is, and consequently, is intimately tied to any psychological process, automatic or volitional, that involves self-knowledge. (p. 389)

In the remaining chapters we consider in detail the psychological processes for which identity and self-concept are relevant.

5

Self-Esteem

Self-esteem is thinking that you are somebody, that you are better than other people, and that you do not let anyone push you around.
—*The mother of one of the authors, when asked what self-esteem is*

Self-esteem is one of those psychological concepts that we encounter frequently in our everyday lives. Everyone seems to have an idea about what it is. Parents want their children to have lots of it, teachers attempt to foster it in their pupils, lawyers and politicians sometimes seem to have too much of it, and clients in therapy have too little. Thus it probably comes as no surprise that self-esteem has been implicated in numerous areas of psychological functioning, including delinquent behaviors (Anderson 1994); substance abuse (Higgins, Clough, and Wallerstedt 1995; Turner 1995); depression (Brown, Andrews, Harris, Adler, and Bridge 1986; Kernis, Grannemann, and Mathis 1991; Kernis et al., in press; Tennen and Herzberger 1987); anger, hostility, and aggressive behavior (Baumeister, Smart, and Boden 1996; Kernis, Grannemann, and Barclay 1989); life satisfaction (Diener and Diener 1995); intimacy and satisfaction in relationships (Griffin and Bartholomew 1994; Rusbult, Morrow, and Johnson 1987); and reactivity to evaluative events (Brown and Dutton 1995; Campbell, Chew, and Scratchley 1991; Kernis, Brockner, and Frankel 1989).

Our focus in this chapter is on the nature of self-esteem and its role in psychological functioning. First, we examine some basic issues and attempt to provide answers to the following questions: What do social psychologists mean by self-esteem? Is self-esteem the same as self-confidence, for example? Can self-esteem vary from self-aspect to self-aspect, such that one can have high self-esteem with respect to some characteristics (e.g., social skills) but low self-esteem with respect to others (physical prowess)? Second, we discuss some of the ways that self-esteem has been measured. Third, we examine what it means to possess high or low self-esteem. Again, opinions differ among psychologists. Interestingly, this difference in opinions has stimulated research and theory on aspects of self-esteem other than whether it is high or low. Accordingly, we discuss these other aspects and show how they can help to resolve apparent controversies and opinion differences. Next, we touch on the origins and functions of self-esteem. Finally, we discuss childhood experiences that can foster optimal self-esteem development.

What Is Self-Esteem?

As is the case with many issues relating to the self, James (1950) provided the grist for a great deal of subsequent theory and research. With respect to the nature of self-esteem, he actually offered two views. In one view, he asserted that self-esteem reflects the ratio of one's "successes" to one's "pretensions" or aspirations. In other words, self-esteem is a summary evaluation that reflects the extent to which a person believes she is performing well in those domains or areas in which she aspires to do well. For example, if Mary wants very much to be a concert violinist, not being selected to her high school orchestra would contribute to her possessing low self-esteem. On the other hand, if Mary wants to play professional soccer and she plays the violin only because her mother forces her to do so, not being selected for the orchestra will have little or no bearing on her self-esteem. Overall self-esteem—how a person generally evaluates himself or herself—stems directly from the sum total of these success/aspiration assessments. Implicit in this view of self-esteem is that it can change. One can perform better or worse on different occasions, or one can take on new areas of importance and drop old ones.

In James's second view, he suggested that self-esteem reflects "a certain average tone of self-feeling which each one of us carries about with him, and which is independent of the objective reasons we may have for satisfaction and discontent" (1950, 306). In other words, self-esteem reflects the average or "baseline" feelings that we have toward ourselves, feelings that include worth, value, liking, and acceptance (see also Savin-Williams and Demo 1983). Instead of relying on specific successes or failures, self-esteem is taken to reflect a general positive or negative orientation toward the self. A person's self-esteem is reflected in his or her answer to the question, Do I like, value, and accept myself? and not to questions such as, Am I good at making friends or making money? Implicit in this view of self-esteem is that it is relatively stable and may be based on factors and processes of which the person is unaware.

Since James proposed these views (1950), each has received considerable attention, as well as some support. In support of the assertion that self-esteem reflects the ratio of successes to aspirations are the following research findings. First, when asked to list attributes that one currently possesses (actual self) and attributes that one would like to ideally possess (ideal self), the more discrepancies that exist between the two lists, the more negative one's feelings toward the self (Morretti and Higgins 1990). Second, children and adults who place high importance on those self-aspects in which they shine and low importance on those self-aspects in which they fare poorly have more favorable feelings toward the self than do people who do otherwise (Harter 1993; Pelham 1995). Third, fluctuations in day-to-day self-judgments of competence correspond to greater fluctuations in global feelings of self-worth among people who place considerable importance on their being competent than among those who do not (Kernis, Cornell, Sun, Berry, and Harlow 1993).

Findings such as these indicate that how people evaluate themselves in specific domains does have implications for their self-esteem. Are these implications powerful enough that we should equate self-esteem with the totality of these more specific self-evaluations (perhaps giving more weight to self-evaluations in domains of high importance)? If so, what about this "average tone of self-feeling" that James proposed, which he presumed to be unrelated to specific evaluations or performances? If it does exist, on what is it based?

Brown (1993) has consistently advocated for conceptualizing self-esteem in terms of global feelings of self-worth, liking, and acceptance that are separate from specific self-evaluations. He argues that to the extent that global self-esteem and specific self-evaluations are related, it is global self-esteem that affects specific self-evaluations, and not the other way around. In other words, how much we like, value, and accept ourselves in general will color how we evaluate our specific qualities such as intelligence, attractiveness, sophistication, and so on. This argument is controversial, partly because it goes against the traditional view of how self-evaluations relate to self-esteem and partly because there seems to be no way to obtain definitive data that would separate one direction of influence over another. Nonetheless, Brown's point that global self-esteem (i.e., feelings of self-worth, liking, and acceptance) is distinct from domain-specific self-evaluations (e.g., competence, attractiveness, popularity) is well-taken. We, as well as most current self-esteem researchers, accept it.

Our feeling is that both directions of influence are likely to occur. Which direction is more important may vary from person to person and dimension to dimension (cf. Crocker and Wolfe 1998a; Harter 1993). Some research supports this bidirectionality of influence viewpoint (Harter and Waters 1991, as cited in Harter 1993; Zumpf and Harter 1989). Specifically, when adolescents are asked about the nature of the link between their physical appearance and self-esteem, some indicate that their assessments of their physical attractiveness precede or determine their global self-esteem, whereas others indicate that their self-esteem determines how much they like how they look. Crocker and Wolfe (1998a) interpret such findings as evidence that people vary in the degree to which their self-esteem is contingent and the basis of the contingency. We present their integrative ideas in more detail later in the chapter.

To appreciate the importance of distinguishing between specific self-evaluations and global self-esteem, or feelings of self-worth, one need only think of a person, who despite all appearances that he is highly competent and proficient in a number of domains, is full of dislike for himself. Sadly, such people are not a complete rarity. Happily, there are also people who are content and satisfied with themselves despite not being a "star" at anything. We return to this distinction between specific self-evaluations and global self-esteem later in the chapter, where we focus on the basis of these global feelings of self-worth.

In concluding this section, we want to emphasize several things. First, people evaluate themselves along a wide range of dimensions that vary in their degree of self-importance. Second, these evaluations relate to, but are not the same as, self-esteem. Third, **self-esteem** refers to *the extent to which an individual likes, values, and accepts himself or herself* (Rogers 1951). Fourth, self-esteem is to be distinguished from related constructs such as self-confidence, or self-efficacy, which refers to beliefs about one's abilities and wherewithal to obtain desired outcomes (Bandura 1997). Self-confidence refers to one's beliefs about oneself, whereas self-esteem refers to the feelings that one has toward oneself (cf. Brown 1993).

Measuring Self-Esteem

Most often, self-esteem is measured by asking people to indicate the extent to which each of a series of potentially self-descriptive statements are, in fact, descriptive of them. The number and content of specific items, as well as what form responses are to take, vary considerably from measure to measure. As a general rule, though, respondents are asked either to indicate the extent to which they agree or disagree with each statement, or to indicate the extent to which each statement is true or characteristic of them. In this section, we briefly describe a few of the most widely known and used self-esteem measures.

The Self-Perception Profile for Children (Harter 1985b) was developed to measure self-evaluations and global self-esteem in elementary school children in grades three and higher. In addition to global self-esteem, this instrument assesses specific self-evaluations in five domains: scholastic competence, athletic competence, social acceptance, physical appearance, and behavioral conduct. Each item describes two different kinds of children; respondents first decide which child they are more like, and then they indicate whether the statement is sort of true or really true of them. For example, one item pertaining to social acceptance is, "Some kids find it hard to make friends, but other kids find it's pretty easy to make friends," and a global self-esteem item reads, "Some kids like the kind of person they are, but other kids often wish they were someone else."

One of the valuable features of this instrument is that it allows researchers to examine which self-evaluations relate most strongly to global self-esteem. Of the five self-evaluative domains mentioned in the previous paragraph, which one do you think relates most strongly to global self-esteem in elementary school children? Before we give you the answer, we want to describe another self-esteem instrument, Rosenberg's (1965) Self-Esteem Scale.

Of all the scales designed to assess self-esteem in adults, the Self-Esteem Scale is perhaps the most widely used. Literally thousands of studies conducted by psychologists, sociologists, and educators have included it. One positive feature of this scale is that it is very brief—only ten items in length, half of which are worded so that agreement indicates high self-esteem, and half so that agreement indicates low self-esteem. Examples of the items are shown in Figure 5.1.

An examination of these items reveals both a considerable strength and a potential liability of the measure (a weakness, by the way, that is shared by virtually all self-esteem measures). On the positive side, the items clearly tap what we mean by global self-esteem, that is, they focus on overall satisfaction and worthiness and not on self-evaluations along specific dimensions (like friendliness or intelligence). On the negative side, the fact that the items so clearly tap self-esteem may prompt people to give responses that reflect well upon them (that they are good people who like themselves),

FIGURE 5.1 Sample Items from the Self-Esteem Scale

On the whole, I am satisfied with myself.
At times I think I am no good at all.[a]
I feel that I have a number of good qualities.
I certainly feel useless at times.[a]
I take a positive view of myself.

NOTE: Respondents indicate the extent to which they agree or disagree with each statement on four- or five-point scales.

[a] Item reverse-scored so that disagreement is given a high score (to reflect high self-esteem).

SOURCE: *Society and the adolescent self-image,* by M. Rosenberg (Princeton, N.J.: Princeton University Press), 17–18.

rather than responses that may not portray them as positively, even though they are more accurate.

Along these lines, research using the Self-Esteem Scale has identified very few people who have scores that are below the scale's midpoint. Some self-esteem researchers have taken this to mean that there may be very few people who truly dislike themselves (e.g., Baumeister, Tice, and Hutton 1989; Leary and Downs 1995). From this vantage point, then, most people with low self-esteem are thought to have predominantly neutral or mildly negative feelings about themselves rather than extremely negative ones. Low self-esteem people who truly loathe themselves are thought to be very few in number. From a different vantage point, given people's general reluctance to respond in a way that reflects poorly on themselves, mildly negative responses on a self-esteem scale may reflect the existence of greater self-directed negativity than a literal interpretation of them may warrant. Which view is more correct? At this point, it is difficult to say. What is safe to say, though, is that the former view is currently more popular among psychologists than the latter view. Regardless of the correct answer, a consideration of the issues it raises has led to a heightened appreciation of the complexities involved in understanding both low and high self-esteem.

Before leaving this section, we return to the question raised earlier: Which self-evaluative domain relates most strongly to global self-esteem? It may surprise you to learn that the answer is "physical appearance." Harter (1993) summarized these findings as follows:

> In study after study, at any developmental level my colleagues and I have examined, including older children, adolescents, college students, and adults (Harter 1990), we have repeatedly discovered that self-evaluations in the domain of physical appearance are inextricably linked to global self-esteem. The correlations between perceived appearance and self-esteem are staggeringly high and robust across the life span, typically between .70 and .80. (p. 95)

There is no denying the relationship between judgments of appearance and global self-esteem that Harter reports. We do wish to note, however, that other self-evaluative domains also relate to global self-esteem. For example, not far behind physical appearance is the extent to which people feel valued and supported by significant others in their lives. Harter (1993) stated that "across numerous studies with older children and adolescents, as well as with college students and adults, we have found that the correlations between perceived support from significant others and self-esteem range from .50 to .65" (p. 99). In addition, other research and theory indicate that the extent to which a person experiences a general sense of mastery (the ability to deal effectively with one's environment) or competence is strongly related to global self-esteem (Deci and Ryan 1995; Wells and Marwell 1976; White 1959).

Overall, then, these three self-evaluative domains—physical appearance, social acceptance, and competence—seem to be among the domains most strongly related to global self-esteem. This is not to deny that there may well be cultural, ethnic, racial, and gender differences in how strongly each of these (as well as other) specific self-evaluative domains relate to global self-esteem. For example, research by Josephs et al. (1992) suggests that, whereas competence may be more important to the self-esteem of men than of women, interpersonal skills and relationships are more important to the self-esteem of women than of men. We now turn to an in-depth examination of the nature of high self-esteem, to be followed by a similar examination of low self-esteem.

The Essence of High Self-Esteem

What does it mean to say that someone has high self-esteem? For some people (like the mother quoted at the beginning of this chapter), to have high self-esteem means that one is very proud of who one is, feels superior to most other people, and is very willing and able to defend against possible threats to one's positive self-view. In other words, people with high self-esteem engage in self-promoting activities (Baumeister, Tice, and Hutton 1989), and they see themselves as "above" most people. Furthermore, high self-esteem people do not like to see (or for other people to see) "chinks in their armor," and they react very strongly to undermine the legitimacy of any information or any person who attempts to cast them in a less than very positive light. That is, people high in self-esteem take on a "circle the wagons" or "defend the fort" mentality as they work to preserve their self-esteem in the face of "attacks" on it.

A variety of research findings can be marshaled in support of this characterization of high self-esteem. First, compared to low self-esteem people, high self-esteem people are more likely to explain their successes in ways that glorify themselves while explaining away their failures by denying responsibility for them—an explanatory pattern referred to as "self-serving" in nature (e.g., Tennen and Herzberger 1987; Zuckerman 1979). Second, after performing poorly or being insulted, it is people with high self-esteem who are especially likely to derogate or criticize others (Crocker et al. 1987; Gibbons and McCoy 1991). Third, being outperformed by someone heightens the desire of high self-esteem people to engage in additional performance comparisons with the same person (Wood et al. 1994), presumably to show that being outperformed was just a "fluke." Fourth, when their egos have been threatened (e.g., by suggesting that they may not be able to perform well under pressure and so should set low goals), people high in self-esteem respond by setting inappropriately difficult and risky goals and go on to compound their dilemma by subsequently performing more poorly than people low in self-esteem (Baumeister, Heatherton, and Tice 1993). When not threatened, high self-esteem people typically set optimal goals for themselves and perform quite well. These and other research findings (e.g., Tice 1991) paint a picture of high self-esteem people which suggests that they are not very secure in their feelings of self-worth and liking. Said differently, these findings suggest that high self-esteem is a precious commodity that must be continually promoted and defended in order to survive.

An alternative view, one that derives from a number of humanistically oriented theories (e.g., Rogers 1959), is that people who have high self-esteem feel that they are worthwhile and valuable individuals, they like and are satisfied with themselves, and they are comfortable with and accepting of their weaknesses. To have high self-esteem, then, is to have positive feelings toward oneself that are built on solid foundations that do not require continual validation or promotion. Moreover, one's feelings of self-worth will not be questioned or threatened with the inevitable adversities that life presents. One will be pleased with one's successes and disappointed with one's failures, but these reactions will not be flavored with the additive "I am better than you, so watch out."

Which view of high self-esteem is the correct one? Our position is that both are correct inasmuch as each characterizes some people with high self-esteem. A full answer to this question, though, requires that we introduce several new concepts. Before doing so, let us consider the nature of low self-esteem.

The Essence of Low Self-Esteem

There are two viewpoints on what it means to have low self-esteem. One perspective, which has predominated for many years (cf. Harter 1983), holds that people low in self-esteem exhibit a wide variety of maladaptive cognitive, emotional, motivational, and behavioral patterns. For example, an abundance of research has shown that low self-esteem people evaluate themselves negatively in many domains, readily accept the truthfulness of unfavorable feedback, are prone to experience a wide range of negative emotions, including anxiety and depression, and exhibit ineffective strategies in the face of adversity (e.g., Brockner 1983; Brown and Dutton 1995; Harter 1993; Kernis, Brockner, and Frankel 1989; Watson and Clark 1984). Among adolescents, low self-esteem has been linked to such things as delinquency, drug abuse, and unsafe sexual practices (Hawkins, Catalano, and Miller 1992), and it appears to be one of a number of factors that are associated with suicidal ideation and behaviors (Harter 1993).

Finally, low self-esteem is implicated in a number of psychological disorders that lead people to seek psychotherapy and other mental health services (Leary, Schreindorfer, and Haupt 1995).

Another perspective has emerged recently that characterizes people with low self-esteem as cautious and uncertain (rather than highly maladjusted) individuals whose behavioral styles are geared toward minimizing exposure of their deficiencies (Baumeister et al. 1989). Proponents of this latter viewpoint assert that the self-evaluations and self-concepts of low self-esteem people are characterized more by uncertainty, confusion, and neutrality than by negativity (Baumeister 1993; Baumeister et al. 1989; Baumgardner 1990; Campbell 1990) and that low self-esteem people embrace their positive self-aspects (Swann, Pelham, and Krull 1989) and engage in some forms of self-protection and self-enhancement when they feel safe to do so (Brown, Collins, and Schmidt 1988; Tice 1991; Wood et al. 1994). These findings suggest that people with low self-esteem are not necessarily miserable people who loathe and despise themselves and who inevitably engage in self-destructive behaviors.

Which of these two views better characterizes low self-esteem is currently a major point of contention among researchers who study self-esteem. It may be noteworthy that most of the research that has supported the "cautious and uncertain" view of self-esteem has involved college students, whereas most of the research that has supported the "self-loathing and maladaptive" view of self-esteem has involved children, adolescents, or "special" populations (e.g., substance abusers, juvenile delinquents, psychotherapy clients). Perhaps the low self-esteem people who reach college take on qualities and utilize strategies that differentiate them from other people with low self-esteem. Alternatively, it may be that only a subset of people with very low self-esteem suffer from extreme self-loathing and maladaptive behavior patterns.

Self-Esteem and Emotional Reactions to Failure

Research has consistently shown that low self-esteem people have more adverse emotional reactions to failure than do high self-esteem people. In fact, when low self-esteem people fail, they are more likely than their high self-esteem counterparts to experience strongly negative emotions—shame, humiliation, and lack of motivation. They are less likely to attribute their current failure to lack of effort (Brown and Dutton 1995; Kernis et al. 1989). Why does this occur? One reason seems to be that people with low self-esteem are more likely to believe that specific failures have negative global implications for who they are as people. That is, if they fail at something, they begin to think that they are stupid, incompetent, and incapable of doing anything right. These thoughts intensify their negative feelings, leaving them demoralized and unmotivated.

The process that characterizes the reactions of low self-esteem people to failure experiences can be depicted as follows:

Failure → "I am so stupid! Can't I do anything right?" → Intense negative emotions, shame, lack of motivation

Of course, some people with low self-esteem may not be very skilled. Objectively, however, there is no hard evidence that low self-esteem people are generally less skilled than their high self-esteem counterparts. This suggests that the tendency for people low in self-esteem to make global negative self-statements after a specific instance of failure (or even after several successive ones) is not justified. Nor, as we have seen, does it contribute to their psychological well-being. This is one instance in which low self-esteem people would benefit from adopting the strategy used by high self-esteem people, who in general are better able to compartmentalize the implications of specific failures (cf. Showers 1995).

Beyond High Versus Low Self-Esteem

A growing number of researchers and theorists are focusing on other aspects of self-esteem. This work, for the most part, is still in its infancy, but many believe that it holds the promise of reconciling divergent viewpoints on the role of self-esteem in psychological functioning (particularly with respect to high self-esteem).

Defensive Versus Genuine High Self-Esteem

Schneider and Turkat (1975) conducted research in which they examined the distinction between "genuine" and "defensive" high self-esteem. *Genuine* high self-esteem people are thought to have genuinely favorable feelings of self-worth, whereas *defensive* high self-esteem people are thought to harbor inner negative self-feelings that they are unwilling to admit, due to high needs for social approval (see also Horney 1950). Because they are unwilling to admit their weaknesses, they may appear to have high self-esteem. Defensive high self-esteem people usually are distinguished from genuine high self-esteem people on the basis of their greater agreement with statements that cast people in a positive light but probably are not true (called "socially desirable responding," Crowne and Marlowe 1960). Because of their greater needs for social approval, "defensively high [self-esteem people] ought to do more than react to success or failure; they ought to engage in active attempts to change their public definition after failure, to gain approval when possible, and to structure social situations to maximize self-enhancement possibilities" (Schneider and Turkat 1975, 129). "On the other hand, a more genuine high self-esteem person should be less concerned to avoid or repudiate failure, since failure is not particularly threatening" (p. 128).

Consistent with these assertions, Schneider and Turkat (1975) found that after a failure experience, defensive high self-esteem people described themselves to others in an extremely positive manner (presumably as a way to garner approval). The same did not occur among genuine high self-esteem people, who apparently had little need to compensate for the failure by altering their self-descriptions. These findings are important because they represent clear support for the assertion that individuals who score high on a self-esteem scale are not all the same.

Explicit and Implicit Self-Esteem

Although people with high self-esteem report that they like themselves, they may simultaneously have negative self-feelings of which they are unaware (and not just that they are unwilling to report, as in defensive high self-esteem). This possibility has been elaborated most clearly by Epstein and Morling (1995), who argue that people actually have two kinds of self-esteem. One kind, called *explicit self-esteem,* refers to feelings of self-worth that people are conscious of possessing. Explicit self-esteem is measured by standard self-esteem scales like Rosenberg's (1965) measure. The second kind, called *implicit self-esteem,* refers to feelings of self-worth that are nonconscious and thus cannot normally be reported. Yet they "seep through" to color people's emotional and behavioral responses. Implicit self-esteem cannot be assessed directly using self-reports. It can only be assessed indirectly, perhaps by examination of people's emotional or nonverbal reactions. There currently is no widely accepted method for measuring implicit self-esteem.

A particularly interesting case exists when a person reports having high self-esteem (explicit high self-esteem) but nonconsciously possesses low feelings of self-worth (implicit low self-esteem). Epstein and Morling (1995) suggested that this person will often react very defensively to potentially negative evaluative information, due to the conflicting implications created by coexisting positive and negative feelings about oneself. This prediction is very similar to what would be predicted for (and was observed in) people with defensive high self-esteem. That is, people who report high self-esteem but simultaneously hold low self-esteem, which they are unwilling (defensive) or unable (implicit) to admit to, would be easily threatened by negative self-relevant information. Furthermore, they would take the steps (perhaps even drastic ones) they feel would allow them to successfully maintain their consciously held positive self-esteem. In contrast, people whose conscious and nonconscious self-feelings are favorable would not be so easily threatened and would have less need to "defend" their self-esteem.

Contingent Versus True Self-Esteem

Yet another distinction is between contingent and true self-esteem (Deci and Ryan 1995). *Contingent self-esteem* is based on achieving specific outcomes, matching specific standards, or meeting specific expectations. According to Deci and Ryan (1995),

> contingent self-esteem refers to feelings about oneself that result from—indeed, are dependent on—matching some standard of excellence or living up to some interpersonal or intrapsychic expectations. A man who feels like a good and worthy person (i.e., has high self-esteem) only when he has just accomplished a profitable business transaction would have contingent self-esteem. If he were very successful, frequently negotiating such deals, he would have a continuing high level of self-esteem; yet that high level would be tenuous, always requiring that he continue to pass the tests of life, always requiring that he match some controlling standard. (p. 32)

Deci and Ryan (1995) portrayed *true self-esteem* quite differently:

> People with true self-esteem, of course, would have goals and aspirations, and they would attempt to accomplish those outcomes by devoting their personal resources to them, often wholeheartedly. And their emotions would surely be affected by the outcomes of their efforts. They would probably feel pleased or excited when they succeed and disappointed when they fail. But their feelings of worth as people would not fluctuate as a function of those accomplishments, so they would not feel aggrandized and superior when they succeed or depressed and worthless when they fail. (p. 33)

In short, contingent self-esteem, unlike true, or secure, feelings of self-worth, requires continual validation.

How can we distinguish between true and contingent self-esteem? One strategy might be to directly ask people how much their feelings of self-worth depend on whether they achieve certain performance levels or satisfy particular goals or expectations. This approach was taken by Crocker and Wolfe (1998a) in a series of studies designed to highlight the various sources of self-esteem for people with contingent self-esteem. Their Contingencies of Self-Esteem Scale (Crocker and Wolfe 1998b) queries respondents concerning nine contingencies: approval, appearance, God's love, love of friends and family, power, self-reliance, social identity, school competency, and virtue. Respondents complete the measure by indicating the degree to which they agree with statements such as "I can't respect myself if others don't respect me" (approval) and "doing something I know is wrong makes me completely lose my self-respect" (virtue).

Initial research with the Contingencies of Self-Esteem Scale produced a number of interesting patterns involving demographic groups. Among college students, women's self-esteem is more contingent on approval, appearance, God's love, and school competency than is men's self-esteem. Comparisons between samples of white, African-American, and Asian students indicate that the self-esteem of African-American students is less contingent on approval, appearance, and school competence than the self-esteem of white and Asian students. African-American students' self-esteem is more contingent on God's love than the self-esteem of white and Asian students, and Asian students' self-esteem is more contingent on self-reliance and social identity than the self-esteem of white and African-American students. More generally, their research indicates that the more contingent self-esteem is on approval, appearance, and self-reliance, the lower it is.

Another means of distinguishing between contingent and true self-esteem would be to assess self-regulatory styles proposed to differentiate between the two forms of self-esteem (Deci and Ryan 1995). We discuss self-regulatory styles at length in Chapter 8. For now, let us just say that people with true self-esteem are thought to choose how to live their lives primarily based on what is personally important to them, what they enjoy, and what they are good at. In contrast, people with contingent self-esteem are thought to live lives that are governed primarily by the demands placed on them by others and by themselves, as well as by rigid application of expectations and standards by which they judge themselves.

Self-Esteem Lability

The self-esteem of some people is highly tied to specific, environmentally based events. For example, Jamie might feel good about herself (have high self-esteem) on a day in which predominantly good things happen (e.g., she gets a raise at work for good performance, she is told that she looks pretty) but feel bad about herself (have low self-esteem) on days in which predominantly bad things happen (i.e., her friend accuses her of being selfish, she has an argument with her boss). Jamie possesses *labile self-esteem.* Research indicates that people with labile self-esteem are prone to experience depression when their lives are filled with negative, stressful events (Butler, Hokanson, and Flynn 1994). Additional implications of possessing labile self-esteem are only beginning to be understood.

Self-Esteem (In)Stability

Related to the concept of self-esteem lability is the concept of self-esteem instability. Self-esteem instability can be conceptualized in terms of long-term or short-term fluctuations (Rosenberg 1986). Viewed as long-term fluctuations, self-esteem instability reflects change in one's baseline or typical feelings of self-worth (i.e., how much do I generally, or typically, like myself?) that occurs "slowly and over an extended period of time" (Rosenberg 1986, 126). For example, some children may experience a drop in self-esteem during the transition from elementary to middle school, which is then followed by a steady but gradual increase in self-esteem through the high school years (O'Malley and Bachman 1983). Also, some people seek professional guidance in order to improve the feelings that they have for themselves. The process of changing one's baseline self-esteem is likely to involve considerable effort, although it is often successful.

Alternatively, self-esteem instability can be viewed as short-term fluctuations in people's current, or immediate, feelings of self-worth (i.e., how much do I like myself at this moment?). These types of changes can be measured daily or even more frequently. Considerable research has shown that people do vary in the extent to which their immediate feelings of self-worth change from one assessment to the other (Kernis and Waschull 1995; Roberts and Monroe 1992; Savin-Williams and Demo 1983; Waschull and Kernis 1996). For some people, feelings of self-worth change little or not at all, whereas for other people they range from very positive feelings to very negative feelings over the course of a very short time. Both long-term and short-term fluctuations in self-esteem are likely to have implications for psychological functioning. The bulk of research, however, has focused primarily on short-term fluctuations (for reviews, see Greenier, Kernis, and Waschull 1995; Kernis 1993; Kernis and Waschull 1995).

Importantly, the tendency to exhibit short-term fluctuations in immediate feelings of self-worth is distinct from whether a person's level of self-esteem is high or low. That is, a person could report either high or low self-esteem and show considerable moment-to-moment fluctuations in his or her current self-feelings (or not). Kernis and his colleagues have argued that unstable self-esteem reflects fragile and vulnerable feelings of self-worth that are subject to the influences of externally provided (e.g., being insulted by one's supervisor) and internally generated (e.g., thinking about one's progress toward important goals) evaluative information. If this information is positive, one's immediate feelings of self-worth are favorable; if the information is negative, one's feelings of self-worth are also negative. In contrast, people with stable self-esteem have feelings of self-worth that are more separable from these specific evaluative experiences. This does not necessarily mean that they have highly favorable feelings of self-worth; in fact, these feelings could be quite negative. Yet they are stable in the sense that they do not change from moment to moment. Before discussing research on unstable self-esteem, we take a step back and reexamine these recent perspectives on self-esteem.

Taking Stock of These Various Positions

A common theme shared by all of these perspectives, summarized in Table 5.1, is that there is more to self-esteem than whether it is high or low. That is, two people may obtain the same high (or low) score on a self-report measure of self-esteem, but the nature of their self-esteem and how it relates to their psychological functioning may be quite different. In some instances, a high score may mask negative feelings that a person has about himself. In the case of defensive high self-esteem, the person is aware of his or her negative self-feelings but is unwilling to admit them to others. In the case of high explicit/low implicit self-esteem, the person is unaware of their existence. In contrast, a person who truly likes himself or herself and does not unconsciously hold negative self-feelings will in general have little reason to feel threatened. Thus, one factor that can distinguish between high self-esteem people with the same score on a self-esteem measure (such as the Self-Esteem Scale) is whether they also hold negative self-feelings that they are unwilling or unable to admit to.

In other instances, a person's high self-esteem might be based on specific outcomes such as achieving a lofty goal, performing at a high level, or receiving a favorable evaluation (contingent self-esteem). Or, a person's self-esteem may be highly affected by the events of a particular day (labile self-esteem). Finally, people may report high self-esteem when asked to base their responses on how they typically feel about themselves, but their im-

TABLE 5.1   Varieties of Self-Esteem

Type of Self-Esteem and Definition	
Defensive high self-esteem	Report positive feelings of self-worth but harbor negative feelings inside
Genuine high self-esteem	Report and feel positive feelings of self-worth
Explicit self-esteem	Conscious feelings of positive or negative self-worth
Implicit self-esteem	Nonconscious feelings of positive or negative self-worth
Contingent self-esteem	Positive feelings of self-worth that are dependent on achieving specific outcomes, meeting expectations, matching standards, etc.
True self-esteem	Secure, positive feelings of self-worth that do not need continual validation
Labile self-esteem	Daily feelings of self-worth that are tied to specific, environmentally based events
Unstable self-esteem	Immediate feelings of self-worth that exhibit considerable short-term fluctuations

mediate feelings of self-worth may undergo considerable short-term fluctuations (unstable self-esteem).

These distinctions or components of self-esteem are not mutually exclusive. In fact, it is probably rare for an individual to possess self-esteem that has not at any point in time been somewhat defensive, contingent, labile, or whatever. For most of us, the issue is "to what extent is our self-esteem . . . ?" rather than "do we or don't we have self esteem that is . . . ?" For instance, the type of high self-esteem suggested by the quote that opened the chapter is likely to be, at least to some extent, defensive, contingent, labile, unstable, and/or accompanied by low implicit self-esteem. It is the presence of these other components of self-esteem that is thought to promote the type of self-aggrandizing and self-protective efforts exhibited by (some) high self-esteem people. In contrast, high self-esteem that does not include these other components is thought to be more secure and well anchored, obviating the need for self-promotion and "counterattacks."

A Research Example

Anger and hostility are often instigated by threats of an interpersonal nature, such as insulting treatment or unfair criticism. In these instances, anger and hostility may serve to ward off other negative self-feelings or restore damaged self-esteem or public self-image (Felson 1984; Feshbach 1970). In addition, the angered person may blame the instigator for making him or her feel bad, thereby making it easier to direct ill will toward the instigator (and away from the self). Given these considerations, do you think that people with high self-esteem more often get angry and hostile toward others than people with low self-esteem, or vice versa?

One possibility is that high self-esteem people are more likely to become angry because they tend to perceive slights as unjustified, and unjustified threats are particularly potent elicitors of anger and hostility (cf. Averill 1982). A second possibility is that low self-esteem people are especially quick to anger because people who already feel negative toward themselves are especially sensitive to an outside threat (cf. Averill 1982; Wills 1981). You may be anticipating that a third view exists as well—that some high self-esteem people would be more prone to anger and hostility than their low self-esteem counterparts, whereas others would be less prone. Specifically, it may be that people with high self-esteem whose self-esteem is fragile and unstable may more frequently react with anger and hostility than people with low self-esteem. But high self-esteem people whose self-esteem is stable and secure may lash out in these ways less often than low self-esteem people.

To test these possibilities, Kernis et al. (1989) asked a group of college students to complete self-report measures of self-esteem level, self-esteem stability, and anger and hostility proneness. Participants reported on the likelihood in general of their becoming angry and hostile, as well as on the likelihood of their responding with anger and hostility in specific situations. The results attest to the importance of qualitative aspects of self-esteem. High and low self-esteem people did not differ in their reported tendencies toward anger and hostility. Thus one cannot say that high self-esteem people get angry and hostile more than low self-esteem people, or that low self-esteem people get angry and hostile more than their high self-esteem counterparts. However, when self-esteem stability was also taken into consideration, people with unstable high self-esteem reported the highest tendencies to become angry and hostile (more than low self-esteem people), whereas people with stable high self-esteem reported the lowest tendencies (and less than low self-esteem people). Whether high self-esteem people were more or less prone than low self-esteem people toward anger and hostility depended on whether their self-esteem was unstable or stable. In short, important individual differences in tendencies to become angry and hostile would have been obscured if both self-esteem level *and* self-esteem stability had not been taken into consideration.

Why Is Self-Esteem So Important?

It may seem self-evident that self-esteem is an important aspect of human beings' experience of themselves. Psychologists have not been satisfied with this as an explanation, however, and they have sought to understand the origins and functions of self-esteem. One prominent view emphasizes that self-esteem "is part of a motivational system directed toward self-preservation in an organism intelligent enough to be aware of its own vulnerabilities and ultimate mortality" (Greenberg, Pyszczynski, and Solomon 1995, 74). In essence, according to this perspective, high self-esteem provides a sense of meaning and value that helps protect people from being paralyzed with terrifying anxiety. A second prominent view (e.g., Leary and Downs 1995) emphasizes the social significance of self-esteem. Specifically, self-esteem is thought to guide the selection of interpersonal strategies that limit the potential for individuals to be excluded from the important social groups and relationships that are essential to their survival. It does so by being exquisitely sensitive to whether a person is being accepted or rejected by others— acceptance promotes positive self-feelings, whereas rejection demotes feelings of self-worth and activates corrective steps. A third prominent view is that self-esteem is a natural by-product of the satisfaction of growth-oriented motives, which underlie the continual honing of skills necessary to deal with an ever changing and demanding environment (Deci and Ryan 1995). This brief discussion does not do justice to the enormous insights regarding esteem and the nature of the human condition afforded by each of these perspectives. Regardless of which view(s) one endorses, this much is clear—self-esteem is important to our mental (and perhaps physical) well-being.

Childhood Experiences
Within the Family and Self-Esteem

We conclude this chapter by focusing briefly on the role of family environment in optimizing self-esteem in children. In what is regarded as a landmark study, Coopersmith (1967) reported on the effects of parental attitudes and child-rearing techniques on the self-esteem of ten- to twelve-year-old boys. The data for this study came from the boys as well as their mothers, all of whom completed questionnaires and were extensively interviewed by a member of the research team. The major findings were summarized by Harter (1983) as follows:

> Parents of boys with high self-esteem more often had the following attitudes and behavioral practices: (1) They were accepting, affectionate, and involved, treating the child's interests and problems as meaningful, and showing genuine concern; (2) They were strict in the sense that they enforced rules carefully and consistently, and sought to encourage children to uphold high standards of behavior; (3) They preferred *noncoercive* kinds of discipline, for example denial of privileges and isolation, and typically discussed the reasons why the child's behavior was inappropriate; (4) They were democratic in the sense that the child's opinions were considered in decisions such as the hour of their bedtime, and the child participated in making family plans. (pp. 337–338)

Although many have accepted these conclusions, this research is not without its strong critics (e.g., Harter 1983; Wylie 1979). Criticisms revolve around such issues as the adequacy of the measures used, the adequacy of statistical analyses that were conducted, and the absence of fathers and daughters as participants. Other studies, though, have also documented the importance to children's high self-esteem and well-being of such things as parental involvement, acceptance, support, and clearly defined limits (e.g., Buri et al. 1988; Gecas and Schwalbe 1986; Grolnick and Ryan 1989).

Recent research also implicates many of these same characteristics in the stability of children's self-esteem (Kernis, Brown, and Brody 1997). For example, compared to children with stable self-esteem, children with unstable self-esteem reported that their fathers were more critical and psychologically controlling (e.g., using guilt-arousing techniques) and less likely to acknowledge their positive behaviors or to show approval by being affectionate or spending time doing something together. In addition, fathers of children with stable high self-esteem were viewed as especially good at problem solving.

The research findings discussed in this section implicate childhood experiences within the family as an important factor influencing self-esteem in children. As we enter a new age in self-esteem research, in which features of self-esteem other than its level are addressed, additional research on the influence of family environment, school environment, and peer groups on the level and quality of self-esteem is needed.

6

Self-Enhancement

High self-esteem has become part of the American Dream.
—Swann (1996, 7)

How people evaluate themselves has important implications for how they think, feel, and behave. But this is only part of the story. People not only evaluate themselves positively or negatively and, thereby, experience the consequences of having low or high self-esteem, but they have a vested interest in maintaining a positive view of themselves. They want to protect themselves against damage to their self-esteem and, occasionally, try to raise their self-esteem above its current level. In short, people appear to possess a **self-enhancement motive**—a psychological drive to maintain, protect, and enhance their self-esteem. To varying degrees, people want to feel good about themselves, and they behave in a variety of ways—both beneficial and dysfunctional—that allow them to see themselves in a reasonably positive light.

The idea that people possess a self-enhancement motive has a long history in the science and practice of psychology. Among the topics addressed by James (1950) in his landmark text *The Principles of Psychology* was the human tendency to strive to feel good about oneself—to experience "self-complacency" and to avoid "self-dissatisfaction." James viewed self-seeking as a fundamental aspect of human nature and suggested that much behavior derives from the fact that each of us believes that "whatever is me is precious . . . whatever is mine must not fail" (p. 318).

At about the same time that James's writings were providing a foundation for scientific psychology in the United States, psychologists in Europe were being influenced by Sigmund Freud's revolutionary ideas about the human psyche. Freud himself paid little attention to the topic of self-esteem, but many of his students did. Alfred Adler (1933), in particular, traced much of human behavior to people's feelings of inferiority. According to Adler, people feel inadequate and inferior when there is a discrepancy between how they think they should be and how they think they really are. Adler did not view these inferiority feelings as inherently bad but rather as a "growth force" that spurs people to develop, grow, and improve. Such feelings motivate them to strive for superiority and perfection in an attempt to feel better about themselves. Feelings of inferiority become a problem only if the strategies people adopt to overcome them create problems for themselves or for others (Manaster and Corsini 1982).

The self-enhancement motive has received a great deal of attention from theorists and researchers in the past few decades. Greenwald (1980) compared the human self to a totalitarian political regime. Just as a totalitarian government controls information to lead its citizens to perceive the government in a particular desired fashion, the ego fabricates and revises information in a way that preserves the individual's desired image of himself. Instead of doing "damage control" to put the government's failures and indiscretions in the best possible light, the *totalitarian ego* misconstrues, fabricates, and revises the truth to hide the ugly facts about us from ourselves.

Researchers have traced a variety of human behaviors—both adaptive and maladaptive—to this fundamental desire to feel good about oneself. In this chapter, we examine the self-enhancement motive and the ways in which it affects people's everyday behavior. We look first at ways in which people react to events that damage their self-esteem and then at ways by which they try preemptively to prevent damage from occurring. We then examine two instances in which the self-enhancement motive seems to go awry—narcissism and impostorism. Finally, we address the question of whether the pervasive quest to feel good about ourselves is adaptive.

Undoing Damage to Self-Esteem: Reactive Strategies

Events that damage self-esteem are a regular and unavoidable part of everyday life. We fail tests or do not perform as well on them as we had expected. We lose athletic competitions. We are denied the job we wanted or, if we get it, are passed over for a promotion or are denied a raise. Our performances sometimes receive only lukewarm reactions from the audience or unenthusiastic reviews by the critics. In innumerable ways, we do things that reveal us to be less competent, informed, reasonable, composed, adjusted, or moral than we would wish. Whatever other consequences these kinds of unpleasant events may have for us, they often undermine our feelings about ourselves, if only temporarily.

The events that undermine our feelings about ourselves are universally unpleasant. Not only are we forced to recognize unflattering facts about ourselves, but we typically feel bad about ourselves—ashamed of how we behaved, if not of who we are. Losses of self-esteem are accompanied by unpleasant feelings such as anxiety, sadness, guilt, and anger, among others.

Given the unpleasantness of the events that damage self-esteem, we should not be surprised that most people who encounter threats to their self-esteem quickly jump to work repairing the wreckage and minimizing further damage. Many fundamental features of human behavior have been traced to the human penchant for preserving self-esteem in the face of esteem-deflating events. In this section, we examine four such strategies: self-serving attributions, sour grapes rationalization, social comparison, and compensatory self-affirmation.

Self-Serving Attributions

Life is complex. Things that happen to us—whether good or bad—are the result of many contributing factors. Likewise, our behavior is determined by many forces that may not even be obvious to us. When we behave in a particular way, often it is not entirely clear precisely why we reacted as we did. Why did your team lose the game when, by all indications, it should have won? Why did you do better—or worse—on the exam than you expected? Why has your romantic partner been a bit aloof lately? Why didn't you get the job you wanted? The answers to such questions about everyday events are often ambiguous, and if we were honest with ourselves, we would often admit that we do not really know why they happened. But rather than throw up our hands in despair over not knowing why such things happen, we nonetheless arrive at explanations, or **attributions**, for them.

Because the causes of many events are not clear-cut, people have a certain degree of latitude in the attributions they make. And, given this latitude, their conclusions are often affected by their personal needs and agendas at the time. People do not necessarily intentionally fabricate explanations that make them feel better about how things turned out. Rather, their perceptions of events are unwittingly biased in ways that suit their psychological needs, including their need to feel good about themselves. Freud (1959) observed that "the ego rejects the unbearable idea together with its associated effect and behaves as if the idea never occurred to the person at all" (p. 72).

A person's feelings about herself will be affected by failure, rejection, disappointment, and inappropriate behavior only to the extent that the person herself feels responsible for the undesired event. People need not feel bad about themselves when negative events are not their fault. If we fail an exam because we were deathly ill when we took the test, if we are passed over for a promotion because the boss's son got it, or if we find ourselves alone on New Year's Eve because our romantic partner is in the hospital, our self-esteem is not likely to be diminished by our bad luck (although we may be upset for other reasons in each case). However, if we fail an exam despite having taken it under ideal circumstances, are passed over for a promotion in favor of someone we view as mediocre, or find ourselves alone on New Year's Eve because our partner cannot stand the sight of us anymore, we would likely suffer a loss of self-esteem.

Given that the effects of events on self-esteem depend on whether or not we feel personally responsible for them, people can limit the damage to their self-esteem by explaining the events in particular ways. Specifically, by limiting their perceived responsibility for negative events, people can protect their self-esteem.

Examples of **self-serving (or ego-protective) attributions** are common. For example, students are likely to claim personal responsibility for scoring well on tests, but they tend to deny that failures are their fault (Forsyth 1986). Many social psychological studies have been conducted on this phenomenon. In these experiments, participants—typically university students—take what they believe is an important test of their ability or personality and then receive bogus feedback indicating that they performed either well or poorly on the test. When asked *why* they performed as they did, participants who thought they did poorly are inclined to point to factors that absolve them of responsibility for the failure (Bradley 1978; Kernis and Grannemann 1990). By attributing their failures to factors outside of their control—such as the unfairness of the test or the distracting testing conditions—people can protect their self-esteem. In contrast, participants who believe they performed well attribute their performance to their own ability, thereby promoting their self-esteem.

Similarly, people working together in groups tend to believe that they are more influential in the group's performance than most other group members when their group succeeds. However, if the group fails, each member feels less responsible for the fiasco than he or she believes most of the other members are (Leary and Forsyth 1987; Schlenker and Miller 1977). Attributing the group's success to oneself while denying responsibility for the group's failure serves each member's need for self-esteem.

Along the same lines, people who are in unhappy marriages tend to blame their marital problems mostly on their spouses, but members of happy couples each take personal credit for how well things are going (Bradbury and Fincham 1990). And, lest we be accused of pointing fingers, we should note that psychologists are also susceptible to self-serving attributions. Research suggests that psychologists and other kinds of therapists attribute client improvement to their own skills as a therapist but blame the client when therapy goes poorly (Roberts and McCready 1987). In all of these examples, people protect their self-esteem by interpreting events in ways that reduce their responsibility for negative events and bolster their self-esteem by attributing responsibility for positive events to themselves (for reviews of the literature on self-serving attributions, see Blaine and Crocker 1993; Zuckerman 1979).

Sour Grapes Rationalization

In Aesop's fable of the sour grapes, a hungry fox saw some clusters of ripe grapes hanging from a high trellis. Although she tried everything imaginable, the fox could not reach the grapes. After exhausting herself trying to get the grapes, she turned away, saying "Those grapes are sour anyway and not as ripe as I thought." Just as the fox reduced her sense of failure and disappointment by concluding that she didn't want the grapes anyway, people downplay the importance of events that threaten their self-esteem.

As noted in the previous chapter, James (1961) observed that our self-esteem depends not only on how good we are at something but on how good we aspire to be. "With no attempt there can be no failure; with no failure, no humiliation. So our self-feeling in this world depends entirely on what we back ourselves to be and do" (p. 168). If we convince ourselves that the outcome we failed to attain was not really important or desirable to us, then we will not feel as bad about ourselves for failing to get it. If we don't care how well we play softball or whether we are an A student or that we don't have a date for the prom, then losing softball games, getting bad grades, and sitting at home on prom night should have little effect on our self-esteem.

To further elaborate on this idea, we consider once again James's (1950) "equation" for self-esteem:

$$\text{Self-Esteem} = \text{Success} \,/\, \text{Pretensions}$$

This equation suggests that self-esteem is highest when our successes exceed our pretensions or aspirations. James noted that "such a fraction may be increased as well by diminishing the denominator as by increasing the numerator. To give up pretensions is as blessed a relief as to get them gratified" (p. 311). In other words, people can maintain their self-esteem either by succeeding or by not aspiring to success.

Although it makes sense that people choose to place greater importance on areas of their lives in which they do well, the interesting thing is that people revise their judgments of an activity's importance or desirability *after* they succeed or fail. Like the fox, they often decide that they really didn't want those things they failed to achieve.

In studies of people's reactions to success and failure, participants have been asked to rate how important it was for them to do well on a test or other task after having learned how well they performed on it. As you might guess, participants who perform poorly in such studies indicate that the task was less important to them than participants who perform well. Not only that, but like Aesop's fox, they actually derogate the quality of the test, saying, for example, that the test did not seem very valid to them. Participants who do well disagree, insisting that the test was a good one (Forsyth and Schlenker 1977). We regularly see this phenomenon in college classrooms when students receive exam grades. Students who receive a high grade think that the test was a fair and valid measure of their knowledge; those who do poorly find innumerable problems with the exam.

The sour grapes effect also occurs when people's self-esteem is damaged by being rejected by others. In a study of people's reactions to social rejection, researchers gave research participants bogus information indicating that other participants had either selected them to be a member of a laboratory group or had indicated that they did not want the participant as a member. When later asked to rate the degree to which they initially had wanted to be selected for the group, participants who had been excluded indicated that they had been less interested in being part of the group than participants who had been selected (Leary, Tambor, Terdal, and Downs 1995, Study 3). In other words, participants who believed they were rejected by the other group members insisted that they didn't want to be a member of the group anyway.

To an outside observer, the sour grapes effect seems transparent. We can easily see that the fox really did want the grapes or that the rejected participant really wanted to be included in the group. But the power of the ego is such that the individual himself comes to believe that the unattained goal was not really important or desirable.

Downward Social Comparison

We saw in Chapter 3 that people's views of themselves are affected by how they believe they compare to other people. Believing oneself to be better than other people is associated with higher self-esteem than believing oneself to be inferior. But how do people decide whom to compare themselves to for purposes of evaluating themselves? To whom do we look as standards for judging how intelligent, attractive, athletic, humorous, or ethical we are? As the poem "The Desiderata of Happiness" expresses it, "always there will be greater and lesser persons than yourself" (Erhmann 1927). One can always feel good by comparing oneself to lesser persons, and one can always feel deficient by comparing to greater ones. How do we choose?

Research suggests that when people want a true and accurate assessment of where they stand on a particular dimension, they compare themselves to people who are more or less like them on other dimensions. If you are a college or university student, you probably think about how you compare to other students at your college rather than to students at other colleges or to people who are not students. For practical purposes, you usually find it most useful to know where you stand relative to others in your own social environment; however, people are not always interested in seeing themselves accurately. In fact, accuracy is sometimes the least of their concerns (Sedikides 1993). When they are motivated to protect their self-esteem, for example, people willingly sacrifice accuracy for information that helps them feel good about themselves. Given that people's self-esteem can be affected by where they stand relative to other people, they can protect their self-esteem by comparing themselves to those who are worse than they are on the relevant dimension; that is, they may engage in **downward social comparison** (Wills 1981; Wood 1989).

In one experiment that investigated the effects of a threat to self-esteem on downward social comparison (Pyszczynski, Greenberg, and LaPrelle 1985), researchers told participants that they had performed well or poorly on a test of social sensitivity. Participants were then given the opportunity to look at other test takers' papers after being led to believe that these other test takers had scored either low or high on the test. Participants who thought they personally had scored well on the test showed little interest in seeing other people's tests; their feelings about themselves were already positive, and they had nothing to gain by knowing how others had performed. Participants who thought they performed poorly on the test wanted to see other people's scores, but only if they thought the others had scored low on the test. They could feel better about themselves by comparing themselves to other low scorers.

The self-serving use of downward social comparison apparently starts at an early age. A study of elementary school children (their average age was 9 years) found that children whose performance got worse over the course of testing preferred to look at the scores of children who performed even worse than they did; however, children whose performances improved looked equally often at the scores of superior and inferior performers (Levine and Green 1984). Again, we see evidence that people whose positive feelings about themselves are in jeopardy tend to engage in downward social comparison.

The general tendency toward downward social comparison allows most people to believe themselves to be better than the average person. On nearly every dimension we might pick—leadership ability, driving skills, physical health, honesty, or whatever—most people think they are better than average. Given that most people cannot be better than average (only 50 percent can be better than average), the fact that most of us think we are special attests to our knack for comparing ourselves to people who are worse than we are.

If we cannot find a comparison group that is worse than we are, we can always fabricate one. People sometimes react to failure by belittling other people, thereby creating a lower standard for self-comparison (Brown and Gallagher 1992). If that doesn't work, they can always misremember how bad they really are. One experiment showed that when research participants had no other way to protect their self-esteem, they remembered their behavior in a more flattering light than it actually occurred. In discussing this study, Klein and Kunda (1993) concluded that "people will go to great lengths to convince themselves that they are superior to others" (p. 737).

Often we compare ourselves not to specific, identifiable individuals but to our sense of what *most other people* are like. This sense is often vague and the comparison group usually ill-defined, but that doesn't stop us from comparing ourselves to this so-called generalized other. In the absence of objective criteria for identifying this imaginary comparison group, people can modify their beliefs about what other people are like to suit their own purposes. For example, when people do poorly on some task, instead of suffering a loss of self-esteem they can conclude that most other people would probably do poorly on it as well.

This tendency for people to overestimate the number of other people who are like them is known as **false consensus**. False consensus occurs in many areas of life, even when self-esteem is not at stake. For example, people tend to overestimate the number of other people who share their attitudes and opinions (see Miller and Prentice 1996). False consensus is more common, however, among people who believe they possess negative characteristics, suggesting that false consensus is exacerbated by threats to self-esteem. People seem to believe that their personal strengths are rare but that their weaknesses are common. For example, people who think they possess negative characteristics—that they are irritable, depressed, or fearful, for example—estimate the number of other people who are also irritable, depressed, or fearful as higher than people who do not see themselves in these negative ways (Ross, Greene, and House 1977; Sanders and Mullen 1983; Suls and Wan 1987). By concluding that plenty of other people are just like them, people who believe they possess negative attributes can feel better about themselves.

Compensatory Self-Affirmation

Another way people can protect their self-esteem in the face of potentially threatening events is to turn their attention to areas in which they fare better. People may cope with one kind of self-threat by affirming unrelated aspects of their selves. The student who fails a test may think about what a successful athlete she is. The rejected lover may dwell on his business successes. The person who has done something immoral may do a good deed to convince herself of her overall integrity. By thinking about aspects of themselves that they regard as positive or by acting in self-affirming ways, people can bolster their sense of self-worth in the face of threats to self-esteem.

According to self-affirmation theory, one function of the self-system is to "sustain a phenomenal experience of the self as adaptively and morally adequate" (Steele 1988, 266). When people encounter a threat to their self-esteem—failure or rejection, for example—their goal is not simply to respond to that particular threat but rather to maintain an overall sense of self-integrity. Thus they may deal with specific threats to esteem by affirming central, valued aspects of themselves. Steele (1988) concluded that "in ego defense, people are concerned with the big picture; they regulate their defensive adaptations to maintain very general conceptions of self-integrity rather than to remedy specific threats. It is the war, not the battle, that orients this system" (p. 289). Even so, evidence suggests that when possible, people prefer to deal directly with the esteem-threatening event rather than affirm themselves on other dimensions (Stone et al. 1997). People may use self-affirmation primarily when more direct means of eliminating threats to self-esteem are not available to them.

The self-affirmation perspective suggests that people with high self-esteem should be less likely to react strongly to threats to self-esteem than people with low self-esteem. In essence, high self-esteem provides people with automatic resources for self-affirmation. "Yes, I screwed this up badly," the high self-esteem person may think, "but I'm actually a very capable and wonderful person on most other dimensions." People with low self-esteem, in contrast, do not have such positive self-views and thus may have to engage in explicit self-affirming behaviors to deal with a particular threat to their self-esteem. An experiment conducted by Steele, Spencer, and Lynch (1993) confirmed this reasoning, with one qualification: High self-esteem participants in their study engaged in less rationalization of undesirable behavior than low self-esteem participants only when they were reminded of the fact that they had high self-esteem (by completing a self-esteem measure). This finding suggests that people must consciously think about their positive features in order to compensate for esteem-damaging experiences.

Preventing Damage to Self-Esteem: Preemptive Strategies

In the preceding section we examined tactics that people use after events have cast undesirable aspersions on their self-esteem. However, people do not always wait for their self-esteem to be damaged before taking action. When they foresee the possibility that an esteem threat may occur, they often take preemptive steps to reduce the impact of the event. Like coastal residents boarding up their windows as a hurricane approaches, people use these strategies to minimize the damage brought about by the impending storm. Seeing the storm on the horizon, they make preparations so that a failure, rejection, or other esteem-deflating events, should they arrive, do as little damage as possible.

People protect their self-esteem most straightforwardly by actively avoiding situations in which their esteem may be damaged. They flee the coastline before the storm even arrives. Generally, we like doing things we are reasonably good at and, when possible, prefer to spend our time engaged in such activities rather than activities that make us feel bad about ourselves. Of course, people cannot always avoid situations that may threaten their self-esteem. When they cannot avoid the esteem-deflating event, people may prepare themselves to confront it. In the following section, we discuss four preemptive strategies for protecting self-esteem: preemptive self-serving attributions, self-handicapping, defensive pessimism, and relationship management.

Preemptive Self-Serving Attributions

People sometimes create attributions for events that have not yet happened—**preemptive self-serving attributions** (also called self-reported handicaps). Even before knowing how they performed on a test (or even before taking the test, for that matter), students who are worried about their grade may think about all of the things that are working against them: There is too much material on the test, the professor's tests are always unfair, I haven't felt well for several days, I had two other tests this week, and so on. Of course, some (or all) of these thoughts may contain an element of truth, or they may be exaggerated. Either way, people seem to be particularly inclined to dredge up these excuses prior to a possible threat to their self-esteem. Should the dreaded failure occur, they are already armed with an arsenal of self-serving explanations.

Interestingly, these preemptive excuses sometimes involve an admission that one's upcoming performance is likely to be hampered by a personal problem, weakness, or deficit of some sort. For example, test-anxious students may stress how anxious they feel when they think that anxiety may prove detrimental to their test performance (Smith, Snyder, and Handlesman 1982). Similarly, shy people may emphasize how nervous they feel if they think that their nervousness can account for how awkwardly they behave in social interactions (Snyder, Smith, Augelli, and Ingram 1985). People will also exaggerate the number of traumatic events they have experienced in their lives if they think that a history of personal trauma will explain poor performance (DeGree and Snyder 1985).

This particular kind of preemptive attribution reflects an interesting trade-off. People appear willing to sacrifice a small amount of self-esteem (by emphasizing how anxious, shy, or traumatized they are, for example) in order to protect their self-esteem in a more important domain. Thus, although they are admitting a problem or weakness, "what is lost in such an admission is not as highly valued as what is protected" (Snyder and Smith 1982, 107).

Behavioral Self-Handicapping

The effectiveness of preemptive attributions or self-reported handicaps in protecting self-esteem hinges on their plausibility. People are limited in the preemptive attributions they may make by what they know to be true about the causes of their own behavior. Truly implausible attributions are not effective in protecting self-esteem. Students who are worried about an upcoming exam may exaggerate in their minds the amount of material to be learned or how nervous they feel the day of the test, but they are unlikely to convince themselves that their minds were emptied of the course material during an alien abduction the night before the exam.

Evidence suggests that under certain circumstances, however, people will create *real* impediments to their own performance, thereby providing them with an objective, fully plausible, esteem-protecting explanation should they fail. When people **self-handicap**, they "attempt to reduce a threat to esteem by actively seeking or creating inhibitory conditions that interfere with performance and, thus, provide a persuasive causal explanation for potential failure (or set the stage for the individual to accept personal credit for success)" (Shepperd and Arkin 1989, 101). With a self-handicap in place, the probability of success is reduced, but people can justifiably attribute failure, should it occur, to the unfavorable circumstances rather than to their own lack of ability, thereby insulating their self-esteem from failure. Of course, should they happen to do well in spite of the self-created hindrance, they can rightfully feel even better about themselves than they would otherwise.

In the original study of self-handicapping (Berglas and Jones 1978), participants waiting to work on an intellectual task were given the choice of taking an experimental drug that either enhanced or impeded intellectual performance. The results showed that participants who had performed well on an earlier task but had reason to doubt that they could repeat their performance preferred to take the drug that supposedly would hurt their score on the upcoming task. Faced with uncertain success on the impending task, they self-handicapped. Presumably, these individuals currently felt good about themselves by virtue of having done well earlier, yet they were concerned that their self-esteem would be hurt if they performed worse on the upcoming task. By taking the performance-inhibiting drug, they had a ready-made self-serving attribution should they fail: "My performance on this task doesn't really reflect my ability; after all, I was hindered by the drug."

Other studies have explored the lengths to which people will go prior to an ego-threatening event to create handicaps to their performance. People who are worried about failure may choose to consume alcohol (Tucker, Vuchinich, and Sobell 1981), work in the presence of highly distracting noise (Shepperd and Arkin 1989), or practice inadequately (Rhodewalt, Saltzman, and Wittmer 1984). In each case, they can later attribute poor performance to something other than their own incompetence—being drunk, the distracting environment, or insufficient practice.

The concept of behavioral self-handicapping helps to explain many self-defeating things that people do. Procrastination is one good example. People procrastinate for many reasons, not the least of which is that they simply have more enjoyable things to do than the dreaded task that they continue to avoid. Yet procrastination may serve as a self-handicapping strategy by fostering attributions that protect self-esteem. A person who puts off doing a task until the last minute and then rushes to meet the deadline may reasonably claim that anything less than an optimal performance was due to the fact that he or she simply did not have enough time. It is far less damaging to one's self-esteem to conclude that one did not allow enough time to complete a task than that one was incapable of doing it well.

Or consider the fact that people often do not practice sufficiently for upcoming performances, whether those performances are athletic, musical, intellectual, or whatever. From an outsider's perspective, this seems irrational; why wouldn't a person practice as much as possible? From the self-handicapper's perspective, however, practicing carries a risk. What attribution must I make if I practice diligently but still do poorly? I must conclude that I am truly incompetent, and my self-esteem will be affected. If I don't practice quite enough, I can always attribute my poor performance to not having practiced sufficiently (Rhodewalt, Salzman, and Wittmer 1984).

Self-handicapping protects self-esteem by obscuring the causes of events. People often do not really want to know why things turned out the way they did if that knowledge will force them to acknowledge undesirable things about themselves.

Buffering the Blow

We noted earlier that self-esteem is affected not only by what people accomplish but by what they *want* to accomplish. You can see this easily by observing students' reactions to receiving grades on a test. Two students may receive the same grade—let's say a C—yet one is delighted and the other is devastated. The difference in their reactions obviously has more to do with their expectations or goals than with the grade itself.

In light of this, people sometimes can protect their self-esteem by lowering their expectations. If the student can convince himself that he does not really aspire to an A, his self-esteem will be less affected if he receives a C. We can view this strategy as a preemptive case of sour grapes, discussed earlier. Rather than conclude that the grapes were sour after trying and failing to get them, people can simply decide that they do not want the grapes beforehand.

Much of the research on this phenomenon has been studied in the context of defensive pessimism. **Defensive pessimism** involves imagining the worst that might happen and then setting low performance expectations. We all know students who, before each and every test, are convinced that they will perform abominably and assert that they will be lucky to eke out a passing grade. By catastrophizing, these students try to prepare themselves for the blow to self-esteem that a bad test grade would bring. Interestingly, students' tendencies toward defensive pessimism appear to be unrelated to their true academic ability or prior performance (Norem and Cantor 1986b). Chronic defensive pessimists are always worried about evaluation, but other people cannot understand why they are so concerned. These are the sorts of students who "go about bemoaning the inevitability of failure, and then rush home to work furiously all night before the exam—even though they have prepared conscientiously all semester and done very well on previous exams" (Norem and Cantor 1990, 49).

The defensive pessimistic strategy appears to help some individuals perform better than they otherwise would. Importantly, such individuals do not simply resign themselves to their fate (as many depressed pessimists do). Rather, by setting low expectations and reflecting on the dangers ahead, people who use defensive pessimism motivate themselves to work harder and manage their anxiety by working through alternatives, options, and possible outcomes (Norem and Illingworth 1993).

Apparently, defensive pessimism does help protect self-esteem in the face of failure. When defensive pessimists fail, they are less inclined to use self-serving attributions to absolve themselves of responsibility (Norem and Cantor 1986a, 1990). Having considered the possibility of failure, they appear somewhat more prepared for it should it occur.

Relationship Management

We have already seen that self-esteem depends on who it is that people compare themselves to, and people who are struggling with a blow to their self-esteem tend to engage in downward social comparison. This fact has interesting and important implications for people's close relationships—specifically their friendships and romantic relationships. People obviously use their friends and relationship partners as sources of social comparison information. Our friends are typically similar to us on many dimensions—age, educational level, attitudes, interests, and so on—and thus provide reasonable targets for comparison (Festinger 1954). We can tell a great deal about where we stand by comparing ourselves to our friends, and people who are close to us play a large role in how we evaluate ourselves.

But consider what this suggests. Because our self-esteem may be threatened when we compare ourselves to people who are "better" than we are, we may prefer to have friends who are not as good as we are (or so we perceive). At the same time, however, it does little for our self-esteem to see ourselves as people who are surrounded by losers. Because we often feel good about being associated with people who are successful, we may want our friends and lovers to be as successful as possible. So what do we do? Do we choose friends who are less intelligent, attractive, athletic, or socially skilled, for example, who can serve as targets of our downward social comparison and protect our self-esteem? Or do we go for the best friends we can find to bolster our self-esteem through association? What determines whether the accomplishments of our friends and partners make us pale by comparison or make us proud to be associated with them?

The **self-evaluation maintenance** model (Tesser 1988) suggests that the answers to these questions depend on the *self-relevance* of the dimension on which people are evaluating themselves. When a particular dimension is relevant or important to a person's identity, he is likely to feel threatened when a friend or romantic partner outperforms him; however, when the dimension is not self-relevant—not important to his identity—the person is not only proud of the other's accomplishments but also may derive some self-esteem from being associated with the successful person. Thus we want our friends, partners, and spouses to do well in life and even to do better than we do—as long as their accomplishments are not in areas that are important to us (Pilkington, Tesser, and Stephens 1991; Tesser, Millar, and Moore 1988).

The picture is complicated, however, by the fact that people realize that, just as their self-esteem is affected by the achievements of their friends and partners, the self-esteem of those friends and partners is likewise affected by their own successes as well. As a result, our pleasure at having performed well is sometimes dampened by knowing that the event has threatened our friend's self-esteem. People are concerned not only about maintaining their own self-esteem but also about maintaining the self-esteem of those with whom they are in close relationships (Beach and Tesser 1995; Sedikides, Campbell, Reeder, and Elliot 1998).

Research suggests that couples implicitly "negotiate" areas of self-relevance to minimize the opportunity for one partner's behavior to indirectly threaten the self-evaluation of the other (Clark and Bennett 1992). For example, they may choose to pursue different domains within the same general area. If they are both ornithologists, one may specialize in studying nesting behavior while the other gravitates to seabird migration. Or they may tend to do self-relevant activities jointly whenever possible, thereby making comparison impossible. If they both fancy themselves gourmet cooks, they may begin to do all of the cooking together. Another option is for one partner to abandon the shared self-relevant activity. Whatever their means of resolving this problem, romantic partners (and friends, to a lesser extent) must figure our how they can pursue their relationship without damaging each other's self-esteem.

Failures of Self-Esteem Maintenance

The self-enhancement motive appears to be a pervasive, fundamental, and nearly universal aspect of human nature. Most people beyond a certain age show some tendency toward protecting their self-esteem; however, the self-esteem system appears to "malfunction" for certain individuals. In this section, we examine two such malfunctions—narcissism (in which a person's self-esteem appears too high) and impostorism (in which it appears too low).

Narcissism: Excessive Self-Esteem

In Greek mythology, Narcissus was the handsome son of the river god Cephissus. In punishment for rejecting the amorous advances of the nymph Echo (who undoubtedly suffered a devastating blow to her self-esteem), Narcissus was made to fall hopelessly in love with his own reflection in a pool of water. As he gazed in love-struck fascination at his own image, Narcissus gradually wasted away.

Both psychology and everyday language have adopted Narcissus' name to refer to people who seem hopelessly in love with themselves. The **narcissistic person** is one who has a grandiose sense of self-importance and very high self-esteem (Emmons 1984; Raskin, Novacek, and Hogan 1991b). Such individuals make highly self-serving attributions; to hear them talk, nothing bad that happens is ever their fault (Hartouni 1992). They also think that, by virtue of their superiority, they are entitled to control, manipulate, and use other people.

Several theorists have suggested that narcissism is, at its core, a means of regulating self-esteem. That is, the grandiosity, social dominance, and exploitation that are characteristic of narcissistic people may be ways of protecting themselves against self-doubt. The narcissistic pattern may develop when parents, perhaps because of their own insecurities, develop an idealized image of their child (Raskin, Novacek, and Hogan 1991a). The parents badly want their child to be attractive, brilliant, charming, and so on, and they convey to the child that he or she is highly special. They strongly reinforce these sorts of behaviors but withdraw their affection when the child behaves in a less admirable way. Thus the child develops with a grandiose but fragile sense of being someone special: "I am an exceptional person, but I must work hard to receive the admiration of others." This inflated idea of self, coupled with self-doubt arising from parental rejection over less-than-exemplary behavior, may form the foundation of narcissism. To sustain self-esteem, the narcissistic person maintains grandiose self-views (often through fantasies about success, glory, and adoration), seeks attention and adoration (by being exhibitionistic and self-serving), and dominates those in his or her social environment (in order to feel important, if not indispensable).

Impostorism: Insufficient Self-Esteem

Given how readily most people create and capitalize on opportunities to foster self-esteem, the impostor phenomenon presents a bit of an enigma. Pauline Clance (Clance and Imes 1978) first identified the impostor phenomenon in the course of psychotherapy with highly successful women who, despite having experienced academic and professional success, reported that they did not feel successful. Although these women were high achievers, they insisted that they were less capable than they appeared. In their view, they had inadvertently fooled other people into believing that they were better than they really were. In fact, they admitted to Clance, they felt like frauds or impostors—hence the label **impostor phenomenon**. Not surprisingly, impostors worry a great deal about being "found out" for the fraud they believe themselves to be. Every new evaluative experience— each test, job interview, presentation—is dreaded as yet another opportunity to reveal their true incompetence.

When they do well at things, impostors tend to feel that their success was not deserved. They tend to make self-deprecating (rather than self-serving) attributions for success, claiming that their successes in life have resulted from good luck or hard work, rather than from their own ability, for instance. They disregard or dispute indications that they may in fact be as intelligent, competent, or skilled as they appear. Clance and Imes (1978) noted that impostors "find innumerable means of negating any external evidence that contradict[s] their belief that they were, in reality, unintelligent" (p. 241). In brief, impostors appear to lack the fundamental motivation to maintain their self-esteem that we have examined in this chapter.

The question arises, however, of whether impostors truly lack a need for self-esteem or whether impostorism is, in fact, simply a different sort of strategy for maintaining self-esteem. Impostors resemble the defensive pessimists discussed earlier in that they openly expect each new evaluative event to end in disaster. This similarity raises the possibility that impostors are simply trying to buffer themselves against possible blows to self-esteem by acknowledging that they are not as good at things as they may appear.

Research also suggests, alternatively, that impostorism may reflect a self-presentational tactic designed to influence the perceptions of others. Two recent studies showed that college students who scored high in impostorism expressed lower expectations for an upcoming performance than low impostors only when they expressed those expectations to other people (Leary, Patton, Orlando, and Wagoner 1997). When they expressed their expectations privately and anonymously, high and low impostors' expectations did not differ. This pattern suggests that impostors' claims that they are not as good as others think and that they are certain to fail are interpersonal strategies aimed at other people rather than privately held beliefs. People who are concerned about negative evaluations may find underplaying previous achievements and lowering others' expectations useful for four reasons.

First, claiming that one's ability is lower than it appears to be may cause others to lower their expectations. If those expectations are successfully lowered, the person is less likely to fail (in the sense of not living up to them) and others are less likely to be disappointed. Second, claiming that one is not as good as one's performance indicates may convey a sense of modesty. As long as self-effacement does not overtly misrepresent one's ability (as in the case of a pool shark), people who understate their abilities are liked better than those who accurately acknowledge their performances (Schlenker and Leary 1982). Third, downplaying one's ability may protect one's image in the face of a potential failure. Should the person fail, at least she will be given credit for having the self-insight to recognize her limitations. Fourth, the self-effacing behavior of impostors may serve to elicit encouragement, support, and nurturance from other people (Jones and Pittman 1982). When seemingly successful individuals express doubts about their ability, others are likely to respond with supportive compliments designed to bolster the individual's confidence. Similarly, when successful people minimize their responsibility for their successes, they can expect others to dispute their self-effacing statements.

Is the Self-Enhancement Motive Adaptive?

When behavioral scientists identify a psychological process as potent and as universal as the self-enhancement motive, they naturally assume that it must serve some important function. If the quest for self-esteem did not somehow enhance the individual's ability to function in daily life, it would not exert such a pervasive and powerful influence on human behavior. Thus many researchers have concluded that it must be adaptive for people to overestimate their ability or importance, perceive the world in ways that maintain self-esteem, and behave in ways that keep self-esteem high.

As reasonable as all this may sound, the evidence regarding whether the self-enhancement motive is adaptive is mixed. In this section, we examine this issue.

The Case for Adaptivity

Many psychologists and laypeople alike have come to believe that high self-esteem is a good thing and that the self-enhancement motive is thus beneficial for keeping self-esteem high. In some circles self-esteem has become regarded as a panacea for personal and societal problems (e.g., Branden 1994). Many counselors and psychotherapists focus on enhancing clients' self-esteem as a way of helping them with problems as varied as shyness, underachievement, alcohol and drug abuse, depression, marital difficulties, test anxiety, and guilt. In addition, many people apparently try to deal with their problems themselves; go to any bookstore and you will see dozens of books that purport to help people raise their (or their friends' or their children's) self-esteem. Furthermore, there are social programs that attempt to lower rates of teenage pregnancy, juvenile delinquency, drug use, and domestic violence by raising the self-esteem of certain target populations. Is self-esteem truly the basis of happiness and psychological adjustment?

Few would doubt that high self-esteem is sometimes beneficial. For example, feeling good about oneself is often the first step toward a difficult goal. The little train engine in the children's story, despite its small size, managed to pull the trainload of toys across the mountain by repeating, "I think I can, I think I can." Likewise, people may be motivated to have high self-esteem because it helps them overcome the paralyzing effects of self-doubt and leads them to pursue difficult and imposing goals.

The self-enhancement motive may also promote certain aspects of mental health. For example, having high self-esteem tends to be associated with happiness and personal contentment, as well as with low anxiety. If nothing else, people may be motivated to preserve their self-esteem because it *feels* good. Having high self-esteem also seems to buffer people against feelings of shame when they fail, and it promotes their ability to cope with difficult circumstances (Greenwald 1980; Taylor and Brown 1988, 1994). Self-esteem is also associated with an ability to care for other people and with a heightened capacity for creative, productive work. In general, people with higher self-esteem are able to devote more attention to others because they are less focused on themselves.

The Case Against Adaptivity

Most researchers acknowledge that self-esteem is sometimes associated with beneficial consequences; however, many point out that the pursuit of high self-esteem is not as uniformly positive as it may first appear. First, it is disadvantageous, if not downright dangerous, to overestimate one's ability or value in many situations. How many people have been hurt or killed, for example, by tackling challenges that were beyond their ability? Given that overestimating one's ability or value can lead to imprudent (if not fatal) decisions, the self-enhancement motive would seem to work against people's survival and reproductive success. One wonders, then, how such a motive could ever have evolved; primitive peoples who overestimated their ability in fighting ferocious animals or leaping over crevasses were less likely to pass along their genes than those who had a more accurate sense of their abilities and worth. Even if the overly confident person is not killed or maimed, high self-esteem is sometimes associated with nonproductive persistence. People with very high self-esteem may undertake hopeless tasks that consume their time and energy because they overestimate their ability and the likelihood of eventual success (McFarlin, Baumeister, and Blascovich 1984).

Second, the motive to protect and enhance one's self-esteem can have a negative impact on one's relationships with other people. Research shows that people do not like those who are viewed as egotistical (Schlenker and Leary 1982). Narcissistic individuals, in particular, are disliked and avoided (Leary, Bednarski, Hammon, and Duncan 1997). Thus the endless search for self-esteem may hurt one's interactions and relationships with other people.

Third, people sometimes pursue self-esteem in ways that are dangerous to themselves or others. In their efforts to feel good about themselves, people may join cults and gangs, or they may go to dangerous extremes to enhance their physical appearance (through excessive dieting or sunbathing, for example). Furthermore, when their efforts are thwarted, people sometimes react with violence to events that damage their self-esteem (Baumeister, Smart, and Boden 1996). For example, one cause of aggression between members of street gangs is one gang's perception that another gang views it as inferior (Jankowski 1991). Similarly, narcissistic people sometimes react to attacks on their ego with extreme aggression, which is termed narcissistic rage.

Finally, some theorists have had difficulty accepting the idea that it is normal, natural, and beneficial for people to be endowed with a psychological mechanism that promotes illusions about themselves and the world (Colvin and Block 1994; Dawes 1994). Presumably, an organism fares best when it accurately perceives the resources and dangers in the world and makes accurate judgments about its own characteristics and capabilities. In addition, the tendency to see oneself in self-serving ways obviates the need for self-improvement. If people always underestimate their own short-comings and failures, they will not be motivated to seek ways to learn and improve.

A Partial Resolution

Research on the benefits of the self-enhancement motive presents a mixed picture. On one hand, high self-esteem is associated with certain desirable outcomes, suggesting that self-enhancement is sometimes beneficial. On the other hand, the self-enhancement motive also has some notable liabilities. This seeming paradox may be resolved, in part, if we adopt a somewhat different perspective on self-esteem. Rather than view the self-enhancement motive as a mechanism for simply bolstering our sense of self-worth and making us feel good about ourselves, we can think of it as a mechanism for maintaining and enhancing interpersonal relationships.

Sociometer theory proposes conceptualizing self-esteem as a psychological meter or gauge that helps people monitor the quality of their relation-ships with other people (Leary and Downs 1995). This approach is based on the assumption that human beings possess a "pervasive drive to form and maintain at least a minimum quantity of lasting, positive, and signifi-cant interpersonal relations" (Baumeister and Leary 1995, 497). Indeed, evolutionary psychologists (e.g., Trivers 1976) suggest that early humans who belonged to social groups were more likely to survive and reproduce than those who felt no internal pressure to live with other people. As a re-sult, all normal human beings have a strong need to belong.

Given the disastrous implications of being rejected or ostracized, early human beings would have developed a mechanism for monitoring, on an ongoing basis, the degree to which other people accepted or rejected them. This psychological mechanism—the sociometer—does three things. First, it continuously monitors the social environment for cues that indicate the possibility of social exclusion. People are very attuned to indications that other people dislike, disapprove, or reject them. Second, it alerts the person when such cues are detected. Like many such "warning systems," the so-ciometer relies on the emotions to do this, grabbing the person's attention through the negative feelings that are associated with threats to self-esteem. Third, it motivates behaviors that decrease the likelihood of exclusion.

According to sociometer theory, the self-esteem system is the cornerstone of this sociometer mechanism. Feelings of self-esteem fluctuate up and down as a function of how accepted or rejected the person feels. Cues that connote acceptance induce high self-esteem; cues that indicate rejection lower self-esteem. When no such cues are present, the person does not have any feelings of self-esteem at all (although such feelings may occur even in private if the person remembers or imagines accepting and rejecting events). Thus self-esteem can be viewed as an ongoing subjective readout of events occurring in the social environment.

Events that affect a person's self-esteem are precisely the ones that would injure the person's acceptance by other people, if they knew about them. Self-esteem is hurt most often by failure, criticism, rejection, and so on— events that have implications for others' acceptance of us. Self-esteem rises when we succeed, we are praised, or we experience another's love—all events that are associated with heightened acceptance (Leary, Tambor, Terdal, and Downs 1995).

Thus the goal of what we traditionally call the self-enhancement motive is not to maintain self-esteem per se but to increase our likelihood of acceptance and to decrease our likelihood of rejection. When people do things to protect their self-esteem, they are often acting in ways that improve their chances of social acceptance. For example, people may make self-serving attributions to absolve themselves of responsibility for failure in other people's eyes to forestall criticism and rejection (Bradley 1978; Leary 1995; Leary and Forsyth 1987). Similarly, people may compensate for esteem-deflating behaviors by behaving in particularly pleasant, prosocial ways, not just to feel good about themselves but to convince others that they are not the failure they may appear to be. Defensive pessimists and impostors may underplay their achievements because they believe that this tactic results in social acceptance.

Sometimes people try to soothe their damaged self-esteem. The emotions associated with lowered self-esteem are often acutely painful, and we sometimes engage in a variety of cognitive shenanigans to mute them. Yet the sociometer perspective suggests that self-esteem itself has a deeper purpose than simply feeling good about oneself and that the self-enhancement motive serves an important interpersonal function in everyday life.

Next, lest we conclude that the only motivated activity of the self-system is the promotion of good feelings about oneself, we proceed to a discussion of other motives that give rise to thought and behavior in service of the self-system.

7

Other Self-Motives

To thine own self be sure, to thine own self be true, and to thine own self be better.

—Sedikides and Stube (1997, 209)

The previous chapter on self-enhancement may have left the impression that human beings are chronic egotists who design their lives in ways that maintain their self-esteem. When that fails, they creatively misconstrue events to support their fragile egos. Clearly, people do often react in self-enhancing ways, but this is only part of the story. Social psychologists have suggested that thoughts, feelings, and behavior are affected by at least three other motivational processes in addition to self-enhancement:

- **Self-consistency.** People are motivated to maintain a consistent image of themselves. They do not like information that contradicts their existing self-image, and they behave in ways that help them maintain a sense of consistency.
- **Self-assessment.** People are motivated to perceive themselves accurately. Because effective living requires that people have a reasonably accurate view of their attributes and abilities, they are motivated to seek valid information about themselves.
- **Self-improvement.** People are motivated to develop and improve. People naturally seek opportunities to better themselves, developing new competencies and pursuing new activities and roles.

In this chapter, we examine the self-motives toward consistency, accuracy, and improvement. We discuss each of the motives in detail, then explore how people resolve conflicts that inevitably arise among them.

Self-Consistency

Psychologists and laypeople alike assume that inconsistency is one benchmark of psychological maladjustment. People who are inconsistent are seen as hypocritical, weak, or even psychologically disturbed. What view do you have of people who change how they behave as they go chameleon-like from one situation to another, for example, professing their religious convictions and then demonstrating behavior that is inconsistent with those convictions a little while later? What do you think of people who express blatantly contradictory attitudes, for example, claiming to be absolutely nonprejudiced while hating members of minority groups? How do you react when people say one thing and then do another?

James (1958) minced no words in his characterization of inconsistent people. He contrasted the psychologically healthy people whose personalities are "harmonious and well balanced" with inconsistent, maladjusted individuals whose "spirit wars with their flesh, they wish for incompatibles, wayward impulses interrupt their most deliberate plans, and their lives are one long drama of repentance and of effort to repair misdemeanors and mistakes" (p. 141). Later, Lecky (1945) built a theory of personality and psychotherapy around the importance of psychological consistency. In his view, well-adjusted, normally functioning people strive for consistency in all aspects of life. "Any idea . . . which is inconsistent with the individual's conception of himself . . . gives rise to an inconsistency which must be removed as promptly as possible" (p. 153).

As James, Lecky, and other writers have noted, self-consistency is important for human well-being because it provides a relatively stable point of reference within a changing environment. Imagine the difficulty you would have making decisions and functioning effectively if your perception of yourself changed each time you received a new piece of information about yourself or had a new experience. Once we have developed an identity, we are motivated to sustain that identity because it gives our lives a sense of order, predictability, and control. We know who we are (or at least we think we do), we know what to expect of ourselves, and we are reassured by this knowledge. Inconsistency, on the other hand, is troubling and discombobulating. Research involving the motivation for consistency has been dominated by two perspectives—cognitive dissonance and self-verification.

Cognitive Dissonance

In the 1950s, Marian Keech, a Michigan psychic, announced that she had been contacted by beings from outer space who told her that they planned to destroy Earth on December 21. Many people left their families, homes, and jobs to join Keech to await the arrival of the aliens. Needless to say, the space travelers did not appear at the designated time, and Earth was not destroyed.

Stop for a moment and try to imagine how the gathered throng would have reacted once they realized that the aliens were not coming. How do you think *you* would have reacted? Would you have returned home quickly and quietly with a concocted story about where you had been for the past few weeks? (After all, you couldn't tell your boss and friends that you had been sitting in a Michigan cornfield waiting for the saucers to arrive, could you?) Would you have been outraged at Keech for having duped you into doing such an absurd thing? Would you have concluded that you were psychologically deranged to have fallen for such a story and checked yourself into a psychiatric clinic? Might you have decided it was better just to move to a new town and start over rather than face the reactions of the people back home?

In fact, Keech's followers did none of these things after their doomsday beliefs were disconfirmed. They became even *more* committed to Keech and her teachings, convinced that their tremendous faith and devotion had forestalled the predicted cataclysm. They called in representatives of the news media and boldly announced that they had saved the Earth from destruction.

This episode is well-known among social psychologists because it was the impetus for cognitive dissonance theory—one of the most influential and widely studied theories in the field (Festinger 1957; Festinger, Riecken, and Schachter 1956). According to **cognitive dissonance theory**, Keech's followers responded to her failed prediction with renewed commitment in order to maintain consistency among their beliefs. If they had admitted that Keech was a lunatic or a false prophet, they would have been forced to accept the conclusion that they were stupid enough to be duped by her crazy message and that they acted irresponsibly, if not ridiculously, when they abandoned their former lives to join her. Such a belief was undoubtedly inconsistent with how they saw themselves, thereby creating a feeling of dissonance. According to the theory, because the dissonance aroused by contradictory thoughts is distressing, people are motivated to restore consistency among their thoughts to reduce it. Thus, by coming to believe that their actions had saved the world, Keech's followers could restore cognitive consistency and eliminate their dissonance: "I am a rational, responsible person, and, yes, I helped to spare the Earth by heeding Mrs. Keech's call." No contradiction, no dissonance, no problem.

Such tactics for reducing dissonance are by no means limited to people who seek contact with aliens. We all occasionally revise our beliefs to retain a sense of consistency. For example, after engaging in behavior that we disapprove of, we often decide that the forbidden action is not really that bad (continuing to disapprove of behaviors that we practice would induce dissonance). We dislike the enemies of our friends (liking them would feel inconsistent). We like things better as we invest more time and effort to get them (working hard to obtain worthless things would contradict our beliefs in our reasonableness). And so on.

Although cognitive dissonance theory is usually regarded as a theory about how people maintain "cognitive balance," it can also be viewed as a theory of self-consistency. In fact, Aronson (1968) proposed that inconsistency must implicate some aspect of the self in order to arouse dissonance. The inconsistencies that people try hardest to avoid are those that involve aspects of themselves—conflicts among different components of their identities or between their identity and their behavior. Over the years, cognitive dissonance theory has moved from being a theory about cognitive consistency per se to being a theory about how people resolve disturbing inconsistencies between their positive views of themselves and the cognition that they have done something foolish, irrational, or immoral.

Research has shown that people experience dissonance only to the extent that they feel responsible for their inconsistent actions (Cooper and Fazio 1984). This is because behaving inconsistently with some aspect of one's self will not violate one's sense of self-consistency unless, for reasons developed in Chapter 3, the person had a certain degree of freedom to act as she did. If we are forced to do something against our will, the inconsistency between our beliefs and our behavior will not cause dissonance or lead us to try to reduce the discrepancy.

Furthermore, Steele and his colleagues have shown that people who behave inconsistently do not show evidence of experiencing dissonance if they are given opportunities to maintain or affirm their self-integrity (Steele 1988; Steele and Liu 1983). These studies suggest that inconsistency threatens something about the self and that, by affirming oneself more generally, the inconsistencies are less troubling. When people are able to bolster their self-images by other means, they are less bothered by inconsistency.

Importantly, recent research suggests that the dissonance processes studied by Western (particularly American) psychologists may not be as prominent in cultures that have a less individualistic view of the self. A study by Heine and Lehman (1997) showed less evidence of dissonance arousal in Japanese than Canadian participants. Among people from cultures that promote an *inter*dependent view of self, inconsistent thoughts about the self appear not to threaten the integrity of the self-system as they do among people from cultures that promote an *in*dependent view of self. Such cross-cultural research is critically important in helping us understand how general self-processes are moderated by cultural factors.

Self-Verification

Another perspective on self-consistency is provided by self-verification theory. According to **self-verification theory,** people are motivated to verify, validate, and sustain their existing self-concepts (Swann 1983, 1990). Unlike cognitive dissonance theory, self-verification theory does not assume that people are motivated to maintain consistency for its own sake. Rather, it suggests that people are motivated toward self-consistency because consistency increases the degree to which they perceive that they can predict and control what happens to them. As prescribed in our definition of the self-system in Chapter 2, we would have a great deal of difficulty behaving effectively if we had no concrete, stable sense of who we were or what we were like. As Swann, Stein-Seroussi, and Giesler (1992) put it, "Because people recognize the central role that stable self-concepts play in negotiating social reality, they come to prefer appraisals that confirm their self-concepts and eschew appraisals that do not" (p. 393).

When people receive information about themselves, they engage in a process of **self-comparison** (Eisenstadt and Leippe 1994). They first compare the information with their self-concept—how they think they really are. If the information is consistent with their self-concept, thereby confirming what they already believe about themselves, the self-comparison process stops. However, if the information is discrepant from how people think they are, they may become upset and anxious, particularly if they cannot dismiss it easily (Eisenstadt and Leippe 1994; Swann 1997). Because information that is inconsistent with people's self-concept is unsettling, they often behave in ways that help them verify their self-concepts.

People try to sustain their self-concept in a number of ways. First, they tend to seek out and interact with people who see them as they see themselves—people whose appraisals of them confirm their self-views. Thus they are reassured that they know themselves well, they expect to have more pleasant interactions with such people, and the social world seems more predictable and controllable (Swann, Stein-Serouss, and Giesler 1992).

On the face of it, the idea that we prefer to interact with people who see us as we see ourselves seems straightforward and noncontroversial. But consider for a moment what this notion implies about the preferences of people who view themselves *negatively*. If people truly prefer to receive self-consistent information, then people with unfavorable views of themselves should prefer to associate with those who think poorly of them.

This counterintuitive implication of self-verification theory has been supported by research. In a study of married couples, Swann, Hixon, and De La Ronde (1992) found, not surprisingly, that people with positive views of themselves expressed more commitment to their marriage if their spouse saw them positively rather than negatively; however, people with negative self-views were more committed to spouses who thought poorly of them (see also Ritts and Stein 1995). Similarly, among people who are strangers to one another, people prefer to interact with people whose views of them are consistent with their own self-concepts; as the theory predicts, people with negative self-views prefer to interact with those who see them negatively (Swann, Hixon, and De La Ronde 1992; Swann, Pelham, and Krull 1989). These findings show that, in some instances, people are willing to forego positive evaluations from others in favor of negative but self-verifying evaluations. Put differently, sometimes the self-verification motive takes precedence over self-enhancement.

People who receive unflattering information that is consistent with their self-concept do not necessarily *like* the negative feedback. Virtually everyone feels better after receiving positive feedback about themselves. Even so, people with an unfavorable self-concept seem to realize that the unfavorable information is more accurate and thus feel more comfortable about receiving it (Shrauger 1975; Swann, Griffin, Predmore, and Gaines 1987).

A second route to self-verification involves behaving in ways that elicit self-verifying reactions from other people. People tend to solicit feedback from others that supports their image of themselves (Pyszczynski, Greenberg, and LaPrelle 1985; Robinson and Smith-Lovin 1992). For example, when people think that others hold inaccurate impressions of them (that is, impressions that are inconsistent with their own self-image), they behave in ways that dispel the other's misconception and reaffirm their view of who they are (Swann and Read 1981). Again, they sometimes do this even if other people's impressions are more favorable than their own self-view.

Third, people may selectively look for, see, and remember more self-confirmatory information than really exists (Swann and Read 1981). Much research has shown that people interpret the information they receive in ways that are consistent with their existing views of self (Shrauger 1982). When information is not consistent with how they see themselves, they may simply dismiss or refute it as inaccurate (Doherty, Weigold, and Schlenker 1990; Shrauger 1982). For example, a person with a negative self-concept may dismiss others' compliments with the thought that "they were just saying that to be nice." People also remember information more easily when it verifies rather than contradicts their self-beliefs (Swann and Read 1981).

These self-verifying biases in how people deal with self-discrepant information allow their self-concepts to remain unaffected by even volumes of contradictory evidence. This is one reason why people's perceptions of themselves are so resistant to change.

Three Caveats

Before leaving the topic of self-consistency, we should mention three caveats to the notion that people are motivated to maintain a consistent, unified sense of self. The first is that people often tolerate major inconsistencies without trying to resolve them and without apparent ill effect. Not only do we often say things we do not believe, but we are all occasional hypocrites who act contrary to our inner beliefs. Sometimes we are deeply troubled by such inconsistencies, but often we are not.

Second, despite the fact that consistency is often regarded as a mark of adjustment, if not a moral virtue (Maslow 1968), being consistent is not always desirable. People must often be able to change their mind and their behavior without being constrained by the feeling that the two should always be the same. Excessive pressures toward self-verification may interfere with healthy changes in attitudes, personality, and behavior (Swann 1997). Furthermore, life is such that people cannot always speak their mind or do what they want. People who are rigidly bound by the self-consistency motive may be seen as tactless and socially inappropriate. Although consistency is sometimes good, rigid adherence to self-image is not.

Third, some theorists have questioned whether people's efforts toward consistency always emerge from an inner motive for self-consistency, as cognitive dissonance theory and self-verification theory suggest. They have suggested that people are often not as bothered about their own inconsistencies as they are about being perceived as inconsistent by other people. Thus what may appear to be an inner drive toward consistency is often an attempt to appear consistent to other people. As we noted, Western culture places a great deal of importance on being consistent. We expect people to be consistent and predictable, and to act in accordance with their personal beliefs. People who are inconsistent may be seen as unpredictable, untrustworthy, or unstable. As a result, people may manage their public impressions in ways that make them appear reasonably consistent to other people (Gergen 1968). Some theorists have even suggested that many of the behaviors that have been attributed to cognitive dissonance are instead the result of people's efforts to avoid appearing inconsistent, stupid, or immoral to other people (Schlenker 1982; Tedeschi, Schlenker, and Bonoma 1971). In support of this idea, studies have shown that people show a greater drive toward consistency when other people are aware of their inconsistent behavior (Schlenker 1985a; Schlenker, Forsyth, Leary, and Miller 1980).

Accurate Self-Assessment

We have seen that people are motivated to maintain their self-esteem as well as their conception of who they are, and that the motives for self-enhancement and self-consistency provide certain psychological benefits. However, both self-enhancement and self-verification have a drawback: They sometimes lead people to misconstrue reality. We may be able to maintain our self-esteem or verify our self-concept only by ignoring, denying, or de-emphasizing feedback that violates our self-esteem or self-image.

The cost of these self-deceptive biases can be high. People who do not see themselves accurately are likely to bungle their lives. Effective living requires knowing what one is like—for good and for bad—and making decisions accordingly. People whose self-perceptions are heavily biased by their need for self-esteem or self-consistency may pursue careers, spouses, and activities that do not really suit them well. They may have difficulty anticipating how they will respond in particular situations and preparing themselves for new situations. They may also be blind to areas in which they need to improve. Furthermore, effective self-regulation requires accurate information about one's attributes and abilities, so that failing to see oneself clearly impedes one's ability to self-regulate. Given the importance of having accurate knowledge about oneself, people possess a motive for accurate self-assessment that involves the desire for objective and accurate information about oneself. According to the **self-assessment perspective**, people are motivated to figure out what they are really like and to reduce their uncertainty about their abilities and other characteristics.

In the landmark text that helped begin the scientific study of human personality, Allport (1937) wrote that "an impartial and objective attitude toward oneself is held to be a primary virtue, basic to the development of all others . . . if any trait of personality is intrinsically desirable, it is the disposition and ability to see oneself in perspective" (p. 422). The importance of having an accurate view of oneself is obvious: A person's effectiveness in life depends on knowing one's strengths and weaknesses and in having an accurate assessment of one's personal characteristics. In fact, some theorists have suggested that human beings, in their search for self-understanding, operate something like everyday scientists. Just as scientists systematically and objectively try to understand the world, people systematically and objectively try to understand themselves and the world in which they live (Kelley 1967; Kelly 1955).

We have already seen that people sometimes distort the truth about themselves in self-enhancing or self-verifying ways. Obviously, then, people do not seek objective truth about themselves at every turn. But the self-assessment perspective reminds us that people are not so determined to feel good about themselves or to maintain self-consistency that they never seek accurate information about themselves or always disregard it once obtained. Nonetheless, they are sometimes caught in a dilemma between obtaining accurate information that will improve their self-understanding and risking the potential of receiving feedback that undermines their self-esteem or contradicts their existing self-concept. The question, then, is, *when* do people seek accurate information about themselves?

The first condition under which people seek accurate information about themselves is relatively straightforward: When people believe that accurate information will reflect favorably on them, they go out of their way to obtain it. In this instance, it is difficult to determine whether people seek self-relevant information because they want to know how they really are (self-assessment) or because it makes them feel good (self-enhancement). The best we can say is that people are particularly interested in obtaining accurate information about themselves when they expect it to be positive rather than negative (reflecting the self-enhancement motive), and that they do not necessarily refrain from seeking information about themselves even when they expect it to be unflattering (Brown 1990).

Interestingly, people appear more willing to seek accurate information, even if it portrays them in a negative light, if they have recently experienced successes or other positive experiences that will buffer their self-esteem against its negative impact. Put differently, people appear to be more willing to face up to their shortcomings in one area if they feel good about themselves in another area. In fact, when facing the possibility of negative feedback, people may prepare themselves psychologically by thinking about their previous successes (Trope and Neter 1994). Thus people are more likely to seek accurate information about themselves when the threat to their self-esteem is minimized.

Second, people are more motivated to self-assess the more uncertain they are about their standing on a particular dimension. People are bothered by uncertainty and are particularly bothered by uncertainty that involves them. When people do not know where they stand on particular dimensions, they seek opportunities to obtain highly diagnostic feedback about themselves (Strube et al. 1986; Trope 1975, 1979; Trope and Ben-Yair 1982). This is particularly true of people who are prone to focus their attention inward on private self-aspects (Franzoi, Davis, and Markwiese 1990).

Third, people sometimes realize that obtaining accurate information about themselves is ultimately of value to them, even if it is unflattering and unpleasant. If they need objective information in order to decide what skills they should improve, the kinds of tasks to undertake in the future, or how much time, effort, or money to invest in certain lines of action, they may decide that the long-term gain of accurate information outweighs the possible short-term pain. Thus even if they could avoid potentially negative feedback, they seek it out nonetheless if it will be of value to them.

In brief, people often want to know the truth about themselves. Under certain circumstances, they seek accurate information even if they think it will hurt their self-esteem or create puzzling inconsistencies in how they see themselves.

Self-Improvement: The Quest for Growth

In the early days of psychology, the prevailing views of human beings—Freud's psychoanalytic theory and Watson's behaviorism—were mostly negative and unflattering. Psychoanalytic theory depicted people as driven by unconscious biological drives, primarily urges involving sex and aggression. All behavior was seen as stemming from people's efforts to satisfy their basic drives in ways that were acceptable to society. In Freud's view, even seemingly creative, benevolent, and selfless actions arose from these primal urges. Behaviorism's view of people was not much better. Human beings were regarded as little more than sophisticated rats or pigeons pushing the levers of life to obtain reinforcement and to avoid punishment. People were viewed as pawns of their environment having no real freedom or free will.

The humanistic perspective arose as a "third force" in psychology to counter what its proponents viewed as the excessively negative views of psychoanalysis and behaviorism. Humanistic psychologists argued that psychoanalysis and behaviorism did not easily account for many of the positive features of human behavior. In their view, phenomena such as love, compassion, curiosity, creativity, ecstasy, and self-fulfillment were not easily explained in terms of either sexual drives or patterns of reinforcement and punishment. It seemed to the humanistic psychologists that human beings possess some inner quality, some aspect of the self, that accounts for these more positive characteristics.

The Actualizing Tendency

A central idea among humanistic psychologists is that, under ideal circumstances, people naturally develop in ways that are increasingly healthy, effective, and fulfilling. Human beings are endowed with an inherent tendency to develop, grow, and improve. This actualizing tendency toward self-improvement is innate and universal, but it can be thwarted by people's experiences. In particular, events that teach people they are not acceptable, lovable, or worthy lead them to conform to others' desires and expectations instead of simply developing along their natural paths (Rogers 1959).

The self plays a central role in this process and thus partly determines the degree to which people develop in ways that they find fulfilling. As we have seen, people's self-concepts are based in part on how they believe others perceive and evaluate them. In fact, our self-concept is affected by other people's perceptions and values as much as it is by how we really are. Inevitably, each of us runs into people—often parents and teachers—who want us to be a particular way, not because that way is truly better for us but rather because of their own preferences. When this happens, we may try to change the way we are to obtain attention, approval, and love. But once this happens, the actualizing tendency becomes stymied. We are sidetracked from being the person we would naturally become to being the person someone else wants us to be. And, in the process, we are neither as happy nor as fulfilled as we would be otherwise. If not forced into the molds constructed by other people and by society at large, however, we will live in ways that not only lead us to improve and grow as individuals but also to contribute to the welfare of others.

In extreme cases, the self that the person creates to obtain acceptance and approval from other people may be quite different from the person's natural inclinations. The person must deny—both to others and to himself—motives, thoughts, and feelings that are incongruent with the self that has been created. For example, a boy who is naturally gentle and empathic may subvert his tender inclinations in order to convince himself and others that he is the rough-and-tumble masculine type that his father expects. People caught in this dilemma are often tense and unhappy without quite understanding why. Furthermore, they tend to function in a restricted and inefficient way because they cannot rely on their genuine, gut-level reactions when making decisions nor capitalize on their natural strengths.

As university professors, we see students in this bind regularly. They come to college pursuing their parents' dreams for them—that they will become a physician or go into business or pursue a graduate degree or whatever. Because they have implicitly accepted their parents' concept of them and have internalized their goals since childhood, these students do not realize that the path they are taking is not of their own choosing. Yet they experience an underlying sense that things are not quite right, that the road they are traveling is somehow not fulfilling. For example, we have seen premed students who detested chemistry and biology, showed no obvious interest in medicine, and talked enthusiastically of their interests in art or religion or social work. But they doggedly and unhappily pursued the premed track because that was what other people expected. Such students have mortgaged their natural interests and inclinations for other people's goals for them.

One need not accept the humanistic assumption of an actualizing tendency to believe that, in their desire to please others, many people pursue paths in life that do not allow them to develop in ways that they find fulfilling. Most people want to grow and improve, but the aspects of themselves that they choose to foster may not be ones that they ultimately find satisfying.

Rogers (1959) called the person who has maximized her potential for personal growth *fully functioning*. Rogers himself pointed out that full-functioning should be regarded as a process rather than a permanent trait that certain superhuman people attain. Fully functioning people are adaptive, meeting new situations in creative and effective ways. Because they see themselves and their lives clearly and accurately, and because they are unencumbered by others' goals for them, fully functioning people make sound choices. They are "in tune" with their basic nature.

Maslow's (1968) studies of *self-actualization* make much the same point. Maslow's basic premise was that people possess an inherent need for self-fulfillment—a drive to become what one has the potential to become. However, in the grand scheme of things, this need for self-actualization is high on the hierarchy of human needs, certainly not one of the basic things that people pursue. Only after more fundamental needs are met—for example, basic physiological needs and needs for safety, love, and esteem—does the self-actualizing motive become prepotent. The implication of this idea is noteworthy: People will be highly motivated toward self-improvement only after more mundane and basic needs are met.

Maslow (1968) devoted a great deal of his time studying individuals who achieved the highest, self-actualizing stage in his hierarchy of motives. He identified a set of characteristics that he believed are common to such people. Self-actualized people are independent and autonomous individuals who, in Maslow's view, remain true to themselves even in the face of rejection and unpopularity (cf. Swann 1997). Because they are not fettered by others' expectations, they tend to be spontaneous and highly creative. Furthermore, they are nondefensive, easily accepting both themselves and other people "warts and all." They also identify with the welfare of other people and are guided by strong ethical convictions, although they are not necessarily religious in the conventional sense. Maslow (1971) wrote that self-actualized people are "our most compassionate, our great improvers and reformers of society, our most effective fighters against injustice, inequality, slavery, cruelty, exploitation" (p. 346). People who embodied these qualities, who were identifed by Maslow as self-actualized, include Thomas Jefferson, Abraham Lincoln, Albert Einstein, Mohandas Gandhi, and Eleanor Roosevelt.

Although the concept of self-actualization is a controversial one and many of Maslow's conclusions about self-actualized people have been challenged (see Whitson and Olczak 1991), his work provides an intriguing perspective on the self. The fully functioning or self-actualized person is paradoxical. On one hand, self-actualized people seem to be strong personalities with a well-defined sense of self. On the other hand, they almost seem to have no self at all in that they lack the self-centeredness and ego defensiveness that characterize most of us. From the perspective of humanistic psychology, this is because self-actualized people have developed the capacity to freely be themselves, without consciously striving to meet either other people's expectations for them or even their own preconceived ideas about what they should be.

Possible Selves

It is not necessary to believe that people are born with an inherent actualizing tendency to assume that people are motivated to develop and improve. Many psychologists who disagree with the premises of humanistic theory nonetheless believe that people strive to improve themselves. Self-improvement carries many rewards in its own right; the better we become at something, the more likely we are to succeed at it and to reap the benefits of success. People often try to improve to obtain rewards and avoid punishments. Furthermore, some theorists have suggested that people are inherently motivated to pursue feelings of competence, mastery, and control (deCharms 1968; Deci and Ryan 1995; White 1959), feelings that often can be attained through self-improvement.

As people grow and change, they are guided, in part, by their *possible selves*—their "ideas of what they might become, what they would like to become, and what they are afraid of becoming" (Markus and Nurius 1986, 954). Just as people have images and ideas of who they are now, they also have images and ideas of what they could become in the future.

These possible selves motivate and guide people's pursuit of goals and typically promote self-improvement. When you watch what you eat because you do not want to become overweight and unhealthy, it is the image of your possible selves—fat versus thin—that guides your behavior. When you work hard in school with an eye toward graduation, you are pulled along, in part, by an idea of your possible desired self (a successfully employed graduate) as well as by your possible undesired self (an unemployed dropout).

Possible selves not only affect behavior relative to future goals, but they also affect how people feel about themselves in the present situation. Simply considering the possibility of desirable possible selves can make people feel good, or bad. Everyone occasionally revels in the imagined future successes of their possible selves or agonizes over the future failures of their "loser" possible selves.

People's possible selves also affect their evaluations of who and what they are presently—their "now self." The meaning that a person attaches to a personally relevant event is affected by its implications for his or her possible selves. Getting divorced, for example, may deal a blow to one's current self-image and self-esteem, but the impact will be far worse if the event conjures up images of a possible self that is rejected and alone far into the future. Similarly, realizing that one has gained a few extra pounds will have quite different effects depending on whether the realization is accompanied by thoughts of a possible self that might again be thin or of a possible self that will always be overweight.

Self-Saturation

People's selves naturally expand and become increasingly complex as they grow; however, if one's self grows and develops unchecked, it can run the risk of becoming *saturated*—filled with as many self-attributes as it can easily contain. Additional efforts to incorporate new abilities, roles, relationships, responsibilities, interests, and activities into the self cause stress. One disadvantage of the general tendency to grow, improve, and develop is that the additional attributes may put strain on the entire system. People who live hurried, harried lives are often experiencing self-saturation. We sometimes say we are stressed-out because we "have too much to do," but the problem is often one of self-saturation. We are trying to maintain too many parts of our selves simultaneously and, like the juggler who tries to juggle too many balls, we inevitably begin to feel that we cannot keep everything going at once.

As noted in our earlier discussion of historical factors and identity, modern technology is partly responsible for the widespread self-saturation we see in Western society (Gergen 1991). Many Americans often look back wistfully at how "simple" life was not too many years ago. At the turn of the twentieth century, a person might have a job, a family, a few other close relationships (most of them confined to the distance of an easy walk from home), and maybe a hobby or an outside interest such as church or synagogue membership. Compare those earlier times to today. We still have our jobs, families, and close relationships, but now most of us pursue many other activities that we view as important parts of ourselves. We are dedicated to regular exercise and recreation, we have numerous hobbies and interests, we slavishly watch our favorite television shows, we are involved in community activities, and so on and so forth. In addition, we maintain ongoing personal and professional relationships with many people via phone, fax, and e-mail; we involve ourselves (at least psychologically) in events that happen all over the world via television; and we easily travel far from home, doing new things and meeting new people, thereby expanding our selves even further.

In the past, people relinquished old relationships when friends moved away; aside from the occasional letter, it was difficult or impossible to visit or maintain direct contact with someone who moved to another town. Today, we maintain relationships with greater and greater numbers of people through phone calls, e-mail, and visits, even over long distances. Gergen (1991) observed that "as we move through life, the cast of relevant characters is ever expanding" (p. 62). Similarly, in professional and business life, we are in real or virtual contact with people all over the globe, whereas such contacts were once limited to a handful of people who worked nearby.

One consequence of self-saturation is what Gergen (1991) called *multiphrenia*—splitting the individual into an excessive number of self-investments. It is not simply that we have too much to do but that each of us regards these many things as important aspects of who we are. As a result, we are hurried and harried, torn among too many competing parts of our selves. The inevitable result is stress. The human nervous system did not evolve with the capacity to sustain a saturated self. Our ancestors may have faced many dangers that we do not, but their daily life was not the busy, fast-paced, stressful ordeal that it is for many modern people. Their selves were far less complex and were certainly not saturated.

The solution for self-saturation, of course, is to jettison some of the excessive parts of ourselves. We reach a point in our development where we cannot reasonably incorporate new components into our selves without dropping other ones. Yet people find this quite difficult. Once an attribute has become part of the self, they have trouble relinquishing that part in favor of new ones.

When Motives Collide

Behavioral researchers generally accept the existence of the four motives we have described in this and the previous chapter—self-enhancement, self-consistency, self-assessment, and self-improvement (Sedikides and Strube 1997). Yet proponents of each theoretical approach tend to see their favorite self-motive as the most important. Self-enhancement theorists view the maintenance of self-esteem as the most important and common of the four motives; self-verification theorists see the drive for verification at every bend; self-assessment theorists point to the overriding importance of accurate self-views; and self-improvement theorists insist that the most fundamental self-relevant motive involves improvement, growth, and development. Furthermore, some proponents of each perspective provide evidence that at least some of the other motives can be subsumed as a special case of their favorite (e.g., Sedikides and Strube 1997; Swann 1996; Trope 1983).

A few efforts have been made to resolve the question of whether some of the motives are more important or more pervasive than the others. Sedikides (1993) conducted six experiments to explore the importance of various self-motives directly. In these studies, participants were asked to choose which of several questions they would most likely ask themselves to find out whether or not they possessed a particular characteristic (such as whether they were kind, unfriendly, unpredictable, or trustworthy). The questions they could choose were designed to reflect one of three self-motives we have discussed—self-enhancement, self-consistency, or accurate self-assessment. The data from these studies showed that participants' selections of questions were influenced most heavily by the self-enhancement motive, followed by self-consistency and finally self-assessment.

This finding is intriguing and perhaps disturbing. Even though participants were instructed to pick questions that would help them find out *what they were really like,* they selected information-seeking strategies that would provide them with feedback that would maintain their self-esteem (self-enhancement) or was consistent with how they already saw themselves (self-consistency) rather than feedback that would most clearly show them how they really were (self-assessment). These results should not be taken to indicate that people never seek accurate information about themselves (Sedikides 1993). As we noted earlier, certain conditions do seem to promote a search for accurate information. Yet the strength of these findings suggests that people (at least people in Western cultures) are often less interested in knowing who they are than in sustaining a positive and/or consistent view of themselves. Certainly there are individual differences in the extent to which one of these motives predominates over the other, although there currently exists little research that has directly addressed this issue.

As we have seen, the motives toward enhancement, consistency, accurate assessment, and improvement all serve important psychological purposes. We have good reasons for self-enhancing, whether to sustain our confidence or to guide our search for social acceptance. Similarly, we could not function effectively if our view of ourselves fluctuated moment by moment and we had no stable, concrete sense of who we were or what we were like; we need to maintain some degree of self-consistency. At the same time, people need to have accurate information about themselves if they are to get by in life and so strive for self-accuracy. And running through all of this appears to be a general motive toward self-improvement. Most of us would not be satisfied if we stayed exactly the same throughout life, never learning anything new, developing new skills, or getting better with time.

Each of the motives serves important functions, but difficulties may arise when they collide, as they often do. For example, sometimes accurate self-information threatens a person's self-esteem or is inconsistent with the person's self-concept. Self-growth may require people to behave in new ways that are very inconsistent with how they have been throughout their life. Such dilemmas can pit motives for esteem, consistency, accuracy, and improvement against one another. At this point, we do not have a good understanding of how people resolve these conflicts. Clearly, a fruitful area of investigation for the future will involve trying to determine the conditions under which each motive tends to operate (Sedikides and Strube 1997).

8

Self-Regulation and Agency

People are proactive, aspiring organisms who have a hand in shaping their own lives.

—Bandura (1997, vii)

You wake up tomorrow morning (some of you before 7 A.M. and others after 11 A.M., but that's another story) and you think about what you are going to do this day. The weather is beautiful, so you consider going for a bike ride, then having lunch at an outdoor cafe, followed by an afternoon of strolling and relaxing in the park. Just as a smile comes to your lips, you suddenly remember that this is the day that you were supposed to take your car into the shop for repairs, get a haircut, and begin working on a project that you have been avoiding. Hmmm . . . what to do?

Why do people decide to engage in certain behaviors and activities but not in others? Do they do what they want to do and enjoy doing or what they feel forced to do? How do people know when they have done something long enough? What makes them decide it is time to "switch gears" and move on to something else? These are the types of questions that we address in this chapter.

Specifically, this chapter is concerned with issues of *agency* and *self-regulation*. By **agency** we mean the extent to which one experiences oneself as "the origin of one's actions," as opposed to feeling like a "pawn of the environment" (deCharms 1968). One who is the "origin" of action experiences a strong sense of choicefulness. On the other hand, one who is a "pawn" is more likely to feel pressure and tension and may feel helpless and out of control. By **self-regulation**, we mean the processes and mechanisms involved in the initiation, persistence, and termination of behavior. Sometimes these processes and mechanisms accompany "choicefulness" and sometimes they do not. In all cases, they involve a temporary focus of attention on the self—self-awareness—so we begin the chapter with a review of theory and research on self-focused attention.

The Role of Self-Awareness in Self-Regulation

People engage in a variety of behaviors that are intended to achieve some goal that they or someone else has set for them. College students, for example, do homework assignments, study, and write papers in order to learn new information and obtain desired grades. Athletes typically submit to year-round training regimens to optimize their performance levels. Teachers prepare for classes by reading new materials, taking notes, and rehearsing. And so on. In each instance, people are striving to attain a certain level of skill or obtain a given outcome, in other words, to reach a certain standard.

How do people know when they have done enough (or as well as they can) to reach these standards? One answer comes from research and theory focusing on the role of heightened self-awareness in psychological functioning (Carver and Scheier 1981; Duval and Wicklund 1972; Prentice-Dunn and Rogers 1983). **Heightened self-awareness** refers to those times when one's conscious attention is directed toward some aspect of the self—one's behavior, mood, physical appearance, bodily functions, physical sensations, and so forth. Sometimes heightened self-awareness confers just that—a heightened awareness of the aspect of the self that is being focused upon. For example, if you direct your attention toward your breathing, you will probably become more aware of sensations—of air passing in and out of your nose, of your chest moving in and out, and so on—that you previously had not noticed. At this point, no standard is activated, so increased awareness of these self-aspects is all that happens. Suppose, however, that you have just run up a long flight of stairs and are feeling out of breath; just then you run into a friend who starts a conversation with you. You have some trouble responding, however, because your quick breathing keeps getting in the way. At this point, the standard of normal breathing is likely to be activated, and you may attempt to match that standard by deliberately attempting to take slower and deeper breaths. As time passes, you recognize that normal breathing has returned and you focus your attention elsewhere.

What we have just described is the operation of a negative, or discrepancy-reducing, feedback loop (Carver and Scheier 1981; Carver, Lawrence, and Scheier 1996; Miller, Galanter, and Pribam 1960; Powers 1973). In essence, a *negative feedback loop* entails reducing a discrepancy between a current value and a reference value, or standard. In our breathing example, the current value is fast, urgent, and shallow breathing, whereas the reference or standard value is slow, relaxed, and deep breathing. If a discrepancy exists between current and reference values, adjustments are made to bring the two values closer together. Successful adjustments reduce or eliminate the discrepancy; unsuccessful adjustments do not reduce or eliminate the discrepancy. If initial adjustments prove unsuccessful, people reassess the likelihood that they will be able to eliminate the discrepancy. If their expectations are favorable, efforts at discrepancy reduction continue. If expectations are unfavorable, people are prone to withdraw either mentally or behaviorally (Scheier and Carver 1988), especially if continued difficulties will pose a threat to self-esteem (Kernis, Zuckerman, Cohen, and Spadafora 1982).

Heightened self-awareness is integral to the process of meeting goals in a couple of ways. First, it can prompt the activation of a given standard or make an existing standard more salient (Kernis et al. 1982). Second, it can activate the process by which current states are compared against a given standard (Carver and Scheier 1982).

A number of studies have shown that heightened self-awareness increases the extent to which people's behaviors conform to standards. A particularly intriguing study was conducted by Beaman, Klentz, Diener, and Svanum (1979) one Halloween night. Trick-or-treaters arrived at an "experimental" house to find a friendly adult who asked them to come inside, where a large bowl filled with desirable candies was highly visible. With precise timing, the phone rang just as the children stepped inside. Before rushing off to answer it, the "experimenter" instructed the youngsters, "Take one candy from the bowl." For half the children, a large mirror was placed strategically behind the bowl (mirror condition), so that they would be forced to see their image as they reached for the candy (recall from Chapter 3 that seeing one's image is one way to heighten self-awareness). For the other children, no mirror was present (no mirror condition). Unknown to all children, a second "experimenter," who was hidden behind a curtain, recorded how many candies children in fact took. The results were somewhat startling. Children in the no-mirror condition typically did not adhere to the instruction to take one candy—some, in fact, literally stuffed their pockets full of goodies. In stark contrast, children in the mirror (self-aware) condition behaved in conformance with the standard, being far more likely to take only one candy, as they had been instructed. Self-awareness clearly enhanced the children's adherence to salient standards.

In the Beaman et al. (1979) study, the standard for appropriate behavior was provided by an external source, in this case the adult "experimenter." Heightened self-awareness also increases conformity to one's own personal standards, as shown by Carver (1975). Participants, who were either in favor of or opposed to the death penalty, were given an opportunity to punish another subject by ostensibly administering electric shocks to this person when a wrong answer was given. In reality, the other subject was an accomplice of the experimenter and no shocks were actually administered. Half the participants in each group viewed their image in a mirror as they "administered" the shocks, the rest did not. When self-awareness was heightened, highly punitive individuals (who favored the death penalty) delivered considerably more intense shocks than did the less punitive individuals (who opposed the death penalty). No differences emerged when self-awareness was not heightened.

Whether the standards or reference values that people seek to conform to are socially provided or personal, important or unimportant, concrete or abstract, specific or broad, the discrepancy-reducing process that we just described is relevant. People periodically compare their existing state to the standard; when they notice a discrepancy, they implement attempts to reduce the discrepancy. If these attempts are unsuccessful, people may reassert themselves or withdraw, depending on how they assess the probability that continued efforts will be successful. In this way, self-regulation proceeds either toward discrepancy reduction or toward withdrawal and abandonment of a particular standard.

Self-Consciousness

A wide variety of situational factors can induce self-awareness—seeing one's image in a mirror, experiencing a sharp change in one's physical state, standing in front of an audience, being videotaped, or hearing one's name called out. Even transitory emotions can induce self-awareness (Sedikides 1992a, 1992b; Wood, Saltzberg, and Goldsamt 1990). Research has shown, however, that apart from these situational factors, people differ in their chronic or habitual tendencies to focus their attention toward themselves. These chronic tendencies to engage in self-awareness (referred to as **self-consciousness** to distinguish from situationally activated self-focus) can be separated into two broad forms (Buss 1980; Fenigstein, Scheier, and Buss 1975; Scheier and Carver 1982). One form—called **private self-consciousness**—involves a heightened tendency to focus one's attention toward those aspects of the self that are covert and hidden from other people, such as one's thoughts, feelings, and motives. The second form—called **public self-consciousness**—involves a heightened tendency to focus one's attention on publicly observable self-aspects, such as one's physical appearance or behavioral style (Fenigstein, Scheier, and Buss 1975). Importantly, people can be high in one form of self-consciousness and low in the other (the correlation between them is modest). That is, people can be highly attentive to internal, covert self-aspects while being inattentive to publicly observable self-aspects. Both tendencies have implications for self-regulation.

Several studies have shown that people who are high in private self-consciousness are more aware of their transient emotions than are people who are low in it (e.g., Scheier 1976; Scheier and Carver 1977) and thus are less easily misled by false information concerning their internal states (Scheier, Carver, and Gibbons 1979). Likewise, people high in private self-consciousness (compared to people low in private self-consciousness) have more elaborate knowledge structures about their traitlike personality characteristics (Hull and Levy 1979; Turner 1980), are more accurate in their self-reports concerning these characteristics (as gauged by how closely these self-reports map onto their actual behaviors; Scheier, Buss, and Buss 1978), and place greater importance on these characteristics (Cheek and Briggs 1982). There are no differences on these characteristics attributable to public self-consciousness.

Compared to people low in public self-consciousness, people high in public self-consciousness place greater importance on social or public aspects of their identity (e.g., gestures, group memberships, appearance; Cheek and Briggs 1982), have more well-consolidated knowledge concerning these particular self-aspects (Turner, Gilliland, and Klein 1981), and are better able to predict the impressions that they will make on others (Tobey and Tunnell 1981). Interestingly, women high in public self-consciousness wear more makeup (both self-reported and as rated via photographs) than do women low in public self-consciousness (Miller and Cox 1981). Finally, high public self-consciousness individuals are more sensitive to instances of social rejection than low public self-consciousness individuals (Fenigstein 1979), and they are more paranoid as well (i.e., they believe that actions are directed toward them when, in fact, this is not the case; Fenigstein and Vanable 1992). There are no differences on these characteristics attributable to private self-consciousness.

Deindividuation: The Absence of Self-Awareness

What happens when situational or other factors prevent people from focusing attention on themselves? Given that self-awareness increases adherence to standards, it seems logical that its absence should be associated with more impulsive, antinormative behaviors. In fact, impulsive behaviors are observed when people are very excited, physiologically aroused, and engaged in activities that draw their attention away from themselves. For example, if you have ever attended a big Thanksgiving or New Year's Day parade (such as Macy's Thanksgiving Day parade in New York or the Rose Bowl parade in Pasadena, Calif.), you know that observing the people watching the parade is as entertaining as watching the people performing in the parade. Uninhibited parade-goers may take off some or even most of their clothing (even in subfreezing weather!), dance heartily with strangers, and even try to join the parade participants. Such impulsivity is generally harmless, but researchers believe that the absence of self-awareness can prompt impulsive behaviors that involve violence and destruction as well (Prentice-Dunn and Rogers 1983).

Deindividuation is the technical term that is used to connote a multifaceted construct that involves (a) the specific environmental conditions (e.g., group involvement, arousing activities) that (b) promote a particular psychological state (e.g., lack of self-awareness, time distortion), which in turn (c) facilitates certain types of behaviors (e.g., uninhibited, impulsive, antinormative) (Diener 1979, 1980; Dipboye 1977; Prentice-Dunn and Rogers 1982; Scheier and Carver 1982; Zimbardo 1969). Let us focus briefly on each of these components of deindividuation.

Environmental Conditions

Deindividuation involves environmental conditions that shift one's attentional focus away from the self and toward the environment (Prentice-Dunn and Rogers 1983). Prentice-Dunn and Rogers (1982) activated an external attentional focus by instructing participants to focus attention outward and not on the self, perform a group task that involved considerable interaction, be in a dimly lit room, listen to loud rock music, and engage in interesting and visually appealing video games. Likewise, Diener (1979) had participants in groups engage in the following activities: sing together; lift a research assistant high into the air; interlock arms and prevent the assistant from breaking into the circle; and listen, clap, sway in unison, and dance to loud African drum music in a dimly lit room.

Intervening Psychological States

These environmental conditions promote alterations in people's experience and a reduction in private self-awareness that is accompanied by decreased self-regulation and self-evaluation. Furthermore, "with a hampered capacity for self-regulation, the individual becomes more responsive to environmental cues for behavioral direction than to internal standards of appropriate conduct" (Prentice-Dunn and Rogers 1983, 159). Research has shown, for example, that people exposed to deindividuating environmental conditions report that time passed quickly, their thoughts were concentrated on the moment or on what was happening around them, their emotions were different from normal, and their thinking was somewhat altered (Prentice-Dunn and Rogers 1982). In addition, they report being less aware of how their mind was working, less alert to mood changes, and less aware of private aspects of self.

Behavioral Consequences

Deindividuation involves impulsive and nonnormative behaviors that are undertaken with little regard to their consequences. Diener (1979) gave his participants a choice between doing relatively inhibited tasks (e.g., crossword puzzles, reading, answering moral dilemma questions, answering comprehension questions about a story) and uninhibited tasks (e.g., playing in mud, finger painting with nose, writing about friends' faults or obscenities, and sucking liquids from a baby bottle). Deindividuated participants spent more time on the uninhibited tasks than did nondeindividuated participants. Prentice-Dunn and Rogers (1982) reported that deindividuated participants delivered greater electric shocks (and thus were more aggressive) than did nondeindividuated participants.

Generally, people report that the experience of deindividuation is a positive one (but see Dipboye 1977, for a discussion of when it is not). Does this mean that directing attention toward the self is an aversive experience? Directing attention toward the self *can* be aversive, but it need not be. When people are depressed, for example, self-directed attention is generally aversive in that it often serves to worsen their symptoms (Pyszczynski and Greenberg 1987; Pyszczynski, Greenberg, Hamilton, and Nix 1991). This is especially the case after failure experiences, when depressed (but not nondepressed) people tend to engage in prolonged self-directed attention (Pyszczynski and Greenberg 1985). That is, failure leads depressed people to focus on their negative self-aspects, which then feeds back into their depressed feelings. More generally, self-awareness can be aversive if the self-aspect being focused on is a fault or a flaw, or is otherwise undesirable (Duval and Wicklund 1972), or if the self-directed attention involves unwanted and intrusive thoughts (Campbell et al. 1996). In fact, some extreme forms of behavior—such as suicide, masochism, drug and alcohol abuse, binge eating—can be thought of as attempts to "escape the self" when focusing on the self is highly aversive (Baumeister 1991).

On the other hand, self-focused attention can be an enriching and enlightening experience, promoting self-exploration, growth, and integration (Kernis and Grannemann 1988), and magnifying positive moods (Scheier and Carver 1977). A key factor in whether self-awareness is aversive or not is whether the individual feels a sense of control over its initiation and termination. Self-directed attention is likely to be a positive experience when people choose to attend to themselves and they feel that they can stop doing so when they want. When self-attention is unwanted and uncontrollable, it is much more likely to be a negative experience (Campbell et al. 1996).

Standards and Goals in Self-Regulation

When people are self-aware, either as a result of an environmental stimulus (e.g., they see themselves in a home video) or because they tend to focus on themselves (i.e., self-consciousness), they are reminded of the standards and goals they have internalized (Carver and Scheier 1982; Duval and Wicklund 1972). Depending on the self-focusing situation or stimulus, different standards or goals will move to the fore, and the impact of coming face-to-face (so to speak) with those standards or goals will vary for different types of standards and for different people.

Standards

According to self-discrepancy theory, standards take the form of **self-guides**, that is, representations that people have about their valued self-aspects (Higgins 1987). Two self-guides are particularly important. *Ideal self-guides* refer to self-aspects that a person (or a significant other) wishes or hopes that he or she would possess. *Ought self-guides* refer to those self-aspects that a person (or a significant other) feels it is his or her duty or obligation to possess. Discrepancies between either of these self-guides and a person's actual attributes have been shown to have implications for a person's emotional experiences. Specifically, discrepancies between the actual self and the ideal self-guide make a person prone to experience dejection-related emotions such as disappointment, sadness, and dissatisfaction. On the other hand, discrepancies between the actual self and the ought self-guide make a person prone to experience agitation-related emotions such as guilt, anxiety, apprehensiveness, and fear (Higgins 1987).

A somewhat different model of the implications of such discrepancies for emotional experience has been developed by Carver and Scheier (1990; Carver, Lawrence, and Scheier 1996). They propose that a critical determinant of emotion is whether or not the *rate* of progress in reducing current state-desired state discrepancies is judged by the person to be adequate. Adequate or better than adequate progress promotes positive affect; less than adequate progress promotes negative affect. In this perspective, the magnitude of the discrepancy is not an important determinant of affect. What is important is whether people feel that their progress toward matching the standard is occurring at a satisfactory rate (Carver et al. 1996; Hsee and Abelson 1991).

Goals

Standards, such as ideal or ought self-guides, are a type of goal toward which people strive. In recent years, goals have been conceptualized in a number of ways by personality and social psychologists.

Possible selves (Markus and Nurius 1986), already described as an element of the self-improvement motive, refer to hoped-for and feared selves that represent what a person could have been and may yet become. For example, a person who desires a possible self as an architect may go to school and intern with an architectural firm as a way of achieving that identity. On the other hand, a social drinker who fears a possible self as an alcoholic may avoid social situations and people that promote alcohol consumption in order to avoid becoming that person. These people regulate their view of themselves by choosing situations and relationships that correspond to goals relevant to identity and self-concept.

Life tasks (Cantor and Kihlstrom 1987) refer to the problems or tasks that people are working on during a particular period in their lives or during a life transition. These problems or tasks reflect the demands of their particular age and sociocultural groups, toward which people devote considerable time and energy as they go about their everyday lives. For college students, examples of life tasks include "doing well at school" (Norem and Cantor 1986a), "being self-sufficient" (Cantor and Zirkel 1990), and "making friends" (Harlow and Cantor 1995). Life tasks are considered normative in nature, that is, everyone (or nearly everyone) of a particular age-group living in a particular culture is thought to have to deal with them; however, people differ in the strategies that they use to successfully deal with these tasks (e.g., defensive pessimism vs. self-handicapping).

Personal projects refer to sets of personally relevant activities or concerns that are intended to achieve some goal (Little 1989). These activities and concerns can range from a trivial, one-shot affair (to lie still on the couch longer than your cat) to an important, long-term pursuit (to raise your kids well). Personal projects differ from life tasks in that they are not necessarily normative or socially dictated—they can be highly idiosyncratic (and even difficult to understand from the perspective of an outsider). Some people, for example, have as a personal project "collecting bags." Never throwing one out, they may employ elaborate sorting and storing strategies, even though most of the bags may never be used again in their lifetime. The personal projects that a person engages in say a lot about who he or she is and so have implications for well-being. Little (1989) notes that "research has shown that well-being is enhanced to the extent that an individual is engaged in projects that are meaningful, structured, supported, perceived to be efficacious, and relatively unstressful" (p. 164).

In a similar vein, Emmons (1986) introduced the construct of **personal strivings**—the goals that a person is typically trying to accomplish in his or her everyday behavior. As in the case of personal projects (and in contrast to life tasks), personal strivings need not be normative or socially mandated. In contrast to personal projects, strivings refer exclusively to recurring goals. In a typical study, people are asked to list ten or more strivings. These strivings may then be analyzed for their content. In addition, people may be asked questions pertaining to each of the strivings.

Emmons and King (1988) investigated the impact of conflict and ambivalence in personal strivings on individuals' physical and psychological well-being. *Conflict* refers to instances in which a person views one striving as interfering with the achievement of other strivings. *Ambivalence* refers to instances in which the person has the desire to achieve and not achieve the same striving; it can be assessed by asking people to estimate how much unhappiness they would feel if they successfully achieved the striving. The results of several studies indicated that both conflict between strivings and ambivalence about specific strivings were negatively related to physical and psychological well-being. Additional findings indicated that strivings that were in conflict with other strivings or that people felt ambivalent about were those that people spent less time acting on but more time thinking about (Emmons and King 1988).

In sum, possible selves, life tasks, personal projects, and personal strivings are ways of conceptualizing the self-relevant goals that people pursue in the course of their everyday lives. Each of these constructs involves both approach and avoidance goals. *Approach goals* involve attempting to achieve a positive outcome, whereas *avoidant goals* involve attempting to avoid a negative outcome. For example, "being fair and honest" is an approach personal striving, whereas "not making people angry" is an avoidance personal striving. Although this distinction may seem subtle, recent research indicates that it has considerable implications for well-being. Specifically, people whose strivings entail primarily approach goals are less depressed, have higher self-esteem, and report greater psychological well-being compared with people whose strivings entail primarily avoidance goals (Coates, Janoff-Bulman, and Alpert 1996; Elliot and Sheldon 1997). Overall, the extent to which goals "fit together" within a person and the strategies that people use to achieve their goals have implications for their emotional and psychological well-being.

Different Goals for Different People

Just as it is clear that all people plan and enact behaviors that are tied to the standards and goals they have adopted, it is clear that different types of standards and goals matter to different people. Two broad classes of standards and goals are those that are *personal,* which have been embraced to such an extent that they are no longer associated with external sources, and those that are *public,* which are firmly rooted outside the person, usually in the form of the desires or wishes of significant others (Higgins 1987). Two traits that affect which class of standards and goals is most influential for different people are self-consciousness and self-monitoring.

Self-Consciousness

Research has shown that, whereas people who are high in public (and low in private) self-consciousness are likely to behave in line with social or externally provided standards, people who are high in private (and low in public) self-consciousness are likely to behave in line with personal, internal standards (Greenberg 1982; Kernis and Reis 1984). In one study, Kernis and Reis gave pairs of research participants an opportunity to earn money. Each member of the pair was led to believe that she or he would be the one to divide up the money that was earned between them. The experimenter activated an equity standard (i.e., that rewards should be proportional to contributions) by stating that allocators might want to take into considera- tion each person's performance (and hence contribution) when dividing up the money. An equality standard (that each person should be paid the same amount regardless of contribution) was activated in a more personal way without any explicit statements on the part of the experimenter. Specifically, the partners were of equal status, and the task and subsequent payoff em- phasized cooperation (not competition), factors that promote equality as an allocation strategy (Reis and Gruzen 1975). In all cases, participants were led to believe that they had performed slightly better than their part- ner and so had contributed more to the amount of money earned. As antic- ipated, public self-consciousness was related to taking more money for the self (an equity standard), whereas private self-consciousness was related to dividing up the money equally. Whereas participants high in private self- consciousness preferred the standard that did not require social comparison or any reference to characteristics of the situation, participants high in pub- lic self-consciousness preferred a standard that required a reference to the behavior of their partner.

Self-Monitoring

The construct of self-monitoring has been the focus of considerable re- search in social psychology since its introduction over twenty years ago (Snyder 1974). Although it has been the subject of considerable contro- versy, particularly with respect to how it is measured (Briggs, Cheek, and Buss 1980; Hoyle and Lennox 1991), it remains of considerable interest to those who study the self because of its implications for self-regulation. Snyder (1987) conceptualized **self-monitoring** as "differences in the extent to which people *monitor* (observe, regulate, and control) the public appear- ances of *self* they display in social situations and interpersonal relation- ships" (pp. 4–5). High self-monitoring people look to the social environ- ment for cues that will help them plan their behavior, whereas low self-monitoring people look within themselves to their attitudes and feel- ings to find behavioral cues (Hoyle and Sowards 1993; Snyder 1989).

The thoughts, feelings, and behaviors of high self-monitoring people (who also tend to be higher in public self-consciousness than their low self- monitoring counterparts) are influenced by standards and goals that arise in the context of social life. As such, their behavior is not strongly tied to their attitudes, and it varies more from situation to situation than the behavior of low self-monitoring people, who view their behavior as an expression of their internalized attitudes and values (Snyder and Monson 1975; Snyder and Tanke 1976). Also, when choosing friends and romantic partners, high self-monitoring people are more influenced than their low self-monitoring counterparts by standards provided by culture and the popular media such as physical attractiveness. Conversely, low self-monitoring people are more interested in the degree to which potential friends or romantic partners reflect internal characteristics such as an agreeable disposition (Snyder, Berscheid, and Glick 1985; Snyder and Simpson 1984). In sum, high self-monitoring people self-regulate in consultation with the social environment, whereas low self-monitoring people routinely consult their privately held values and opinions when planning and enacting behavior (Hoyle and Sowards 1993).

Self-awareness and related constructs are central to self-regulation, a fundamental activity of the self-system. Apart from self-awareness, people would lack a conscious basis for planning and evaluating the impact of their behavior. Yet self-awareness alone is not sufficient to explain the various ways by which people control themselves and their environment. Building on our discussion of self-awareness and self-regulation, we now turn to the broader issues of human agency and determination.

Agency, Self-Determination, and Self-Regulatory Styles

"Give me liberty or give me death!"

Humanitarians, politicians, revolutionaries, philosophers, and psychologists have long been concerned with issues related to human freedom. As children pass through the so-called terrible twos, they strive to assert their independence from the wishes and demands of their parents. Adult workaholics, despite deriving little pleasure from their jobs, cannot seem to do anything else. In fact, much of human behavior seems to involve a balancing act between acting purely on the basis of one's own wishes and desires and incorporating the norms, rules, and restrictions of others.

One of this century's most prominent psychologists, B. F. Skinner, argued that human behavior can be explained entirely on the basis of environmentally based reinforcement and punishment contingencies. That is, people engage in behaviors for which they have previously been reinforced, and they refrain from behaviors for which they have previously been punished. From this point of view, people do not make choices concerning the initiation, maintenance, and termination of their behavior (e.g., Skinner 1971). During the 1950s and 1960s Skinner's views dominated psychological research and theory; however, with the cognitive revolution in psychology, the pendulum has swung from an almost exclusive focus on the environment to a systematic focus on characteristics of people that give rise to their behavior.

Behaviors that are strictly (or primarily) under the influence of reinforcement and punishment contingencies certainly exist. The saying "once burned, twice shy" is aptly descriptive of such instances. More generally, people often do things in order to gain tangible (e.g., money or material goods) or psychological (e.g., praise, compliments) rewards. At the same time, people seem often to engage in behaviors in the absence of such environmentally based rewards. How are these latter behaviors to be accounted for? Are they due to environmentally based rewards that observers just cannot see? Or are they due to other factors?

Extrinsic Versus Intrinsic Motivation

An important distinction can be made between behaviors that are extrinsically motivated and behaviors that are intrinsically motivated. *Extrinsically motivated behaviors* are those that are undertaken in order to obtain a reward or avoid a punishment. In contrast, *intrinsically motivated behaviors* are undertaken because they are fun, enjoyable, and/or interesting to do. They occur in the absence of any apparent external reward, and they serve to foster optimal development of the self (Deci 1975). How important is it to be intrinsically motivated?

The most comprehensive perspective on the importance of intrinsic motivation to psychological functioning can be found in Deci and Ryan's (1985) **self-determination theory**. According to Deci and Ryan, people have three primary psychological needs: the need for competence; the need for autonomy, or self-determination; and the need for relatedness. For optimal development to occur, satisfaction of these basic needs is thought to be paramount. Here we focus on the need for autonomy (for a discussion of the other two needs, see Deci and Ryan 1985, 1991). The need for autonomy encompasses people's desires to be agentic. That is, people want to feel that they are the origin of their actions, which they freely choose to engage in. How do people go about satisfying their need for autonomy? The answer provided by Deci and Ryan is that people do so by engaging in intrinsically motivated activity.

A number of factors can foster or inhibit the extent to which people are intrinsically motivated to engage in a particular activity. These factors can reside in the activity itself, can be a part of the context in which the activity is undertaken, or can reflect aspects of the person herself.

Enhancing Intrinsic Motivation

One factor that can foster people's interest and enjoyment, thereby promoting their intrinsic motivation, is the *degree of challenge* inherent in a given activity. Specifically, people are more intrinsically motivated to engage in activities that are optimally challenging than they are to do things that are too difficult or too easy (Csikszentmihalyi 1975; Deci 1975). Optimally challenging activities are those that provide opportunities for learning, growth, and development—they stimulate the person's senses, physical capabilities, and/or thought processes. Optimal challenge is a very individualized concept. What constitutes an optimal challenge for one person may be too much or too little for another. Moreover, what is optimally challenging to an individual at a given point in time may become routine and boring with repeated encounters. A second factor that can enhance intrinsic motivation is that the activity be undertaken by choice rather than by force or coercion (Zuckerman et al. 1978). A third factor is that performance or progress-relevant information be provided in a way that is not highly evaluative or threatening. Activities and contexts in which people can monitor their performance or progress in a nonpressured way tend to foster greater intrinsic interest than do activities or contexts in which the focus is on performing up to a certain standard or expectation. This is true even if the standard is achieved or the expectation is matched (Ryan 1982).

Undermining Intrinsic Motivation

Just as there are factors that can enhance intrinsic motivation, there are factors that can undermine it as well. Being forced to do an activity predictably undermines intrinsic motivation (Zuckerman et al. 1978). Also, intrinsic motivation often suffers when people perform under time pressures or when the performance context is highly evaluative in nature (Amabile, DeJong, and Lepper 1976). Offering rewards can also undermine intrinsic motivation, as described in the following fable:[1]

> In a little Southern town where the Klan was riding again, a Jewish tailor had the temerity to open his little shop on the main street. To drive him out of the town, the Kleagle of the Klan sent a gang of little ragamuffins to annoy him. Day after day they stood at the entrance of his shop. "Jew! Jew!" they hooted at him. The situation looked serious for the tailor. He took the matter so much to heart that he began to brood and spent sleepless nights over it. Finally out of desperation he evolved a plan.
>
> The following day when the little hoodlums came to jeer at him, he came to the door and said to them, "From today on any boy who calls me 'Jew' will get a dime from me." Then he put his hand in his pocket and gave each boy a dime.

---

[1]Deci and Ryan (1985) quoted this fable in a similar context.

Delighted with their booty, the boys came back the following day and began to shrill, "Jew! Jew!" The tailor came out smiling. He put his hand in his pocket and gave each of the boys a nickel, saying, "A dime is too much—I can only afford a nickel today." The boys went away satisfied because, after all, a nickel was money too.

However, when they returned the next day to hoot at him, the tailor gave them only a penny each.

"Why do we get only a penny today?" they yelled.

"That's all I can afford."

"But two days ago you gave us a dime, and yesterday we got a nickel. It's not fair, mister."

"Take it or leave it. That's all you're going to get!"

"Do you think we're going to call you 'Jew' for one lousy penny?"

"So don't!"

And they didn't.[2]

Research has shown that rewards are most likely to undermine intrinsic motivation if they are given in a controlling manner. "Controlling rewards are experienced by the recipient as pressure to think, feel, or behave in specified ways" (Deci and Ryan 1985, 95). Parents who reward their children for good grades may unwittingly undermine their children's intrinsic motivation for school-related activities. This is especially likely if the opportunity to obtain rewards is shrouded in pressure to do well. ("If you get all As, as we expect you to, we will give you $20. If you get a B or lower, we will be very disappointed and you will not get any money.") Importantly, rewards that are given in a noncontrolling manner, simply to signify good performance, generally maintain or even enhance intrinsic motivation. ("That's a great report card. You deserve a break from schoolwork. Here's some money—go have fun at the arcade.") (See Deci and Ryan 1985 for a summary of the literature.)

Factors that undermine people's interest and enjoyment in activities can also have deleterious effects on their creativity (Amabile 1983). When focused on earning rewards or avoiding punishments, people tend to do precisely what they need to do to meet the deadline, get the grade, or receive the reward or evaluation—and little more. Instead of letting their minds go and mulling over various possible solutions, people are more likely to be thinking in terms such as, "How can I do this in the quickest way? What is the professor looking for? What is the simplest way to do this?"

As college professors, we sometimes see this type of overemphasis on the part of our students. During a review session, if most of the questions run

---

[2]From *A Treasury of Jewish Folklore,* ed. N. Ausable (1948; New York: Crown, 1976), 440. Reprinted with permission.

along certain lines, such as, "Are we responsible for this material for the exam?" "Will you be asking about ... ?" "Do we have to know ... ?" this is a clue that our students may be more extrinsically than intrinsically motivated. What can we as professors do? It certainly helps if the material we are covering is interesting and fun to learn, but this is not always something that we can control. In almost every course there is material that is important for our students to learn, even if it is not inherently interesting. Even here, though, we can attempt to convey the material in a way that is optimally challenging—not so easy as to be trivial and not so difficult as to be impenetrable. Moreover, we can try to create a range of modules or projects from which students can choose instead of arbitrarily assigning them to one and only one. Also, we can emphasize to our students the benefits of approaching studying and completing assignments as challenges that can broaden their knowledge, not just as means to obtain particular grades. In this regard, going through the course material regularly, but at one's own pace, is likely to be less stressful (and more intrinsically rewarding) than waiting until right before an exam to pore over mountains of material for the first time. Also, we can create an in-class environment that encourages active involvement and flexibility on the part of both students and teachers. If we are successful, most students will enjoy our classes more and will get more out of them.

Despite professors' best efforts, however, there inevitably will be students who hold onto the view that "I will learn this only if I need it to do well in this class." Hopefully these students do take an interest in something (though it may not be our course) and are able to experience the benefit of being intrinsically motivated. Their experience of doing something even though they really do not want to is not an isolated one—it is a basic component of everyday life. As Ryan (1991) states:

> Despite the importance of intrinsic motivation to human behavior and development, much of our social behavior, ritual, and value- or duty-driven action is originally neither intrinsically motivated nor spontaneous. It is thus relevant to examine the extent to which behaviors that have their origins in social contingencies and external (interpersonal) regulations can come to be experienced as autonomous or self-determined. (p. 216)

One way to approach this issue is to examine the types of reasons that people have for engaging in various kinds of activities. As Ryan and Connell (1989) have shown, these reasons reflect self-regulatory processes that vary in the extent to which they involve self-determination (see also Sheldon and Kasser 1995, from which some of the following reasons were taken). *External reasons* reflect the absence of self-determination—activities are undertaken only when another person requests them, with implicit or explicit rewards or punishments accompanying the request. ("I do it because something about my external situation forces me to do it; I do it because somebody else wants me to or because I will get something from somebody if I do.") *Introjected reasons* involve only minimal self-determination—they reflect an "internally controlling state in which affective and self-esteem contingencies are applied to enforce or motivate an adopted value or set of actions" (Ryan, Rigby, and King 1993, 587). Furthermore, introjected self-regulation is characterized by "self and other approval based pressures" (p. 586). It promotes behaviors that "are performed because one 'should' do them, or because not doing so might engender anxiety, guilt, or loss of self-esteem" (p. 587). Introjected reasons are reflected in statements such as, "I force myself to do it to avoid feeling guilty or anxious" and "I do it because I am supposed to do it." *Identified reasons* reflect greater self-determination—one personally and freely identifies with the importance of the activity. ("I do it because it ties into my personal values and beliefs." "I do it because I feel that doing it will help me grow or develop in a way that is personally important to me.") Finally, *intrinsic reasons* reflect the prototype of self-determined regulation. ("I do it because of the pleasure and fun of doing it. I do it because of the interest and enjoyment of doing it.")

We opened this chapter with two possible sets of activities that a person might undertake on any given day. One set involved clearly enjoyable activities (e.g., walking through the park), whereas the other set involved activities resembling chores (e.g., washing the car). A person who freely chooses the more enjoyable set would presumably offer intrinsic reasons for doing so. He would be acting with a great deal of self-determination (i.e., agency). What about a person who decides to tackle the other activities? This decision could involve external, introjected, or identified self-regulatory processes. If the person was undertaking them merely to gain favor in another person's eyes, extrinsic self-regulation would be operative. If the primary reason was to avoid feeling guilty or anxious, introjected self-regulation would be operative and the person would be only minimally self-determining. Greater self-determination would be felt by the person whose choice was based on an appreciation of the importance of having a clean car (e.g., to remove remnants of acid rain), getting a haircut (e.g., a neat appearance is important), and undertaking a particular task (e.g., the knowledge gained would be beneficial).

Research indicates that self-determined regulation (i.e., identified and intrinsic) is positively related to psychological well-being. In a study by Sheldon and Kasser (1995), participants generated a list of personal strivings. They then indicated the extent to which they pursued them for each of four reasons, corresponding to each of the reason categories just discussed. A "striving self-determination" score was created in which higher scores reflected greater striving self-determination. Across two separate studies, findings indicated that greater striving self-determination was related to more positive daily mood, greater life satisfaction, higher self-esteem, greater psychological vitality, and fewer conflicts among one's self-roles, as well as less role-related distress.

Another recent study examined the relation between self-esteem stability and self-regulatory styles, using measures similar to those employed by Sheldon and Kasser (1995). Importantly, the more unstable the individuals' self-esteem, the less self-determined were their self-regulatory styles (Kernis, Paradise, Whitaker, Wheatman, and Goldman 1997). People with unstable self-esteem, compared to people with stable self-esteem, also reported greater feelings of tension and pressure when reflecting on how they felt while engaged in striving-related behavior. One interpretation of these findings is that the absence of self-determined regulation underlies or promotes fragility in one's immediate feelings of self-worth. Future research will undoubtedly shed additional light on the directional nature of the link between unstable self-esteem and self-regulatory styles.

These studies implicate self-regulatory styles in psychological well-being. Moreover, they indicate that people vary in the extent to which they engage in activities for intrinsic versus extrinsic reasons. Other research indicates that the extent to which people's goals and aspirations reflect intrinsic or extrinsic concerns is important to an understanding of their well-being. Specifically, several studies (e.g., Kasser and Ryan 1993, 1995) have shown that people whose aspirations are primarily extrinsic in nature (e.g., financial success, fame and recognition, or physical attractiveness) are more depressed and anxious and are lower in global functioning and self-actualization than are people whose goals are primarily intrinsic in nature (e.g., self-acceptance and personal growth, having close relationships, helping others). Thus, on a number of different fronts, the importance of intrinsic motivation and self-determination to well-being is evident.

Afterword

To deal with the phenomena of selfhood, psychology has to be a historical and cultural science, as well as a biological one.
—*Smith (1978, 1053)*

Philosophers and scientists have long debated what it is about human beings that distinguishes them from the rest of the animal kingdom. What attributes do people possess that make them so different from even their closest relatives on the phylogenetic scale? Scholars once maintained that human beings are unique in their ability to make and use tools, but this belief fell by the wayside when it was discovered that other animals—chimpanzees and elephants, for example—sometimes turn ordinary objects into functional tools. Another proposed distinction was that only human beings use language, thus permitting the communication necessary for major cultural achievements. However, researchers later found that animals as different as bees and whales use very complex systems of communication and that certain animals can even learn to use human language. So the question remains: What makes human beings different from other animals?

One promising answer to this question is that human beings have a much more highly developed *self* than any other animal. Although researchers have shown that many of the great apes have a rudimentary sense of self (Gallup 1977), no other animal can engage in the sophisticated types of self-referent thought and self-regulated behavior that we can. This unique ability to think consciously about ourselves appears to underlie many of the complex behaviors that we regard as uniquely human.

Because we have a self, we can purposefully remember what we did yesterday and consciously plan for what we will do tomorrow. We can imagine ourselves in situations that do not exist and thus can consider in our minds the consequences of various things we might do. We can intentionally seek information about what we are like, ponder over who and what we are, and then regulate our behavior on the basis of who we think we are and who we want to become. With the help of our self, we can deliberately change our bad habits and plot new directions in life. We even defend our self-images against information that contradicts them or makes us feel bad about ourselves, and we can think about how we are perceived by other people and adjust our behavior to convey the impressions we want them to have of us.

The highest human achievements involve these abilities, all of which require a highly developed self. Without a self, we would have no literature, no philosophy, no formal educational systems, no government, and no religion. We could not plan weeks or years ahead to work toward either self-improvement or the betterment of our society. Put simply, civilization as we know it could not exist if human beings did not have selves.

Despite the fact that the human self has played a role in these remarkable achievements, the human capacity for self-thought has come at a high price. Much unhappiness in life—our anxiety, depression, and guilt, for example—springs from our ability to ruminate about the past, fret about the present, and worry about the future. Because we have a self, we can obsess over imagined problems as well as worry about real ones. We live much of our lives inside our own heads, creating unnecessary misery and missing out on the real world as our selves chatter away at us. Often these thoughts distress us so much that we seek to escape them through such means as drinking, binge eating, or even suicide (Baumeister 1991). Our conflicts with one another go beyond skirmishes over territory, food, and mates to fights over abstract self-created ideas and disagreements about who we are. We hate and reject other people because they are *not like us,* a distinction that obviously requires a self. In fact, people have died defending their identity.

So the self is very much a mixed bag—a source of human achievement and accomplishment, yet an instigator of harm and unhappiness. The objective for behavioral researchers who study the self, it seems to us, is to facilitate our understanding of the self so that we can maximize its contributions to human well-being and minimize its capacity to create misery. The theories and research that have formed the backbone of this book have already moved us well along toward this goal. Compared to what social psychologists knew only twenty-five years ago, our current understanding of the self is immense. Yet much is left to do, and we hope that researchers will not only continue the many lines of research we have described but strike out in new directions as well.

In doing so, one of the greatest challenges will be to determine the degree to which the self-processes that we have discussed in this book are characteristic of all human beings or are peculiar to the Western research subjects who have participated in most of the studies that have been conducted. Virtually all of the theories and research studies that constitute our knowledge about the self have come from researchers in Western, industrialized countries, predominately the United States, Canada, and Great Britain. Yet

Eastern cultures have a decidedly different view of the self. Perhaps most importantly, Western cultures edify the individual self whereas Eastern cultures do not. (Indeed, the goal of Eastern religions—for example, Buddhism and Hinduism—is to eliminate the influence of the self.) These cultural differences suggest that our current knowledge of the self may be incomplete and one-sided, and they highlight the importance of cultural psychology in contributing to our understanding of the self.

The solution is not simply to replicate previous research using participants from non-Western cultures (although that is important). The challenge is to determine whether the conceptualizations of the self that have guided our research to date have any basis outside of European and American culture. This is a formidable challenge because researchers' own preexisting assumptions about the self hinder their ability to see the self as it exists in other cultures (Gergen 1985). Our hunch is that much existing theory and research is indeed directly applicable to people of all cultures but that certain important differences will emerge as well. Only a great deal of research will help us determine which features of the self represent human universals and which are culture specific.

Most psychologists would likely agree that the self ranks among the most important constructs in human psychology (certainly among the top ten). Not only does much of human activity utilize our unique ability to think about ourselves, but it would be difficult to understand fully most human behavior without reference to processes that involve self-referent thought, identity, self-related motives, and self-regulation. Human beings are not really human without their selves, and scientific psychology is not complete without an understanding of how the human self works. The following words from M. Brewster Smith's eloquent presidential address to members of the American Psychological Association are as apropos today as they were when spoken two decades ago:

> If psychology can come to deal more directly and coherently with the phenomena of human selfhood, it should gain in competence to play an essential role in interpreting humankind to itself and in supporting people in their struggles to gain a measure of self-direction in their lives. As an endangered species and an endangering one, we need, collectively, all the self-understanding and self-direction that we can muster. (Smith 1978, 1062)

References

Adler, A. 1933. On the origins of the striving for superiority and of social interest. *International Journal of Individual Psychology* 11: 257–263.

Alexander, N. C., and G. W. Knight. 1971. Situated identities and social psychological experimentation. *Sociometry* 34: 65–82.

Allport, G. W. 1937. *Personality: A psychological interpretation*. New York: Holt.

Allport, G. W. 1943. The ego in contemporary psychology. *Psychological Review* 50: 451–479.

Allport, G. W. 1954. The historical background of modern social psychology. In *Handbook of social psychology*, edited by G. Lindzey, 1:3–56. Cambridge, Mass.: Addison-Wesley.

Allport, G. W. 1955. *Becoming*. New Haven: Yale University Press.

Allport, G. W. 1961a. Introduction to *William James/Psychology: The briefer course*, edited by G. W. Allport, xiii-xxiii. New York: Harper Torchbooks.

Allport, G. W. 1961b. *Pattern and growth in personality*. New York: Holt, Rinehart, and Winston.

Allport, G. W. 1968. The historical background of modern social psychology. In *The handbook of social psychology*, edited by G. Lindzey and E. Aronson, 1–80. 2d ed. Reading, Mass.: Addison-Wesley.

Altschule, M. D. 1957. *Roots of modern psychiatry*. New York: Grune.

Amabile, T. M. 1983. *The social psychology of creativity*. New York: Springer-Verlag.

Amabile, T. M., W. DeJong, and M. R. Lepper. 1976. Effects of externally imposed deadlines on subsequent intrinsic motivation. *Journal of Personality and Social Psychology* 34: 92–98.

American Psychological Association Committee. 1918. Definitions and delimitations of psychological terms. *Psychological Bulletin* 15: 89–95.

Anderson, E. 1994. The code of the streets. *Atlantic Monthly*, May, 81–94.

Anthony, C. P., and G. A. Thibodeau. 1984. *Structure and function of the body*. 7th ed. St. Louis: Times Mirror/Mosby.

Arkin, R. M., and A. H. Baumgardner. 1985. Self-handicapping. In *Basic issues in attribution theory and research*, edited by J. H. Harvey and G. Weary, 169–202. New York: Academic.

Aronson, E. 1968. Dissonance theory: Progress and problems. In *The cognitive consistency theories: A source book*, edited by R. Abelson, E. Aronson, W. McGuire, T. Newcomb, M. Rosenberg, and P. Tannenbaum, 5–27. Chicago: Rand McNally.

Aronson, E. 1969. The theory of cognitive dissonance: A current perspective. In *Advances in experimental social psychology*, edited by L. Berkowitz, 4:1–34. New York: Academic.

Attneave, F. 1954. Some informational aspects of visual perception. *Psychological Review* 61: 183–193.

Attneave, F. 1959. *Applications of information theory to psychology: A summary of basic concepts, methods, and results.* New York: Holt-Dryden.

Averill, J. R. 1982. *Anger and aggression: An essay on emotion.* New York: Springer-Verlag.

Backman, C. W., and P. F. Secord. 1962. Liking, selective interaction, and misperception in congruent interpersonal relations. *Sociometry* 25: 231–235.

Backman, C. W., P. F. Secord, and J. R. Pierce. 1963. Resistance to change in the self-concept as a function of consensus among significant others. *Sociometry* 26: 102–111.

Baldwin, M. W. 1992. Relational schemas and the processing of social information. *Psychological Bulletin* 112: 461–484.

Baldwin, M. W., and J. G. Holmes. 1987. Salient private audiences and awareness of the self. *Journal of Personality and Social Psychology* 53: 1087–1098.

Baldwin, M. W., and L. Sinclair. 1996. Self-esteem and "if-then" contingencies of interpersonal acceptance. *Journal of Personality and Social Psychology* 71: 1130–1141.

Bandura, A. 1997. *Self-efficacy: The exercise of control.* New York: Freeman.

Bargh, J. A. 1982. Attention and automaticity in the processing of self-relevant information. *Journal of Personality and Social Psychology* 43: 425–436.

Baumeister, R. F. 1982. A self-presentational view of social phenomena. *Psychological Bulletin* 91: 3–26.

Baumeister, R. F. 1986. *Identity: Cultural change and the struggle for self.* New York: Oxford University Press.

Baumeister, R. F. 1987. How the self became a problem: A psychological review of historical research. *Journal of Personality and Social Psychology* 52: 163–176.

Baumeister, R. F. 1988. Masochism as escape from self. *Journal of Sex Research* 25: 28–59.

Baumeister, R. F. 1990. Suicide as escape from self. *Psychological Review* 97: 90–113.

Baumeister, R. F. 1991. *Escaping the self: Alcoholism, spirituality, masochism, and other flights from the burden of selfhood.* New York: Basic Books.

Baumeister, R. F. 1993. Understanding the inner nature of low self-esteem: Uncertain, fragile, protective, and conflicted. In *Self-esteem: The puzzle of low self-regard,* edited by R. F. Baumeister, 201–218. New York: Plenum.

Baumeister, R. F., T. F. Heatherton, and D. M. Tice. 1993. When ego threats lead to self-regulation failure: Negative consequences of high self-esteem. *Journal of Personality and Social Psychology* 64: 141–156.

Baumeister, R. F., and M. R. Leary. 1995. The need to belong: Desire for interpersonal attachments as a fundamental human motivation. *Psychological Bulletin* 117: 497–529.

Baumeister, R. F., L. Smart, and J. M. Boden. 1996. Relation of threatened egotism to violence and aggression: The dark side of high self-esteem. *Psychological Review* 103: 5–33.

Baumeister, R. F., D. M. Tice, and D. G. Hutton. 1989. Self-presentation motivations and personality differences in self-esteem. *Journal of Personality* 57: 547–579.

Baumgardner, A. H. 1990. To know oneself is to like oneself: Self-certainty and self-affect. *Journal of Personality and Social Psychology* 58: 1062–1072.

Beach, S. R. H., and A. Tesser. 1995. Self-esteem and the extended self-evaluation maintenance model: The self in social context. In *Efficacy, agency, and self-esteem*, edited by M. H. Kernis, 145–170. New York: Plenum.

Beaman, A. L., B. Klentz, E. Diener, and S. Svanum. 1979. Self-awareness and transgression in children: Two field studies. *Journal of Personality and Social Psychology* 37: 1835–1846.

Beck, A. T. 1967. *Depression: Clinical, experimental, and theoretical aspects*. New York: Harper and Row.

Becker, E. 1962. *The birth and death of meaning*. New York: Free Press.

Becker, E. 1973. *The denial of death*. New York: Free Press.

Bem, D. 1972. Self-perception theory. In *Advances in experimental social psychology*, edited by L. Berkowitz, 6:1–62. New York: Academic.

Berger, P. L. 1963. *Invitation to sociology*. Garden City, N.Y.: Anchor.

Berger, P. L., and T. Luckmann. 1967. *The social construction of reality*. Garden City, N.Y.: Anchor.

Berglas, S., and E. E. Jones. 1978. Drug choice as a self-handicapping strategy in response to noncontingent success. *Journal of Personality and Social Psychology* 36: 405–417.

Blaine, B., and J. Crocker. 1993. Self-esteem and self-serving biases in reactions to positive and negative events. In *Self-esteem: The puzzle of low self-regard*, edited by R. F. Baumeister, 55–85. New York: Plenum.

Block, J. 1961. Ego-identity, role variability, and adjustment. *Journal of Consulting and Clinical Psychology* 25: 392–397.

Bower, G. H., and S. G. Gilligan. 1979. Remembering information related to one's self. *Journal of Research in Personality* 13: 420–432.

Bowlby, J. 1969. *Attachment and loss*. Vol. 1, *Attachment*. New York: Basic Books.

Box, G. E. P. 1979. Robustness in the strategy of scientific model building. In *Robustness in statistics*, edited by R. L. Launer and G. N. Wilkinson, 201–236. New York: Academic.

Bradbury, T. N., and F. C. Fincham. 1990. Attributions and behavior in marital interaction. *Journal of Personality and Social Psychology* 63: 613–628.

Bradley, G. W. 1978. Self-serving biases in the attribution process: A reexamination of the fact or fiction question. *Journal of Personality and Social Psychology* 36: 56–71.

Branden, N. 1994. *Six pillars of self-esteem*. New York: Bantam.

Briggs, S. R., J. M. Cheek, and A. H. Buss. 1980. An analysis of the self-monitoring scale. *Journal of Personality and Social Psychology* 38: 679–686.

Brockner, J. 1983. Low self-esteem and behavioral plasticity: Some implications. In *Review of personality and social psychology*, edited by L. Wheeler and P. Shaver, 4:237–271. Beverly Hills, Calif.: Sage.

Brown, G. W., B. Andrews, T. Harris, Z. Adler, and L. Bridge. 1986. Social support, self-esteem, and depression. *Psychological Medicine* 16: 813–831.

Brown, J. D. 1990. Evaluating one's abilities: Shortcuts and stumbling blocks on the road to self-knowledge. *Journal of Experimental Social Psychology* 26: 149–167.

Brown, J. D. 1993. Self-esteem and self-evaluation: Feeling is believing. In *Psychological perspectives on the self,* edited by J. Suls, 4:27–58. Hillsdale, N.J.: Erlbaum.

Brown, J. D., R. L. Collins, and G. W. Schmidt. 1988. Self-esteem and direct versus indirect forms of self-enhancement. *Journal of Personality and Social Psychology* 55: 445–453.

Brown, J. D., and K. A. Dutton. 1995. The thrill of victory, the complexity of defeat: Self-esteem and people's emotional reactions to success and failure. *Journal of Personality and Social Psychology* 68: 712–722.

Brown, J. D., and F. M. Gallagher. 1992. Coming to terms with failure: Private self-enhancement and public self-effacement. *Journal of Experimental Social Psychology* 28: 3–22.

Brown, J. D., N. J. Novick, K. A. Lord, and J. M. Richards. 1992. When Gulliver travels: Social context, psychological closeness, and self-appraisals. *Journal of Personality and Social Psychology* 62: 717–727.

Buber, M. 1958. *I and Thou.* New York: Scribner's. Originally published in 1923.

Buri, J. R., P. A. Louiselle, T. M. Misukanis, and R. A. Mueller. 1988. Effects of parental authoritarianism and authoritativeness on self-esteem. *Personality and Social Psychology Bulletin* 14: 271–282.

Burns, M. 1990. Ten steps to self-esteem. *Essence* 21: 57–58.

Buss, A. H. 1980. *Self-consciousness and social anxiety.* San Francisco: Freeman.

Butler, A. C., J. E. Hokanson, and H. A. Flynn. 1994. A comparison of self-esteem lability and low self-esteem as vulnerability factors for depression. *Journal of Personality and Social Psychology* 66: 166–177.

Cacioppo, J. T., G. G. Berntson, and S. L. Crites Jr. 1996. Social neuroscience: Principles of psychophysiological arousal and response. In *Social psychology: Handbook of basic principles,* edited by E. T. Higgins and A. W. Kruglanski, 72–101. New York: Guilford.

Campbell, J. D. 1990. Self-esteem and clarity of the self-concept. *Journal of Personality and Social Psychology* 59: 538–549.

Campbell, J. D., B. Chew, and L. S. Scratchley. 1991. Cognitive and emotional reaction to daily events: The effects of self-esteem and self-complexity. *Journal of Personality* 59: 473–506.

Campbell, J. D., and B. Fehr. 1990. Self-esteem and perceptions of conveyed impressions: Is negative affectivity associated with greater realism? *Journal of Personality and Social Psychology* 58: 122–133.

Campbell, J. D., P. D. Trapnell, S. J. Heine, I. M. Katz, L. F. Lavallee, and D. R. Lehman. 1996. Self-concept clarity: Measurement, personality correlates, and cultural boundaries. *Journal of Personality and Social Psychology* 70: 141–156.

Cannon, W. B. 1929. Organization for physiological homeostasis. *Physiological Review* 9: 399–431.

Cantor, N., and J. F. Kihlstrom. 1985. Social intelligence: The cognitive basis of personality. In *Review of personality and social psychology,* edited by P. Shaver, 6:15–33. Beverly Hills, Calif.: Sage.

Cantor, N., and J. F. Kihlstrom. 1987. *Personality and social intelligence.* Englewood Cliffs, N.J.: Prentice-Hall.

Cantor, N., and S. Zirkel. 1990. Personality, cognition, and purposive behavior. In *Handbook of personality: Theory and research,* edited by L. A. Pervin, 135–164. New York: Guilford.

Carlson, C. R. 1988. Cardiovascular functioning. Unpublished manuscript, University of Kentucky, Lexington.

Carver, C. S. 1975. Physical aggression as a function of objective self-awareness and attitudes toward punishment. *Journal of Experimental Social Psychology* 11: 510–519.

Carver, C. S., J. W. Lawrence, and M. F. Scheier. 1996. A control-process perspective on the origins of affect. In *Striving and feeling: Interactions among goals, affect, and self-regulation,* edited by L. L. Martin and A. Tesser, 53–78. Hillsdale, N.J.: Erlbaum.

Carver, C. S., and M. F. Scheier. 1981. *Attention and self-regulation: A control theory approach to human behavior.* New York: Springer-Verlag.

Carver, C. S., and M. F. Scheier. 1982. Control theory: A useful conceptual framework for personality—social, clinical, and health psychology. *Psychological Bulletin* 92: 111–135.

Carver, C. S., and M. F. Scheier. 1990. Origins and functions of positive and negative affect: A control-process view. *Psychological Review* 97: 19–35.

Caspi, A., and T. E. Moffitt. 1993. When do individual differences matter? A paradoxical theory of personality coherence. *Psychological Inquiry* 4: 247–271.

Charters, W. W., and T. M. Newcomb. 1952. Some attitudinal effects of experimentally increased salience of a membership group. In *Readings in social psychology,* edited by G. E. Swanson, T. M. Newcomb, and E. L. Hartley, 415–420. 2d ed. New York: Holt.

Cheek, J. M., and S. R. Briggs. 1982. Self-consciousness and aspects of identity. *Journal of Research in Personality* 16: 401–408.

Clance, P. P., and S. A. Imes. 1978. The impostor phenomenon in high achieving women: Dynamics and therapeutic intervention. *Psychotherapy: Theory, Research, and Practice* 15: 241–247.

Clark, M. S., and M. E. Bennett. 1992. Research on relationships: Implications for mental health. In *The social psychology of mental health,* edited by D. N. Ruble, P. R. Constanzo, and M. E. Oliveri, 166–198. New York: Guilford.

Coates, E. J., R. Janoff-Bulman, and N. Alpert. 1996. Approach versus avoidance goals: Differences in self-evaluation and well-being. *Personality and Social Psychology Bulletin* 22: 1057–1067.

Collins, A. M., and E. F. Loftus. 1975. A spreading-activation theory of semantic processing. *Psychological Review* 82: 407–428.

Colvin, C. R., and J. Block. 1994. Do positive illusions foster mental health? An examination of the Taylor and Brown formulation. *Psychological Bulletin* 116: 3–20.

Combs, A., and D. Snygg. 1959. *Individual behavior.* 2d ed. New York: Harper.

Condillac, E. B. 1930. *Traité des sensations.* Translated by G. Carr. London: Favell. Originally published in 1754.

Cooley, C. H. 1902. *Human nature and the social order.* New York: Scribner's.

Cooley, C. H. 1908. A study of the early use of self-words by a child. *Psychological Review* 15: 339–357.

Cooley, C. H. 1925. *Social organization: A study of the larger mind*. New York: Scribner's.

Cooper, J., and R. H. Fazio. 1984. A new look at dissonance theory. In *Advances in experimental social psychology*, edited by L. Berkowitz, 17:229–266. New York: Academic.

Coopersmith, S. 1967. *The antecedents of self-esteem*. San Francisco: Freeman.

Crocker, J., L. L. Thompson, K. M. McGraw, and C. Ingerman. 1987. Downward comparison, prejudice, and evaluations of others: Effects of self-esteem and threat. *Journal of Personality and Social Psychology* 52: 907–916.

Crocker, J., and C. T. Wolfe. 1998a. Contingencies of worth. Unpublished manuscript, University of Michigan.

Crocker, J., and C. T. Wolfe. 1998b. Determining the sources of self-esteem: The Contingencies of Self-Esteem Scale. Unpublished manuscript, University of Michigan.

Crowne, D. P., and D. Marlowe. 1960. A new scale of social desirability independent of psychopathology. *Journal of Consulting Psychology* 24: 349–354.

Csikszentmihalyi, M. 1975. *Beyond boredom and anxiety*. San Francisco: Jossey-Bass.

Damon, W., and D. Hart. 1986. Stability and change in children's self-understanding. *Social Cognition* 4: 102–118.

Dawes, R. M. 1994. *House of cards: Psychology and psychotherapy built on myth*. New York: Free Press.

Deaux, K. 1993. Reconstructing social identity. *Personality and Social Psychology Bulletin* 19: 4–12.

Deaux, K., and B. Major. 1987. Putting gender into context: An interactive model of gender-related behavior. *Psychological Review* 94: 369–389.

deCharms, R. 1968. *Personal causation: The internal-affective determinants of behavior*. New York: Academic.

Deci, E. L. 1975. *Intrinsic motivation*. New York: Plenum.

Deci, E. L., and R. M. Ryan. 1985. *Intrinsic motivation and self-determination in human behavior*. New York: Plenum.

Deci, E. L., and R. M. Ryan. 1991. A motivational approach to self: Integration in personality. In *Nebraska symposium on motivation: Perspectives on motivation*, edited by N. J. Arnold and D. Levine, 38:237–288. Lincoln: University of Nebraska Press.

Deci, E. L., and R. M. Ryan. 1995. Human agency: The basis for true self-esteem. In *Efficacy, agency, and self-esteem*, edited by M. H. Kernis, 31–50. New York: Plenum.

DeGree, C. E., and C. R. Snyder. 1985. Adler's psychology of use today: Personal history of traumatic life events as a self-handicapping strategy. *Journal of Personality and Social Psychology* 48: 1512–1519.

DePaulo, B. M., D. A. Kenny, C. W. Hoover, W. Webb, and P. V. Oliver. 1987. Accuracy of person perception: Do people know what kinds of impressions they convey? *Journal of Personality and Social Psychology* 52: 303–315.

Descartes, R. 1962. *Discourse on method*. Translated by E. Anscombe and P. T. Geach. London: Nelson. Work originally published in 1637.

Descartes, R. 1986. *Meditations on First Philosophy.* Translated by R. Rubin. Claremont, Calif.: Areté. Work originally published in 1641.

DeSteno, D., and P. Salovey. 1997. Structural dynamism in the concept of self: A flexible model for a malleable concept. *Review of General Psychology* 1: 389–409.

Deutsch, F. M., and M. E. Mackesy. 1985. Friendship and the development of self-schemas: The effects of talking about others. *Personality and Social Psychological Bulletin* 11: 399–408.

Devine, P. 1989. Stereotypes and prejudice: Their automatic and controlled components. *Journal of Personality and Social Psychology* 56: 5–18.

Dewey, J. 1887. *Psychology.* New York: Scribner's.

Dewey, J. 1890. On some current conceptions of the term "Self." *Mind* 15: 58–74.

Diener, E. 1979. Deindividuation, self-awareness, and disinhibition. *Journal of Personality and Social Psychology* 37: 1160–1171.

Diener, E. 1980. Deindividuation: The absence of self-awareness and self-regulation in group members. In *Psychology of group influence,* edited by P. B. Paulus, 209–242. Hillsdale, N.J.: Erlbaum.

Diener, E., and M. Diener. 1995. Cross-cultural correlates of life satisfaction. *Journal of Personality and Social Psychology* 68: 653–663.

Dipboye, R. L. 1977. Alternative approaches to deindividuation. *Psychological Bulletin* 84: 1057–1075.

Dixon, T. M., and R. F. Baumeister. 1991. Escaping the self: The moderating effect of self-complexity. *Personality and Social Psychology Bulletin* 17: 363–368.

Doherty, K., M. F. Weigold, and B. R. Schlenker. 1990. Self-serving interpretations of motives. *Personality and Social Psychology Bulletin* 16: 485–495.

Donahue, E. M., R. W. Robins, B. W. Roberts, and O. P. John. 1993. The divided self: Concurrent and longitudinal effects of psychological adjustment and social roles on self-concept differentiation. *Journal of Personality and Social Psychology* 64: 834–846.

Duval, S., and R. A. Wicklund. 1972. *A theory of objective self-awareness.* New York: Academic.

Eisenstadt, D., and M. R. Leippe. 1994. The self-comparison process and self-discrepant feedback: Consequences of learning you are what you thought you were not. *Journal of Personality and Social Psychology* 67: 611–626.

Elliot, A. J., and K. M. Sheldon. 1997. Avoidant achievement motivation: A personal goals analysis. *Journal of Personality and Social Psychology* 73: 171–185.

Emmons, R. A. 1984. Factor analysis and construct validity of the Narcissistic Personality Inventory. *Journal of Personality Assessment* 48: 291–300.

Emmons, R. A. 1986. Personal strivings: An approach to personality and subjective well-being. *Journal of Personality and Social Psychology* 51: 1058–1068.

Emmons, R. A., and L. A. King. 1988. Conflict among personal strivings: Immediate and long-term implications for psychological and physical well-being. *Journal of Personality and Social Psychology* 54: 1040–1048.

Emmons, R. A., and L. A. King. 1989. Personal striving differentiation and affective reactivity. *Journal of Personality and Social Psychology* 56: 478–484.

Epstein, R., and J. Koerner. 1986. The self-concept and other daemons. In *Psychological perspectives on the self,* edited by J. Suls and A. G. Greenwald 3:27–53. Hillsdale, N.J.: Erlbaum.

Epstein, S. 1973. The self-concept revisited: Or a theory of a theory. *American Psychologist* 28: 404–416.

Epstein, S. 1980. The self-concept: A review and the proposal of an integrated theory of personality. In *Personality: Basic aspects and current research,* edited by E. Staub, 82–132. Englewood Cliffs, N.J.: Prentice-Hall.

Epstein, S., and B. Morling. 1995. Is the self motivated to do more than enhance and/or verify itself? In *Efficacy, agency, and self-esteem,* edited by M. H. Kernis, 9–30. New York: Plenum.

Erhmann, M. 1927. The desiderata of happiness. In the public domain.

Erikson, E. H. 1959. *Identity and the life cycle.* New York: International Universities Press.

Fazio, R. H., E. A. Effrein, and V. J. Falender. 1981. Self-perception following social interaction. *Journal of Personality and Social Psychology* 41: 232–242.

Felson, R. B. 1984. Patterns of aggressive social interaction. In *Social psychology of aggression: From individual behavior to social interaction,* edited by A. Mummendey, 107–126. Berlin: Springer-Verlag.

Fenigstein, A. 1979. Self-consciousness, self-attention, and social interaction. *Journal of Personality and Social Psychology* 37: 75–86.

Fenigstein, A. 1987. On the nature of public and private self-consciousness. *Journal of Personality* 55: 543–554.

Fenigstein, A., M. G. Scheier, and A. H. Buss. 1975. Public and private self-consciousness: Assessment and theory. *Journal of Consulting and Clinical Psychology* 43: 522–528.

Fenigstein, A., and P. A. Vanable. 1992. Paranoia and self-consciousness. *Journal of Personality and Social Psychology* 62: 129–138.

Feshbach, S. 1970. Aggression. In *Carmichael's manual of child psychology,* edited by P. H. Mussen, 2:159–259. New York: Wiley.

Festinger, L. 1954. A theory of social comparison processes. *Human Relations* 7: 117–140.

Festinger, L. 1957. *A theory of cognitive dissonance.* Evanston, Ill.: Row, Peterson.

Festinger, L., H. W. Riecken, and S. Schachter. 1956. *When prophecy fails.* Minneapolis: University of Minnesota Press.

Forsyth, D. R. 1986. An attributional analysis of students' reactions to success and failure. In *The social psychology of education,* edited by R. Feldman, 17–38. New York: Cambridge University Press.

Forsyth, D. R., and B. R. Schlenker. 1977. Attributing the causes of group performance: Effects of performance quality, task importance, and future testing. *Journal of Personality* 45: 220–236.

Franzoi, S. L., M. H. Davis, and B. Markwiese. 1990. A motivational explanation for the existence of private self-consciousness differences. *Journal of Personality* 58: 641–659.

Freud, S. 1959. The defence neuro-psychoses. Translated by J. Rickman. In *Sigmund Freud: Collected papers,* edited by E. Jones. Vol. 1. New York: Basic Books. Originally published in 1894.

Froming, W. J., G. R. Walker, and K. J. Lopyan. 1982. Public and private self-awareness: When personal attitudes conflict with societal expectations. *Journal of Experimental Social Psychology* 18: 476–487.

Fromm, E. 1956. *The art of loving*. New York: Harper and Row.

Gallup, G. G., Jr. 1977. Self-recognition in primates: A comparative approach to the bidirectional properties of consciousness. *American Psychologist* 32: 329–338.

Gecas, V., and M. L. Schwalbe. 1986. Parental behavior and adolescent self-esteem. *Journal of Marriage and the Family* 48: 37–46.

Geertz, C. 1975. On the nature of anthropological understanding. *American Scientist* 63: 47–53.

Gergen, K. J. 1968. Personal consistency and the presentation of self. In *The self in social interaction,* edited by C. Gordon and K. J. Gergen, 299–308. New York: Wiley.

Gergen, K. J. 1971. *The concept of self*. New York: Holt, Rinehart, and Winston.

Gergen, K. J. 1972. Multiple identity: The healthy, happy human being wears many masks. *Psychology Today* 5: 31–35, 64–66.

Gergen, K. J. 1985. The social constructivist movement in modern psychology. *American Psychologist* 40: 266–275.

Gergen, K. J. 1991. *The saturated self*. New York: Basic Books.

Gergen, K. J., and M. M. Gergen. 1988. Narrative and the self as relationship. In *Advances in experimental social psychology,* edited by L. Berkowitz, 21:17–56. New York: Academic.

Gibbons, F. X., and S. B. McCoy. 1991. Self-esteem, similarity, and reactions to active versus passive social comparisons. *Journal of Personality and Social Psychology* 60: 414–424.

Goffman, E. 1959. *Presentation of self in everyday life*. Garden City, N.Y.: Doubleday/Anchor.

Graziano, W. G., L. A. Jensen-Campbell, and J. F. Finch. 1997. The self as a mediator between personality and adjustment. *Journal of Personality and Social Psychology* 73: 392–404.

Greenberg, J. 1982. Self-image versus impression management in adherence to distributive justice standards: The influence of self-awareness and self-consciousness. *Journal of Personality and Social Psychology* 44: 5–19.

Greenberg, J., and T. Pyszczynski. 1985. Compensatory self-inflation: A response to the threat to self-regard of public failure. *Journal of Personality and Social Psychology* 49: 273–280.

Greenberg, J., T. Pyszczynski, and S. Solomon. 1986. The causes and consequences of the need for self-esteem: A terror management theory. In *Public self and private self,* edited by R. F. Baumeister, 189–207. New York: Springer-Verlag.

Greenberg, J., T. Pyszczynski, and S. Solomon. 1995. Toward a dual-motive depth psychology of self and social behavior. In *Efficacy, agency, and self-esteem,* edited by M. H. Kernis, 73–100. New York: Plenum.

Greenier, K. G., M. H. Kernis, and S. B. Waschull. 1995. Not all high or low self-esteem people are the same: Theory and research on stability of self-esteem. In *Efficacy, agency, and self-esteem,* edited by M. H. Kernis, 51–71. New York: Plenum.

Greenwald, A. G. 1980. The totalitarian ego: Fabrication and revision of personal history. *American Psychologist* 35: 603–618.

Greenwald, A. G., F. S. Bellezza, and M. R. Banaji. 1988. Is self-esteem a central ingredient of the self-concept? *Personality and Social Psychology Bulletin* 14: 34–45.

Greenwald, A. G., and A. R. Pratkanis. 1984. The self. In *Handbook of social cognition*, edited by S. Wyer and T. K. Srull, 129–178. Hillsdale, N.J.: Erlbaum.

Greenwald, A. G., and D. Ronis. 1978. Twenty years of cognitive dissonance: Case study of the evolution of a theory. *Psychological Review* 85: 53–57.

Griffin, D. W., and K. Bartholomew. 1994. Models of the self and other: Fundamental dimensions underlying measures of adult attachment. *Journal of Personality and Social Psychology* 67: 430–445.

Grolnick, W. S., and R. M. Ryan. 1989. Parent styles associated with children's self-regulation and competence in school. *Journal of Educational Psychology* 81: 143–154.

Hales, S. 1985. The inadvertent rediscovery of the self in social psychology. *Journal for the Theory of Social Behaviour* 15: 237–282.

Haney, C., C. Banks, and P. Zimbardo. 1973. Interpersonal dynamics in a simulated prison. *International Journal of Criminology and Penology* 1: 69–97.

Hardin, C. D., and E. T. Higgins. 1996. Shared reality: How social verification makes the subjective objective. In *Handbook of motivation and cognition*, edited by R. M. Sorrentino and E. T. Higgins, 3:28–84. New York: Guilford.

Harlow, R. E., and N. Cantor. 1995. Overcoming a lack of self-assurance in an achievement domain: Creating agency in real life. In *Efficacy, agency, and self-esteem*, edited by M. H. Kernis, 171–196. New York: Plenum.

Harter, S. 1983. Developmental perspectives on the self-system. In *Handbook of child psychology: Social and personality development*, edited by M. Hetherington, 4:275–385. New York: Wiley.

Harter, S. 1985a. Competence as a dimension of self-evaluation: Toward a comprehensive model of self-worth. In *The development of the self*, edited by R. L. Leahy, 55–121. London: Academic.

Harter, S. 1985b. *Manual for the self-perception profile for children.* Denver: University of Denver Press.

Harter, S. 1990. Adolescent self and identity development. In *At the threshold: The developing adolescent*, edited by S. S. Feldman and G. R. Elliot, 352–387. Cambridge: Harvard University Press.

Harter, S. 1993. Causes and consequences of low self-esteem in children and adolescents. In *Self-esteem: The puzzle of low self-regard*, edited by R. F. Baumeister, 87–106. New York: Plenum.

Harter, S., S. Bresnick, H. A. Bouchey, and N. R. Whitesell. 1997. The development of multiple role-related selves during adolescence. *Development and Psychopathology* 9: 835–853.

Harter, S., and P. Waters. 1991. Correlates of the directionality of perceived physical appearance and global self-worth. Unpublished manuscript, University of Denver.

Hartouni, Z. S. 1992. Effects of narcissistic personality organization on causal attributions. *Psychological Reports* 71: 1339–1346.

Hawkins, J. D., R. F. Catalano, and J. Y. Miller. 1992. Risk and protective factors for alcohol and other drug problems in adolescence and early adulthood: Implications for substance abuse programs. *Psychological Bulletin* 112: 64–105.

Heine, S. J., and D. R. Lehman. 1997. Culture, dissonance, and self-affirmation. *Personality and Social Psychology Bulletin* 23: 389–400.

Hermans, H. J. M. 1996. Voicing the self: From information processing to dialogical interchange. *Psychological Bulletin* 119: 31–50.

Higgins, E. T. 1987. Self-discrepancy: A theory relating self and affect. *Psychological Review* 94: 319–340.

Higgins, E. T. 1996. Knowledge activation: Accessibility, applicability, and salience. In *Social psychology: Handbook of basic principles*, edited by E. T. Higgins and A. W. Kruglanski, 133–168. New York: Guilford.

Higgins, E. T., E. Van Hook, and D. Dorfman. 1988. Do self-attributes form a cognitive structure? *Social Cognition* 6: 177–207.

Higgins, P. G., D. H. Clough, and C. Wallerstedt. 1995. Self-esteem of pregnant substance abusers. *Maternal-Child Nursing Journal* 23: 75–81.

Hilgard, E. R. 1949. Human motives and the concept of self. *American Psychologist* 4: 374–382.

Hinkley, K., and A. M. Andersen. 1996. The working self-concept in transference: Significant-other activation and self-change. *Journal of Personality and Social Psychology* 71: 1279–1295.

Hobbes, T. 1948. *Leviathan*. Oxford: Blackwell. Originally published in 1651.

Hoelter, J. W. 1985. The structure of self-conception: Conceptualization and measurement. *Journal of Personality and Social Psychology* 49: 1392–1407.

Hoffman, C., I. Lau, and D. R. Johnson. 1986. The linguistic relativity of person cognition: An English-Chinese comparison. *Journal of Personality and Social Psychology* 51: 1097–1105.

Honeycutt, J. M., and J. Patterson. 1997. Affinity strategies in relationships: The role of gender and imagined interactions in maintaining liking among college roommates. *Personal Relationships* 4: 35–46.

Horney, K. 1950. *Neurosis and human growth: The struggle toward self-realization*. New York: Norton.

Hoyle, R. H. 1988. Effects of basic features of social situations on four aspects of self-esteem: The social nature of self-appraisal. *Dissertation Abstracts International* 49: 12B. University Microfilms 88–23: 436.

Hoyle, R. H. 1991. Evaluating measurement models in clinical research: Covariance structure analysis of latent variable models of self-conception. *Journal of Consulting and Clinical Psychology* 59: 67–76.

Hoyle, R. H., and R. D. Lennox. 1991. Latent structure of self-monitoring. *Multivariate Behavioral Research* 26: 511–540.

Hoyle, R. H., and B. A. Sowards. 1993. Self-monitoring and the regulation of social experience: A control-process model. *Journal of Social and Clinical Psychology* 12: 280–306.

Hsee, C. K., and R. P. Abelson. 1991. Velocity relation: Satisfaction as a function of the first derivative of outcome over time. *Journal of Personality and Social Psychology* 60: 341–347.

Hull, J. G., and A. S. Levy. 1979. The organizational functions of the self: An alternative to the Duval and Wicklund model of self-awareness. *Journal of Personality and Social Psychology* 37: 756–768.

Iberall, A. S. 1987. On rivers. In *Self-organizing systems: The emergence of order*, edited by F. E. Yates, 33–52. New York: Plenum.

Ip, G. W. M., and M. H. Bond. 1995. Culture, values, and the spontaneous self-concept. *Asian Journal of Psychology* 1: 29–35.

James, W. 1950. *The principles of psychology*. Vol. 1. New York: Dover. Originally published in 1890.

James, W. 1958. *The varieties of religious experience.* New York: New American Library. Originally published in 1902.

James, W. 1961. *Psychology: The briefer course.* New York: Harper Torchbooks. Originally published in 1892.

Jankowski, M. S. 1991. *Islands in the streets: Gangs and American urban society.* Berkeley: University of California Press.

Jones, E. E. 1964. *Ingratiation: A social psychological analysis.* New York: Appleton-Century-Crofts.

Jones, E. E., and S. Berglas. 1978. Control of attributions about the self through self-handicapping strategies: The appeal of alcohol and the role of underachievement. *Personality and Social Psychology Bulletin* 4: 200–206.

Jones, E. E., and H. B. Gerard. 1967. *Foundations of social psychology.* New York: Wiley.

Jones, E. E., and T. S. Pittman. 1982. Toward a general theory of strategic self-presentation. In *Psychological perspectives on the self,* edited by J. Suls, 1:231–262. Hillsdale, N.J.: Erlbaum.

Jones, E. E., F. Rhodewalt, S. C. Berglas, and A. Skelton. 1981. Effects of strategic self-presentation on subsequent self-esteem. *Journal of Personality and Social Psychology* 41: 407–421.

Jordan, A., and D. A. Cole. 1996. Relation of depressive symptoms to the structure of self-knowledge in children. *Journal of Abnormal Psychology* 105: 530–540.

Josephs, R. A., H. R. Markus, and R. W. Tafarodi. 1992. Gender and self-esteem. *Journal of Personality and Social Psychology* 63: 391–402.

Kant, I. 1934. *Critique of pure reason.* Translated by N. A. Smith. London: Macmillan. Originally published in 1781.

Kasser, T., and R. M. Ryan. 1993. A dark side of the American dream: Correlates of financial success as a central life aspiration. *Journal of Personality and Social Psychology* 65: 410–422.

Kasser, T., and R. M. Ryan. 1996. Further examining the American dream: Differential correlates of intrinsic and extrinsic goals. *Personality and Social Psychology Bulletin* 22: 280–287.

Kelley, H. H. 1967. Attribution theory in social psychology. In *Nebraska Symposium on Motivation,* edited by D. Levine, 15:192–240. Lincoln: University of Nebraska Press.

Kelly, G. A. 1955. *The psychology of personal constructs.* New York: Norton.

Kernis, M. H. 1993. The roles of stability and level of self-esteem in psychological functioning. In *Self-esteem: The puzzle of low self-regard,* edited by R. F. Baumeister, 167–182. New York: Plenum.

Kernis, M. H., J. Brockner, and B. S. Frankel. 1989. Self-esteem and reactions to failure: The mediating role of overgeneralization. *Journal of Personality and Social Psychology* 57: 707–714.

Kernis, M. H., A. C. Brown, and G. H. Brody. 1997. Fragile self-esteem in children and its associations with perceived patterns of parent-child communication. Unpublished manuscript, University of Georgia.

Kernis, M. H., D. P. Cornell, C. R. Sun, A. J. Berry, and T. Harlow. 1993. There's more to self-esteem than whether it is high or low: The importance of stability of self-esteem. *Journal of Personality and Social Psychology* 65: 1190–1204.

Kernis, M. H., and B. D. Grannemann. 1988. Private self-consciousness and perceptions of self-consistency. *Personality and Individual Differences* 5: 897–902.

Kernis, M. H., and B. D. Grannemman. 1990. Excuses in the making: A test and extension of Darley and Goethals' model. *Journal of Experimental Social Psychology* 26: 333–349.

Kernis, M. H., B. C. Grannemann, and L. C. Barclay. 1989. Stability and level of self-esteem as predictors of anger arousal and hostility. *Journal of Personality and Social Psychology* 56: 1013–1023.

Kernis, M. H., B. D. Grannemann, and L. C. Barclay. 1992. Stability of self-esteem: Assessment, correlates, and excuse making. *Journal of Personality* 60: 621–644.

Kernis, M. H., B. C. Grannemann, and L. C. Mathis. 1991. Stability of self-esteem as a moderator of the relation between level of self-esteem and depression. *Journal of Personality and Social Psychology* 61: 80–84.

Kernis, M. H., A. Paradise, D. Whitaker, S. Wheatman, and B. Goldman. 1997. Self-esteem stability, self-concept clarity, and self-regulatory styles. Unpublished manuscript, University of Georgia.

Kernis, M. H., and H. T. Reis. 1984. Self-awareness, self-consciousness, and adherence to internal versus normative standards of justice behavior. *Journal of Personality* 52: 58–70.

Kernis, M. H., and S. B. Waschull. 1995. The interactive roles of stability and level of self-esteem: Research and theory. In *Advances in experimental social psychology*, edited by M. P. Zanna, 27:93–141. San Diego, Calif.: Academic.

Kernis, M. H., C. R. Whisenhunt, S. B. Waschull, K. D. Greenier, A. J. Berry, C. E. Herlocker, and C. A. Anderson. In press. Multiple facets of self-esteem and their relations to depressive symptoms. *Personality and Social Psychology Bulletin*.

Kernis, M. H., M. Zuckerman, A. Cohen, and S. Spadafora. 1982. Persistence following failure: The interactive role of self-awareness and the attributional basis for negative expectancies. *Journal of Personality and Social Psychology* 43: 1184–1191.

Kihlstrom, J. F., and N. Cantor. 1984. Mental representations of the self. In *Advances in experimental social psychology*, edited by L. Berkowitz, 17:1–47. New York: Academic.

Kihlstrom, J. F., N. Cantor, J. S. Albright, B. R. Chew, S. B. Klein, and P. M. Niedenthal. 1988. Information processing and the study of the self. In *Advances in experimental social psychology*, edited by L. Berkowitz, 21:145–178. New York: Academic.

Kitayama, S., H. R. Markus, H. Matsumoto, and V. Norasakkunkit. 1997. Individual and collective processes in the construction of the self: Self-enhancement in the United States and self-criticism in Japan. *Journal of Personality and Social Psychology* 72: 1245–1267.

Klein, S. B., and J. F. Kihlstrom. 1986. Elaboration, organization, and the self-reference effect in memory. *Journal of Experimental Psychology: General* 115: 26–38.

Klein, S. B., and J. Loftus. 1993. The mental representation of trait and autobiographical knowledge about the self. In *Advances in social cognition*, edited by T. K. Srull and R. S. Wyer Jr., 5:1–49. Hillsdale, N.J.: Erlbaum.

Klein, W. M., and Z. Kunda. 1993. Maintaining self-serving social comparisons: Biased reconstruction of one's past behaviors. *Personality and Social Psychology Bulletin* 19: 732–739.

Kolditz, T. A., and R. W. Arkin. 1982. An impression management interpretation of the self-handicapping strategy. *Journal of Personality and Social Psychology* 43: 492–502.

Kruglanski, A. W., N. Miller, and R. G. Geen. 1996. Introduction to the special issue on the self and social identity. *Journal of Personality and Social Psychology* 71: 1061.

Kuhn, M. H., and T. S. McPartland. 1954. An empirical investigation of self-attitudes. *American Sociological Review* 19: 68–76.

Kuiper, N. A., P. A. Derry, and M. R. MacDonald. 1982. Self-reference and person perception in depression: A social cognition perspective. In *Integrations of clinical and social psychology*, edited by G. Weary and H. Mirels, 79–103. New York: Oxford.

Kuiper, N. A., and L. J. Olinger. 1986. Dysfunctional attitudes and a self-worth contingency model of depression. In *Advances in cognitive-behavioral research and therapy*, edited by P. C. Kendall, 115–142. Orlando, Fla.: Academic.

Kuiper, N. A., and T. B. Rogers. 1979. Encoding of personal information: Self-other differences. *Journal of Personality and Social Psychology* 37: 499–514.

Kunda, Z. 1987. Motivated inference: Self-serving generation and evaluation of causal theories. *Journal of Personality and Social Psychology* 53: 636–647.

Laing, R. D. 1965. *The divided self: An existential study in sanity and madness.* Baltimore: Penguin. Originally published in 1959.

Lasch, C. 1992. For shame: Why Americans should be wary of self-esteem. *The New Republic* 207: 29–34.

Leary, M. R. 1995. *Self-presentation: Impression management and interpersonal behavior.* Boulder: Westview.

Leary, M. R., R. Bednarski, D. Hammon, and T. Duncan. 1997. Blowhards, snobs, and narcissists: Interpersonal reactions to excessive egotism. In *Aversive interpersonal behaviors*, edited by R. M. Kowalski, 111–131. New York: Plenum.

Leary, M. R., and D. L. Downs. 1995. Interpersonal functions of the self-esteem motive: The self-esteem system as a sociometer. In *Efficacy, agency, and self-esteem*, edited by M. H. Kernis, 123–144. New York: Plenum.

Leary, M. R., and D. R. Forsyth. 1987. Attributions of responsibility for collective endeavors. In *Group processes*, edited by C. Hendrick, 167–188. Newbury Park, Calif.: Sage.

Leary, M. R., and R. M. Kowalski. 1990. Impression management: A literature review and two-component model. *Psychological Bulletin* 107: 34–47.

Leary, M. R., K. M. Patton, A. E. Orlando, and W. F. Wagoner. 1997. The impostor phenomenon: Self-perceptions, reflected appraisals, and interpersonal strategies. Unpublished manuscript, Wake Forest University.

Leary, M. R., L. S. Schreindorfer, and A. L. Haupt. 1995. The role of self-esteem in emotional and behavioral problems. *Journal of Social and Clinical Psychology* 14: 297–314.

Leary, M. R., E. S. Tambor, S. J. Terdal, and D. L. Downs. 1995. Self-esteem as an interpersonal monitor: The sociometer hypothesis. *Journal of Personality and Social Psychology* 68: 518–530.

Lecky, P. 1945. *Self-consistency: A theory of personality.* Long Island, N.Y.: Island Press.

Levine, J. M., and S. M. Green. 1984. Acquisition of relative performance information: The roles of intrapersonal and interpersonal comparison. *Personality and Social Psychology Bulletin* 10: 385–393.

Levy, B. 1996. Improving memory in old age through implicit self-stereotyping. *Journal of Personality and Social Psychology* 71: 1092–1107.

Lewis, M. 1992. Will the real self or selves please stand up? *Psychological Inquiry* 3: 123–124.

Linville, P. W. 1985. Self-complexity and affective extremity: Don't put all of your eggs in one cognitive basket. *Social Cognition* 3: 94–120.

Linville, P. W. 1987. Self-complexity as a cognitive buffer against stress-related depression and illness. *Journal of Personality and Social Psychology* 52: 663–676.

Little, B. 1989. Personal projects analysis: Trivial pursuits, magnificent obsessions, and the search for coherence. In *Personality psychology: Recent trends and emerging directions*, edited by D. Buss and N. Cantor, 15–31. New York: Springer-Verlag.

Locke, J. 1960. *Concerning human understanding.* London: Oxford University Press. Work originally published in 1690.

Malle, B. F., and L. M. Horowitz. 1995. The puzzle of negative self-views: An explanation using the schema concept. *Journal of Personality and Social Psychology* 68: 470–484.

Manaster, G. J., and R. J. Corsini. 1982. *Individual psychology: Theory and practice.* Itasca, Ill.: Peacock.

Markus, H. 1977. Self-schemata and processing information about the self. *Journal of Personality and Social Psychology* 35: 63–78.

Markus, H. 1983. Self-knowledge: An expanded view. *Journal of Personality* 51: 543–565.

Markus, H. R., and S. Cross. 1990. The interpersonal self. In *Handbook of personality: Theory and research*, edited by L. A. Pervin, 576–608. New York: Guilford.

Markus, H. R., and S. Kitayama. 1991. Culture and the self: Implications for cognition, emotion, and motivation. *Psychological Review* 98: 224–253.

Markus, H. R., and Z. Kunda. 1986. Stability and malleability of the self-concept. *Journal of Personality and Social Psychology* 51: 858–866.

Markus, H., and P. Nurius. 1986. Possible selves. *American Psychologist* 41: 954–969.

Markus, H., and K. Sentis. 1982. The self in information processing. In *Psychological perspectives on the self*, edited by J. Suls, 1:41–70. Hillsdale, N.J.: Erlbaum.

Markus, H., J. Smith, and R. L. Moreland. 1985. Role of the self-concept in the perception of others. *Journal of Personality and Social Psychology* 49: 1494–1512.

Markus, H., and E. Wurf. 1987. The dynamic self-concept: A social-psychological perspective. *Annual Review of Psychology* 38: 299–337.

Marsh, H. W., and R. J. Shavelson. 1985. Self-concept: Its multifaceted, hierarchical structure. *Educational Psychologist* 20: 107–125.

Maslow, A. 1968. *Motivation and personality.* 3d ed. New York: Harper.

Maslow, A. 1971. *The farther reaches of human nature.* New York: Viking.

McAdams, D. P. 1995. What do we know when we know a person? *Journal of Personality* 63: 365–396.

McAdams, D. P. 1996. Personality, modernity, and the storied self: A contemporary framework for studying persons. *Psychological Inquiry* 7: 295–321.

McAdams, D. P., A. Diamond, E. de St. Aubin, and E. Mansfield. 1997. Stories of commitment: The psychosocial construction of generative lives. *Journal of Personality and Social Psychology* 72: 678–694.

McFarlin, D. B., R. F. Baumeister, and J. Blascovich. 1984. On knowing when to quit: Task failure, self-esteem, advice, and nonproductive persistence. *Journal of Personality* 52: 138–155.

McGuire, W. J., and C. V. McGuire. 1981. The spontaneous self-concept as affected by personal distinctiveness. In *Self-concept: Advances in theory and research*, edited by M. D. Lynch, A. A. Norem-Hebeisen, and K. Gergen, 147–171. New York: Ballinger.

McGuire, W. J., and C. V. McGuire. 1982. Significant others in self space: Sex differences and developmental trends in social self. In *Psychological perspectives on the self*, edited by J. Suls, 1:71–96. Hillsdale, N.J.: Erlbaum.

McGuire, W. J., C. V. McGuire, P. Child, and T. A. Fujioka. 1978. Salience of ethnicity in the spontaneous self-concept as a function of one's ethnic distinctiveness in the social environment. *Journal of Personality and Social Psychology* 36: 511–520.

McGuire, W. J., and A. Padawer-Singer. 1976. Trait salience in the spontaneous self-concept. *Journal of Personality and Social Psychology* 33: 743–754.

McKenzie, K. S., and R. H. Hoyle. 1996. A self-administered measure of self-complexity. Paper presented at the annual meeting of the Midwestern Psychological Association, Chicago, May.

Mead, G. H. 1914. The psychological bases of internationalism. *Survey* 33: 604–607.

Mead, G. H. 1934. *Mind, self, and society.* Chicago: University of Chicago Press.

Mead, G. H. 1982. 1927 class lectures in social psychology. In *The individual and the social self*, edited by D. L. Miller, 106–175. Chicago: University of Chicago Press. Originally published in 1927.

Mill, J. S., ed. 1878. *Analysis of the phenomena of the human mind.* Vol. 2. 2d ed. London: Longmans, Green, Reader, and Dyer.

Miller, D. T., and D. A. Prentice. 1996. The construction of social norms and standards. In *Social psychology: Handbook of principles*, edited by E. T. Higgins and A. W. Kruglanskipp, 799–829. New York: Guilford.

Miller, G. A., E. Galanter, and K. H. Pribram. 1960. *Plans and the structure of behavior.* New York: Holt, Rinehart, and Winston.

Miller, L. C., and C. L. Cox. 1981. *Public self-consciousness and makeup use: Individual differences in preparational tactics.* Paper presented at the Annual Meeting of the American Psychological Association, Los Angeles, August.

Miller, R. L., and J. M. Suls. 1977. Affiliation preferences as a function of attitude and ability similarity. In *Social comparison processes: Theoretical and empirical perspectives*, edited by R. L. Miller and J. M. Suls, 103–123. New York: Wiley.

Montemayor, R., and M. Eisen. 1977. The development of self-conceptions from childhood to adolescence. *Developmental Psychology* 13: 314–319.

Morgan, H. J., and R. Janoff-Bulman. 1994. Positive and negative self-complexity: Patterns of adjustment following traumatic versus non-traumatic life experiences. *Journal of Social and Clinical Psychology* 13: 63–85.

Morretti, M. M., and E. T. Higgins. 1990. Relating self-discrepancy to self-esteem: The contribution of discrepancies beyond actual-self ratings. *Journal of Experimental Social Psychology* 26: 108–123.

Morse, S., and K. Gergen. 1970. Social comparison, self-consistency, and the presentation of self. *Journal of Personality and Social Psychology* 16: 148–156.

Neisser, U. 1976. *Cognition and reality.* San Francisco: Freeman.

Neisser, U. 1988. Five kinds of self-knowledge. *Philosophical Psychology* 1: 35–59.

Nelson, K. 1993. The psychological and social origins of autobiographical memory. *Psychological Science* 4: 7–14.

Niedenthal, P. M., and D. R. Beike. 1997. Interrelated and isolated self-concepts. *Personality and Social Psychology Review* 1: 106–128.

Niedenthal, P. M., M. B. Setterlund, and M. B. Wherry. 1992. Possible self-complexity and affective reactions to goal-relevant evaluation. *Journal of Personality and Social Psychology* 63: 5–16.

Nisbett, R. E., and T. D. Wilson. 1977. Telling more than we can know: Verbal reports on mental processes. *Psychological Review* 84: 231–259.

Norem, J., and N. Cantor. 1986a. Anticipatory and post hoc cushioning strategies: Optimism and defensive pessimism in "risky" situations. *Cognitive Therapy and Research* 10: 347–362.

Norem, J., and N. Cantor. 1986b. Defensive pessimism: "Harnessing" anxiety as a motivation. *Journal of Personality and Social Psychology* 52: 1208–1217.

Norem, J., and N. Cantor. 1990. Capturing the "flavor" of behavior: Cognition, affect, and interpretation. In *Affect and social behavior,* edited by B. S. Moore and A. M. Isen, 39–63. Cambridge: Cambridge University Press.

Norem, J., and K. S. S. Illingworth. 1993. Strategy-dependent effects of reflecting on self and tasks: Some implications of optimism and defensive pessimism. *Journal of Personality and Social Psychology* 65: 822–835.

Norem, J. K. 1989. Cognitive strategies as personality: Effectiveness, specificity, flexibility, and change. In *Personality psychology: Recent trends and emerging directions,* edited by D. Buss and N. Cantor, 45–60. New York: Springer-Verlag.

Ogilvie, D. M. 1987. The undesired self: A neglected variable in personality research. *Journal of Personality and Social Psychology* 52: 379–385.

Ogilvie, D. M., and R. D. Ashmore. 1991. Self-with-other representation as a unit of analysis in self-concept research. In *The relational self,* edited by R. C. Curtis, 282–314. New York: Guilford.

O'Malley, P. M., and J. G. Bachman. 1983. Self-esteem: Change and stability between ages 13 and 23. *Developmental Psychology* 19: 256–268.

Oyserman, D., and H. R. Markus. 1990. Possible selves and delinquency. *Journal of Personality and Social Psychology* 59: 112–125.

Pelham, B. W. 1995. Self-investment and self-esteem: Evidence for a Jamesian model of self-worth. *Journal of Personality and Social Psychology* 69: 1141–1150.

Pelham, B. W., and S. B. Swann Jr. 1989. From self-conceptions to self-worth: On the sources and structure of global self-esteem. *Journal of Personality and Social Psychology* 57: 672–680.

Pelham, B. W., and J. O. Wachsmuth. 1995. The waxing and waning of the social self: Assimilation and contrast in social comparison. *Journal of Personality and Social Psychology* 69: 825–838.

Pepitone, A. 1968. An experimental analysis of self-dynamics. In *The self in social interaction,* edited by C. Gordon and K. Gergen, 347–354. New York: Wiley.

Pilkington, C. J., A. Tesser, and D. Stephens. 1991. Complementarity in romantic relationships: A self-evaluation maintenance perspective. *Journal of Social and Personal Relationships* 8: 481–504.

Plato. 1951. *Phaedo.* Translated by F. J. Church. New York: Liberal Arts. Written in the fourth century B.C.

Popper, K., and J. C. Eccles. 1977. *The self and its brain.* New York: Springer International.

Powers, W. T. 1973. *Behavior: The control of perception.* Chicago: Aldine.

Pratkanis, A. R., and A. G. Greenwald. 1985. How shall the self be conceived? *Journal for the Theory of Social Behaviour* 15: 311–329.

Prentice-Dunn, S., and R. W. Rogers. 1982. Effects of deindividuating situational cues and aggressive models on subjective deindividuation and aggression. *Journal of Personality and Social Psychology* 43: 503–513.

Prentice-Dunn, S., and R. W. Rogers. 1983. Deindividuation in aggression. In *Aggression: Theoretical and empirical reviews,* edited by R. G. Geen and E. Donnerstein, 2:155–172. New York: Academic.

Prince, M. 1929. *Clinical and experimental studies in personality.* Cambridge, Mass.: Sci-Art.

Pyszczynski, T., and J. Greenberg. 1985. Depression and preference for self-focusing stimuli after success and failure. *Journal of Personality and Social Psychology* 49: 1066–1075.

Pyszczynski, T., and J. Greenberg. 1987. Self-regulatory perseveration and the depressive self-focusing style: A self-awareness theory of reactive depression. *Psychological Bulletin* 102: 122–138.

Pyszczynski, T., J. Greenberg, J. Hamilton, and G. Nix. 1991. On the relationship between self-focused attention and psychological disorder: A critical reappraisal. *Psychological Bulletin* 110: 538–543.

Pyszczynski, T., J. Greenberg, and J. LaPrelle. 1985. Social comparison after success and failure: Biased search for information consistent with a self-serving conclusion. *Journal of Experimental Social Psychology* 21: 195–211.

Rank, O. 1936. *Will therapy.* New York: Norton.

Raskin, R., J. Novacek, and R. Hogan. 1991a. Narcissism, self-esteem, and defensive self-enhancement. *Journal of Personality* 59: 19–38.

Raskin, R., J. Novacek, and R. Hogan. 1991b. Narcissistic self-esteem management. *Journal of Personality and Social Psychology* 60: 911–918.

Reid, A., and K. Deaux. 1996. Relationship between social and personal identities: Segregation or integration? *Journal of Personality and Social Psychology* 71: 1084–1091.

Reis, H. T., and J. Gruzen. 1975. On mediating equity, equality, and self-interest: The role of self-presentation in social exchange. *Journal of Experimental Social Psychology* 12: 487–503.

Rhee, E., J. Uleman, H. Lee, and R. Roman. 1995. Spontaneous self-descriptions and ethnic identities in individualistic and collectivistic cultures. *Journal of Personality and Social Psychology* 69: 142–152.

Rhodewalt, F., J. C. Madrian, and S. Cheney. 1998. Narcissism, self-knowledge organization, and emotional reactivity: The effect of daily experiences on self-esteem and affect. *Personality and Social Psychology Bulletin* 24: 75–87.

Rhodewalt, F., A. T. Saltzman, and J. Wittmer. 1984. Self-handicapping among competitive athletes: The role of practice in self-esteem protection. *Basic and Applied Social Psychology* 5: 197–210.

Ribot, T. 1895. *The diseases of personality.* Chicago: Open Court.

Ritts, V., and J. R. Stein. 1995. Verification and commitment in marital relationships: An exploration of self-verification theory in community college students. *Psychological Reports* 76: 383–386.

Roberts, J. E., and V. McCready. 1987. Different clinical perspectives of good and poor therapy sessions. *Journal of Speech and Hearing Research* 30: 335–342.

Roberts, J. E., and S. M. Monroe. 1992. Vulnerable self-esteem and depressive symptoms: Prospective findings comparing three alternative conceptualizations. *Journal of Personality and Social Psychology* 62: 804–812.

Robinson, D. T., and L. Smith-Lovin. 1992. Selective interaction as a strategy for identity maintenance: An affect control model. *Social Psychology Quarterly* 55: 12–28.

Rogers, C. R. 1951. *Client-centered therapy.* New York: Houghton-Mifflin.

Rogers, C. R. 1959. A theory of therapy, personality and interpersonal relationships, as developed in the client-centered framework. In *Psychology: A study of a science,* edited by S. Koch, 3:184–256. Toronto: McGraw-Hill.

Rogers, T. B. 1977. Self-reference in memory: Recognition of personality items. *Journal of Research in Personality* 11: 295–305.

Rogers, T. B. 1981. A model of the self as an aspect of the human information processing system. In *Personality, cognition and social interaction,* edited by N. Cantor and J. F. Kihlstrompp, 193–214. Hillsdale, N.J.: Erlbaum.

Rogers, T. B., N. A. Kuiper, and W. S. Kirker. 1977. Self-reference and the encoding of personal information. *Journal of Personality and Social Psychology* 35: 677–688.

Rogers, T. B., P. J. Rogers, and N. A. Kuiper. 1979. Evidence for the self as a cognitive prototype: The "false alarms effect." *Personality and Social Psychology Bulletin* 5: 53–56.

Rosenberg, M. 1965. *Society and the adolescent self-image.* Princeton, N.J.: Princeton University Press.

Rosenberg, M. 1973. Which significant others? *American Behavioral Scientist* 16: 829–860.

Rosenberg, M. 1979. *Conceiving the self.* New York: Basic Books.

Rosenberg, M. 1986. Self-concept from middle childhood through adolescence. In *Psychological perspectives on the self,* edited by J. Suls and A. G. Greenwald, 3:107–136. Hillsdale, N.J.: Erlbaum.

Rosenberg, M. 1988. Self-objectification: Relevance for the species and society. *Sociological Forum* 3: 548–565.

Rosenberg, M. 1990. Reflexivity and emotions. *Social Psychology Quarterly* 53: 3–12.

Ross, L., D. Greene, and P. House. 1977. The false consensus effect: An egocentric bias in social perception and attribution processes. *Journal of Experimental Social Psychology* 13: 279–301.

Rusbult, C. E., G. D. Morrow, and D. J. Johnson. 1987. Self-esteem and problem-solving behavior in close relationships. *British Journal of Social Psychology* 26: 293–303.

Ryan, R. M. 1982. Control and information in the intrapersonal sphere: An extension of cognitive-evaluation theory. *Journal of Personality and Social Psychology* 43: 450–461.

Ryan, R. M. 1991. The nature of the self in autonomy and relatedness. In *The self: Interdisciplinary approaches,* edited by J. Strauss and G. R. Goethals, 208–238. New York: Springer-Verlag.

Ryan, R. M., and J. P. Connell. 1989. Perceived locus of causality and internalization: Examining reasons for acting in two domains. *Journal of Personality and Social Psychology* 57: 749–761.

Ryan, R. M., S. Rigby, and K. King. 1993. Two types of religious internalization and their relations to religious orientations and mental health. *Journal of Personality and Social Psychology* 65: 586–596.

Safran, J. D. 1990. Towards a refinement of cognitive therapy in light of interpersonal theory: I. Theory. *Clinical Psychology Review* 10: 87–103.

Salovey, P. 1992. Mood-induced self-focused attention. *Journal of Personality and Social Psychology* 62: 699–707.

Sande, G. N., G. R. Goethals, and C. E. Radloff. 1988. Perceiving one's own traits and others': The multifaceted self. *Journal of Personality and Social Psychology* 54: 13–20.

Sanders, G. S., and B. Mullen. 1983. Accuracy in perceptions of consensus: Differential tendencies of people with majority and minority status. *European Journal of Social Psychology* 13: 57–70.

Sartre, J. P. 1956. *Being and nothingness.* Translated by H. E. Barnes. Secaucus, N.J.: Citadel. Originally published in 1943.

Savin-Williams, R. C., and D. H. Demo. 1983. Situational and transituational determinants of adolescent self-feelings. *Journal of Personality and Social Psychology* 44: 824–833.

Scheier, M. F. 1976. Self-awareness, self-consciousness, and angry aggression. *Journal of Personality* 44: 627–644.

Scheier, M. F., A. H. Buss, and D. M. Buss. 1978. Self-consciousness, self-report of aggressiveness, and aggression. *Journal of Research in Personality* 12: 133–140.

Scheier, M. F., and C. S. Carver. 1977. Self-focused attention and the experience of emotion: Attraction, repulsion, elation, and depression. *Journal of Personality and Social Psychology* 35: 625–636.

Scheier, M. F., and C. S. Carver. 1981. Private and public aspects of the self. In *Review of personality and social psychology,* edited by L. Wheeler, 2:189–216. Beverly Hills, Calif.: Sage.

Scheier, M. F., and C. S. Carver. 1983. Two sides of the self: One for you and one for me. In *Psychological perspectives on the self,* edited by J. Suls and A. G. Greenwald, 2:123–157. Hillsdale, N.J.: Erlbaum.

Scheier, M. F., and C. S. Carver. 1988. A model of behavioral self-regulation: Translating intention into action. In *Advances in experimental social psychology,* edited by L. Berkowitz, 21:303–346. New York: Academic.

Scheier, M. F., C. W. Carver, and F. X. Gibbons. 1979. Self-directed attention, awareness of bodily states, and suggestibility. *Journal of Personality and Social Psychology* 37: 1576–1588.

Schlenker, B. R. 1980. *Impression management: The self-concept, social identity, and interpersonal relations.* Monterey, Calif.: Brooks/Cole.

Schlenker, B. R. 1982. Translating actions into attitudes: An identity-analytic approach to the explanation of social conduct. In *Advances in experimental social psychology,* edited by L. Berkowitz, 15:193–247. New York: Academic.

Schlenker, B. R. 1985a. Identity and self-identification. In *The self and social life,* edited by B. R. Schlenker, 65–99. New York: McGraw-Hill.

Schlenker, B. R., ed. 1985b. *The self and social life.* New York: McGraw-Hill.

Schlenker, B. R., D. R. Forsyth, M. R. Leary, and R. S. Miller. 1980. A self-presentational analysis of the effects of incentives on attitude change following counterattitudinal behavior. *Journal of Personality and Social Psychology* 39: 553–577.

Schlenker, B. R., and M. R. Leary. 1982. Audiences' reactions to self-enhancing, self-denigrating, and accurate self-presentations. *Journal of Experimental Social Psychology* 18: 89–104.

Schlenker, B. R., and R. S. Miller. 1977. Egotism in groups: Self-serving biases or logical information processing? *Journal of Personality and Social Psychology* 10: 755–764.

Schneider, D. J., and D. Turkat. 1975. Self-presentation following success or failure: Defensive self-esteem models. *Journal of Personality* 43: 127–135.

Schopenhauer, A. 1948. *The world as will and idea.* London: Routledge and Kegan Paul. Originally published in 1819.

Schwarz, N., H. Bless, F. Strack, G. Klumpp, H. Rittenauer-Schatka, and A. Simons. 1991. Ease of retrieval as information: Another look at the availability heuristic. *Journal of Personality and Social Psychology* 61: 195–202.

Schwartz, R. M. 1986. The internal dialogue: On the asymmetry between positive and negative coping thoughts. *Cognitive Therapy and Research* 10: 591–605.

Scott, W. A. 1969. Structure of natural cognitions. *Journal of Personality and Social Psychology* 12: 261–278.

Sedikides, C. 1992a. Attentional effects on mood are moderated by self-conception valence. *Personality and Social Psychology Bulletin* 18: 580–584.

Sedikides, C. 1992b. Mood as a determinant of attentional focus. *Cognition and Emotion* 6: 129–148.

Sedikides, C. 1993. Assessment, enhancement, and verification determinants of the self-evaluation process. *Journal of Personality and Social Psychology* 65: 317–338.

Sedikides, C., W. K. Campbell, G. D. Reeder, and A. J. Elliot. 1998. The self-serving bias in relational context. *Journal of Personality and Social Psychology* 74: 378–386.

Sedikides, C., and J. J. Skowronski. 1997. The symbolic self in evolutionary context. *Personality and Social Psychology Review* 1: 80–102.

Sedikides, C., and M. J. Strube. 1995. The multiply motivated self. *Personality and Social Psychology Bulletin* 21: 1330–1335.

Sedikides, C., and M. J. Strube. 1997. Self-evaluation: To thine own self be good, to thine own self be sure, to thine own self be true, and to thine own self be better. In *Advances in experimental social psychology,* edited by M. P. Zanna, 29:209–269. New York: Academic.

Segal, Z. V., J. E. Hood, B. F. Shaw, and E. T. Higgins. 1988. A structural analysis of the self-schema construct in major depression. *Cognitive Therapy and Research* 12: 471–485.

Segal, Z. V., and D. D. Vella. 1990. Self-schema in major depression: Replication and extension of a priming methodology. *Cognitive Therapy and Research* 14: 161–176.

Shannon, C. E., and W. Weaver. 1949. *The mathematical theory of communication.* Urbana: University of Illinois Press.

Shavelson, R. J., J. J. Hubner, and G. C. Stanton. 1976. Self-concept: Validation of construct interpretations. *Review of Educational Research* 46: 407–441.

Sheldon, K. M., and T. Kasser. 1995. Coherence and congruence: Two aspects of personality integration. *Journal of Personality and Social Psychology* 68: 531–543.

Shepperd, J. A., and R. M. Arkin. 1989. Determinants of self-handicapping: Task importance and the effects of preexisting handicaps on self-generated handicaps. *Personality and Social Psychology Bulletin* 15: 101–112.

Showers, C. 1992a. Compartmentalization of positive and negative self-knowledge: Keeping bad apples out of the bunch. *Journal of Personality and Social Psychology* 62: 1036–1049.

Showers, C. 1992b. Evaluatively integrative thinking about characteristics of the self. *Personality and Social Psychology Bulletin* 18: 719–729.

Showers, C. 1995. The evaluative organization of self-knowledge: Origins, process, and implications for self-esteem. In *Efficacy, agency and self-esteem,* edited by M. H. Kernis, 101–122. New York: Plenum.

Showers, C. J., and K. C. Kling. 1996. Organization of self-knowledge: Implications for recovery from sad mood. *Journal of Personality and Social Psychology* 70: 578–590.

Showers, C. J., and C. D. Ryff. 1996. Self-differentiation and well-being in a life transition. *Personality and Social Psychology Bulletin* 22: 448–460.

Shrauger, J. S. 1975. Responses to evaluation as a function of initial self-perceptions. *Psychological Bulletin* 82: 581–596.

Shrauger, J. S. 1982. Selection and processing of self-evaluative information. In *Integrations of clinical and social psychology,* edited by G. Weary and H. L. Mirels, 128–153. New York: Oxford University Press.

Shrauger, J. S., and T. J. Schoeneman. 1979. Symbolic interactionist view of self-concept: Through the looking glass darkly. *Psychological Bulletin* 86: 549–573.

Shweder, R. A. 1982. Beyond self-constructed knowledge: The study of culture and morality. *Merrill-Palmer Quarterly* 28: 41–69.

Sidis, B., and S. P. Goodhart. 1904. *Multiple personality: An experimental investigation into the nature of human individuality.* Englewood Cliffs, N.J.: Prentice-Hall.

Simon, B., G. Pantaleo, and A. Mummenday. 1995. Unique individual or interchangeable group member? The accentuation of intragroup differences versus similarities as an indicator of the individual self versus the collective self. *Journal of Personality and Social Psychology* 69: 106–119.

Skinner, B. F. 1971. *Beyond freedom and dignity.* New York: Knopf.

Smith, H. S., and L. H. Cohen. 1993. Self-complexity and reactions to a relationship breakup. *Journal of Social and Clinical Psychology* 12: 367–384.

Smith, M. B. 1978. Perspectives on selfhood. *American Psychologist* 33: 1053–1063.

Smith, T. W., C. R. Snyder, and M. M. Handlesman. 1982. On the self-serving function of a wooden leg: Test anxiety as a self-handicapping strategy. *Journal of Personality and Social Psychology* 42: 314–321.

Snyder, C. R., and E. T. Higgins. 1988. Excuses: Their effective role in the negotiation of reality. *Psychological Bulletin* 104: 23–35.

Snyder, C. R., and T. W. Smith. 1982. Symptoms as self-handicapping strategies: On the virtues of old wine in a new bottle. In *Integration of clinical and social psychology,* edited by G. Weary and H. L. Mirels, 104–127. New York: Oxford University Press.

Snyder, C. R., T. W. Smith, R. W. Augelli, and R. E. Ingram. 1985. On the self-serving function of social anxiety: Shyness as a self-handicapping strategy. *Journal of Personality and Social Psychology* 48: 970–980.

Snyder, M. 1974. Self-monitoring of expressive behavior. *Journal of Personality and Social Psychology* 30: 526–537.

Snyder, M. 1979. Self-monitoring processes. In *Advances in experimental social psychology,* edited by L. Berkowitz, 12:85–128. New York: Academic.

Snyder, M. 1987. *Public appearances/private realities: The psychology of self-monitoring.* New York: Freeman.

Snyder, M., E. Berscheid, and P. Glick. 1985. Focusing on the exterior and the interior: Two investigations of the initiation of personal relationships. *Journal of Personality and Social Psychology* 48: 1427–1439.

Snyder, M., S. Gangestad, and J. A. Simpson. 1983. Choosing friends as activity partners: The role of self-monitoring. *Journal of Personality and Social Psychology* 45: 1061–1072.

Snyder, M., and T. C. Monson. 1975. Persons, situations, and the control of social behavior. *Journal of Personality and Social Psychology* 32: 637–644.

Snyder, M., and J. A. Simpson. 1984. Self-monitoring and dating relationships. *Journal of Personality and Social Psychology* 47: 1281–1291.

Snyder, M., and E. D. Tanke. 1976. Behavior and attitude: Some people are more consistent than others. *Journal of Personality* 44: 510–517.

Steele, C. M. 1988. The psychology of self-affirmation: Sustaining the integrity of the self. In *Advances in experimental social psychology,* edited by L. Berkowitz, 21:261–302. New York: Academic.

Steele, C. M. 1992. Race and the schooling of Black Americans. *Atlantic Monthly,* April, 68–80.

Steele, C. M., and T. J. Liu. 1983. Dissonance processes as self-affirmation. *Journal of Personality and Social Psychology* 45: 5–19.

Steele, C. M., S. J. Spencer, and M. Lynch. 1993. Self-image resilience and dissonance: The role of affirmational processes. *Journal of Personality and Social Psychology* 64: 885–896.

Stern, D. N. 1985. *The interpersonal world of the infant.* New York: Basic Books.

Stone, J., A. W. Wiegand, J. Cooper, and E. Aronson. 1997. When exemplification fails: Hypocrisy and the motive for self-integrity. *Journal of Personality and Social Psychology* 72: 54–65.

Stroop, J. R. 1935. Studies of interference in serial verbal reactions. *Journal of Experimental Psychology* 18: 643–662.

Strube, M. J., C. L. Lott, G. M. Le-Xuan-Hy, J. Oxenberg, and A. K. Deichmann. 1986. Self-evaluation of abilities: Accurate self-assessment versus biased self-enhancement. *Journal of Personality and Social Psychology* 51: 16–25.

Stryker, S. 1977. Developments in two social psychologies. *Sociometry* 40: 145–160.

Stryker, S. 1987. Stability and change in self: A structural symbolic interactionist explanation. *Social Psychology Quarterly* 50: 44–55.

Sullivan, H. S. 1953. *The interpersonal theory of psychiatry.* New York: Norton.

Suls, J. 1982. *Psychological perspectives on the self.* Vol. 1. Hillsdale, N.J.: Erlbaum.

Suls, J. 1993. *Psychological perspectives on the self.* Vol. 4. Hillsdale, N.J.: Erlbaum.

Suls, J., and A. G. Greenwald. 1983. *Psychological perspectives on the self.* Vol. 2. Hillsdale, N.J.: Erlbaum.

Suls, J., and A. G. Greenwald. 1986. *Psychological perspectives on the self.* Vol. 3. Hillsdale, N.J.: Erlbaum.

Suls, J., and C. K. Wan. 1987. In search of the false-uniqueness phenomenon: Fear and estimates of social consensus. *Journal of Personality and Social Psychology* 52: 211–217.

Swann, W. B., Jr. 1983. Self-verification: Bringing social reality into harmony with the self. In *Psychological perspectives on the self,* edited by J. Suls and A. G. Greenwald, 2:33–66. Hillsdale, N.J.: Erlbaum.

Swann, W. B., Jr. 1985. The self as architect of social reality. In *The self and social life,* edited by B. R. Schlenker, 100–125. New York: McGraw-Hill.

Swann, W. B., Jr. 1990. To be adored or to be known? The interplay of self-enhancement and self-verification. In *Motivation and cognition,* edited by R. M. Sorrentino and E. T. Higgins, 2:408–448. New York: Guilford.

Swann, W. B., Jr. 1996. *Self-traps: The elusive quest for higher self-esteem.* New York: W. H. Freeman.

Swann, W. B., Jr. 1997. The trouble with change: Self-verification and allegiance to self. *Psychological Science* 8: 177–180.

Swann, W. B., Jr., J. J. Griffin, S. Predmore, and E. Gaines. 1987. The cognitive-affective crossfire: When self-consistency confronts self-enhancement. *Journal of Personality and Social Psychology* 52: 881–889.

Swann, W. B., Jr., and C. A. Hill. 1982. When our identities are mistaken: Reaffirming self-conceptions through social interaction. *Journal of Personality and Social Psychology* 43: 59–66.

Swann, W. B., Jr., J. G. Hixon, and C. De La Ronde. 1992. Embracing the bitter "truth": Negative self-concepts and marital commitment. *Psychological Science* 3: 118–121.

Swann, W. B., Jr., B. W. Pelham, and D. S. Krull. 1989. Agreeable fancy or disagreeable truth? Reconciling self-enhancement and self-verification. *Journal of Personality and Social Psychology* 57: 782–791.

Swann, W. B., Jr., and S. J. Read. 1981. Self-verification processes: How we sustain our self-conceptions. *Journal of Experimental Social Psychology* 17: 351–373.

Swann, W. B., Jr., A. Stein-Seroussi, and R. B. Giesler. 1992. Why people self-verify. *Journal of Personality and Social Psychology* 62: 392–401.

Tajfel, H., and J. C. Turner. 1986. The social identity theory of intergroup behavior. In *Psychology of intergroup relations,* edited by S. Worchel and W. Austin, 7–24. Chicago: Nelson-Hall.

Taylor, S. E., and J. D. Brown. 1988. Illusion and well-being: A social psychological perspective on mental health. *Psychological Bulletin* 103: 193–210.

Taylor, S. E., and J. D. Brown. 1994. Positive illusions and well-being revisited: Separating fact from fiction. *Psychological Bulletin* 116: 21–27.

Taylor, S. E., E. Neter, and H. A. Wayment. 1995. Self-evaluation processes. *Personality and Social Psychology Bulletin* 12: 1278–1287.

Tedeschi, J. T., B. R. Schlenker, and T. V. Bonoma. 1971. Cognitive dissonance: Private ratiocination or public spectacle? *American Psychologist* 26: 685–695.

Tennen, H., and S. Herzberger. 1987. Depression, self-esteem, and the absence of self-protective attributional biases. *Journal of Personality and Social Psychology* 52: 72–80.

Tesser, A. 1988. Toward a self-evaluation model of social behavior. In *Advances in experimental social psychology,* edited by L. Berkowitz, 21:181–227. New York: Academic.

Tesser, A., M. Millar, and J. Moore. 1988. Some affective consequences of social comparison and reflection processes: The pain and pleasure of being close. *Journal of Personality and Social Psychology* 54: 49–61.

Tetlock, P. D., and A. S. R. Manstead. 1985. Impression management vs. intrapsychic explanations in social psychology: A useful dichotomy? *Psychological Review* 92: 59–77.

Tice, D. M. 1991. Esteem protection or enhancement? Self-handicapping motives and attributions differ by trait self-esteem. *Journal of Personality and Social Psychology* 60: 711–725.

Tice, D. M. 1992. Self-concept change and self-presentation: The looking glass self is also a magnifying glass. *Journal of Personality and Social Psychology* 63: 435–451.

Tice, D. M., J. L. Butler, M. B. Muraven, and A. M. Stillwell. 1995. When modesty prevails: Differential favorability of self-presentation to friends and strangers. *Journal of Personality and Social Psychology* 69: 1120–1138.

Tobey, E. L., and G. Tunnell. 1981. Predicting our impressions on others: Effects of public self-consciousness and acting, a self-monitoring subscale. *Personality and Social Psychology Bulletin* 7: 661–669.

Trafimow, D., H. C. Triandis, and S. G. Goto. 1991. Some tests of the distinction between private self and collective self. *Journal of Personality and Social Psychology* 60: 649–655.

Triandis, H. C. 1989. The self and social behavior in differing cultural contexts. *Psychological Review* 96: 506–520.

Trivers, R. 1976. Foreword to *The selfish gene,* edited by R. Dawkins. New York: Oxford University Press.

Trope, Y. 1975. Seeking information about one's own ability as a determinant of choice among tasks. *Journal of Personality and Social Psychology* 32: 1004–1013.

Trope, Y. 1979. Uncertainty-reducing properties of achievement tasks. *Journal of Personality and Social Psychology* 37: 1505–1518.

Trope, Y. 1983. Self-assessment in achievement behavior. In *Psychological perspectives on the self,* edited by J. Suls and A. G. Greenwald, 2:93–121. Hillsdale, N.J.: Erlbaum.

Trope, Y., and E. Ben-Yair. 1982. Task construction and persistence as means of self-assessment of abilities. *Journal of Personality and Social Psychology* 42: 637–645.

Trope, Y., and E. Neter. 1994. Reconciling competing motives in self-evaluation: The role of self-control in feedback seeking. *Journal of Personality and Social Psychology* 66: 646–657.

Tucker, J. A., R. E. Vuchinich, and M. B. Sobell. 1981. Alcohol consumption as a self-handicapping strategy. *Journal of Abnormal Psychology* 90: 220–230.

Turner, J. C., M. A. Hogg, P. J. Oakes, S. D. Reicher, and S. M. Wetherell. 1987. *Rediscovering the social group: A self-categorization theory.* Oxford, England: Blackwell.

Turner, R. G. 1980. Self-consciousness and memory of trait terms. *Personality and Social Psychology Bulletin* 6: 273–277.

Turner, R. G., L. Gilliland, and H. M. Klein. 1981. Self-consciousness, evaluation of physical characteristics, and physical attractiveness. *Journal of Research in Personality* 15: 182–190.

Turner, S. 1995. Alcoholic women's self-esteem. *Alcoholism Treatment Quarterly* 12: 109–116.

Vallacher, R. R., and D. M. Wegner. 1985. *A theory of action identification.* Hillsdale, N.J.: Erlbaum.

Viney, L. 1969. Self: The history of a concept. *Journal of the History of the Behavioral Sciences* 5: 349–359.

Waschull, S. B., and M. H. Kernis. 1996. Level and stability of self-esteem as predictors of children's intrinsic motivation and reasons for anger. *Personality and Social Psychology Bulletin* 22: 4–13.

Watson, D., and L. A. Clark. 1984. Negative affectivity: The disposition to experience aversive emotional states. *Psychological Bulletin* 96: 465–490.

Wegner, D. M., and R. R. Vallacher, eds. 1980. *The self in social psychology.* New York: Oxford University Press.

Wells, G. E., and G. Marwell. 1976. *Self-esteem: Its conceptualization and measurement.* Beverly Hills, Calif.: Sage.

White, R. W. 1959. Motivation reconsidered: The concept of competence. *Psychological Review* 66: 297–335.

Whitson, E. R., and P. V. Olczak. 1991. Criticisms and polemics surrounding the self-actualization construct: An evaluation. In *Handbook of self-actualization,* edited by A. Jones and R. Crandall, 75–95. San Rafael, Calif.: Select.

Wicklund, R. A. 1979. The influence of self-awareness on human behavior. *American Scientist* 67: 187–193.

Wicklund, R. A., and P. M. Gollwitzer. 1982. *Symbolic self-completion*. Hillsdale, N.J.: Erlbaum.

Wicklund, R. A., and P. M. Gollwitzer. 1987. The fallacy of the public-private distinction. *Journal of Personality* 55: 491–523.

Wiener, N. 1948. *Cybernetics*. New York: Wiley.

Wills, T. A. 1981. Downward comparison principles in social psychology. *Psychological Bulletin* 90: 245–271.

Wood, J. V. 1989. Theory and research concerning social comparison of personal attributes. *Psychological Bulletin* 106: 231–248.

Wood, J. V., M. Giordano-Beech, K. L. Taylor, J. L. Michela, and V. Gaus. 1994. Strategies of social comparison among people with low self-esteem: Self-protection and self-enhancement. *Journal of Personality and Social Psychology* 67: 713–731.

Wood, J. V., J. A. Saltzberg, and L. A. Goldsamt. 1990. Does affect induce self-focused attention? *Journal of Personality and Social Psychology* 58: 899–908.

Woolfolk, R. L., J. Novalany, M. A. Gara, L. A. Allen, and M. Polino. 1995. Self-complexity, self-evaluation, and depression: An examination of form and content within the self-schema. *Journal of Personality and Social Psychology* 68: 1108–1120.

Wylie, R. C. 1974. *The self-concept: A review of methodological considerations and measuring instruments* Rev. ed. Vol. 1. Lincoln: University of Nebraska Press.

Wylie, R. C. 1979. *The self-concept*. Vol. 2. Lincoln: University of Nebraska Press.

Yates, F. E., ed. 1987. *Self-organizing systems: The emergence of order*. New York: Plenum.

Zimbardo, P. G. 1969. The human choice: Individuation, reason and order versus deindividuation, impulse and chaos. In *Nebraska symposium on motivation*, edited by N. J. Arnold and D. Levine, 17:237–307. Lincoln: University of Nebraska Press.

Zuckerman, M. 1979. Attribution of success and failure revisited, or: The motivational bias is alive and well in attribution theory. *Journal of Personality* 47: 245–287.

Zuckerman, M., J. Porac, D. Lathin, R. Smith, and E. L. Deci. 1978. On the importance of self-determination for intrinsically motivated behavior. *Personality and Social Psychology Bulletin* 4: 443–446.

Zumpf, C. L., and S. Harter. 1989. *Mirror, mirror on the wall: The relationship between appearance and self-worth in adolescent males and females*. Paper presented at the Annual Meeting of the Society for Research in Child Development, Kansas City, Missouri.

Index